MILLICENT AKWELEY
CORNELIUS ANNOR
CRYSTAL YAYRA ANTHONY
ATSOUPÉ
SOULEIMANE BARRY
AMOAKO BOAFO
APLERH-DOKU BORLABI
ALEXANDRE DIOP
KIMATHI DONKOR
MATTHEW EGUAVOEN
BOUVY ENKOBO
BASIL KINCAID
TURIYA MAGADLELA
GASTINEAU MASSAMBA
JAMES MISHIO
CHRISTOPHER MYERS
EVERLYN NICODEMUS
JEAN DAVID NKOT
BOLUWATIFE OYEDIRAN
AFIA PREMPEH
OTIS KWAME KYE QUAICOE
JOSIE LOVE ROEBUCK
ERIC ADJEI TAWIAH
TESFAYE URGESSA

THE NEW AFRICAN PORTRAITURE.
Shariat Collections.

KUNST HALLE KREMS

Verlag der Buchhandlung Walther und Franz König, Köln

CONTENTS / INHALT

FOREWORD AND ACKNOWLEDGMENTS

FLORIAN STEININGER

The New African Portraiture: Shariat Collections is the first comprehensive exhibition of current trends in figurative painting from Africa and the African diaspora presented at the Kunsthalle Krems. A new self-confidence, empowerment, and body positivity are evident in the artistic positions on display. Of particular importance are the preferred genres of figure and portrait. Image themes include one's identity, one's fellow human beings, family, everyday scenes, political contexts and cultural settings, lifestyle and fashion, as well as heroes of people of color.

The Black body has been marginalized throughout art history, where it was mainly represented in the background and from a colonialist-motivated viewpoint, painted by Western artists. The positions presented in Krems reveal a wide range of painterly and pictorial-collage-like contributions—from realistic-scenic to expressionist-iconic imagery. Most of the artists were born in Africa, but some live and work in Europe or the US. Within Africa, Ghana forms a central focus as an emerging hub of current figurative painting. It was possible to win over Ekow Eshun as exhibition curator. The London-based journalist, author, and curator has family roots in Ghana. In his 2005 memoir *Black Gold of the Sun*: *Searching for Home in England and Africa*, he reflects on his identity and cultural connections to Africa and England.

The art presented in the exhibition is largely drawn from the collection of Amir and Shahrokh Shariat, whose recent collecting activities have focused on current figurative art in Africa.

Such an exhibition requires the support of numerous contributors. My sincere thanks go to Amir and Shahrokh Shariat, the lenders of the exhibition, as well as to Eva Kovač, production manager of the Shariat Collections, who helped oversee the project on the collectors' behalf. I would also like to express my sincere gratitude to all the artists involved in the exhibition, who have shown us their trust and confidence in the exhibition project.

VORWORT UND DANK

The New African Portraiture. Shariat Collections ist die erste umfangreiche Schau aktueller Tendenzen figurativer Malerei aus Afrika und der afrikanischen Diaspora, die in der Kunsthalle Krems präsentiert wird. Ein neues Selbstbewusstsein, Empowerment und Körperpositivität sind in den gezeigten künstlerischen Positionen zu erkennen. Von besonderer Bedeutung sind die bevorzugten Genres Figur und Porträt. Die Themen der Bilder sind die eigene Identität, nahestehende Menschen, die Familie, alltägliche Szenen, politische Kontexte und kulturelle Verortung, Lifestyle und Mode sowie Held:innen der People of Color.

Der Schwarze Körper war in der Kunstgeschichte marginalisiert, meist im Hintergrund und aus einem kolonialistisch motivierten Blick dargestellt, von westlichen Kunstschaffenden gemalt. Die in Krems vertretenen Positionen zeigen eine große Bandbreite an malerischen und bildnerisch-collagehaften Beiträgen - von realistisch-szenischen bis expressionistisch ikonischen. Die Schöpfer:innen sind großteils in Afrika geboren, leben und arbeiten jedoch teilweise in Europa und den USA. Innerhalb Afrikas wird ein Fokus auf Ghana gelegt, ein aufstrebendes Zentrum der aktuellen figurativen Malerei. Für die Ausstellung konnte Ekow Eshun als Kurator gewonnen werden. Der in London lebende Journalist, Autor und Kurator hat familiäre Wurzeln in Ghana. In seinen 2005 erschienenen Memoiren *Black Gold of the Sun. Searching for Home in England and Africa* reflektiert er seine Identität und seine kulturellen Bezüge zu Afrika und England.

Die in der Ausstellung gezeigte Kunst stammt großteils aus der Sammlung von Amir und Shahrokh Shariat, die sich in ihrer Sammlertätigkeit in letzter Zeit auf aktuelle figurative Kunst in Afrika konzentrieren.

Solch eine Ausstellung bedarf der Unterstützung vieler. Mein großer Dank geht an Amir und Shahrokh Shariat, die Leihgeber der Ausstellung, sowie an Eva Kovač, Production Manager der Shariat Collections, die das Projekt von Seiten der Sammler mitbetreut hat. Mein herzlicher Dank richtet sich auch an alle Kunstschaffenden der Ausstellung, die uns und dem Ausstellungsprojekt mit Vertrauen und Engagement entgegengetreten sind.

My special thanks go to Ekow Eshun, exhibition curator and catalog co-editor, whose wealth of expertise was essential to shaping the exhibition *The New African Portraiture*.

For their cooperation on the publication, I would like to thank Walther König from Verlag der Buchhandlung Walther und Franz König, Cologne; Alexander Rendi for his intuitive and skillful design of the catalog; as well as all the authors whose contributions provide a deep insight into the current situation of African figurative painting. Thanks are also due to the Collection Michael Ballack for the loan of a work as well as a generous donation to the production of the catalog. I am also grateful for Dr. Andreas Huber's financial support of the exhibition project.

Sincere thanks also go to the entire team at the Kunsthalle Krems and the Kunstmeile Krems, in particular managing director Julia Flunger-Schulz; head of exhibition and catalog management Elke Pehamberger-Müllner; project manager Elisabeth Kainberger and Helene Heiß; and catalog editor Philipp Emanuel Missaghi. Thanks also to the marketing and communications department headed by Sigrid Wilhelm; Elisabeth Zettl, deputy head of marketing and communications/tourism; Martina Hackel, head of the events department; Nicole Pröll and Stephanie Schmitzer responsible for development; Isabell Fiedler, head of art education and visitor service; and the entire art education team, in particular Claudia Pitnik; Reinhard Kern, head of facility management; and the installation team.

Finally, the Kunsthalle Krems would like to thank the main sponsors, the State of Lower Austria; the Austrian Federal Ministry for Arts, Culture, Civil Service, and Sport; the City of Krems and the Freunde der Kunstmeile Krems association, whose financial support contributed to the realization of the exhibition, catalog, and art-education projects.

Mein besonderer Dank geht an Ekow Eshun, Kurator der Ausstellung und Mitherausgeber des Kataloges, der mit seiner umfassenden Expertise die Ausstellung *The New African Portraiture* gestaltet hat.

Für die Kooperation in Zusammenhang mit der Publikation bedanke ich mich bei Walther König vom Verlag der Buchhandlung Walther und Franz König, Köln, und bei Alexander Rendi, der das Buch mit viel Sensibilität und Wissen gestaltet hat, sowie bei sämtlichen Autor:innen, die mit ihren Beiträgen einen tieferen Einblick in die aktuelle Situation der afrikanischen figurativen Malerei geben. Gedankt sei Michael Ballack für seine Werkleihgabe sowie seine generöse Spende für die Katalogproduktion. Ebenso geht mein Dank an Dr. Andreas Huber, der mit seiner Spende das Ausstellungsprojekt unterstützt.

Herzlicher Dank gebührt dem gesamten Team der Kunsthalle Krems beziehungsweise der Kunstmeile Krems, vor allem der operativen Geschäftsführerin Julia Flunger-Schulz, der Leiterin des Ausstellungs- und Katalogmanagements Elke Pehamberger-Müllner, der Projektleiterin Elisabeth Kainberger, Helene Heiß und dem Katalogredakteur Philipp Emanuel Missaghi. Zu danken ist auch der Abteilung für Marketing und Kommunikation unter der Leitung von Sigrid Wilhelm, Elisabeth Zettl, der stellvertretenden Leiterin für Marketing und Kommunikation/Tourismus, Martina Hackel, der Leiterin der Abteilung Events, Nicole Pröll und Stephanie Schmitzer verantwortlich für das Development, Isabell Fiedler, der Leiterin von Kunstvermittlung und Besucherservice, und dem gesamten Kunstvermittlungsteam, insbesondere Claudia Pitnik, Reinhard Kern, dem Leiter des Facility Managements, sowie dem Aufbauteam.

Schließlich bedankt sich die Kunsthalle Krems sehr herzlich bei den Hauptfördergebern, dem Land Niederösterreich, dem Bundesministerium für Kunst, Kultur, öffentlichen Dienst und Sport, der Stadt Krems und dem Verein der Freunde der Kunstmeile Krems, die durch ihr finanzielles Engagement zur Realisierung der Ausstellung und des Kataloges sowie von Kunstvermittlungsprojekten beigetragen haben.

INTRODUCTION

EKOW ESHUN

The New African Portraiture is a group exhibition bringing together leading figures from a generation of thrilling figurative artists of African origin. Focusing on the African continent and diaspora, the exhibiting artists explore complex questions of identity, aesthetics, and art history. Through compelling portraiture, their work invites an examination of how the Black figure has often been misrepresented or overlooked in the Western painting tradition.

The elegant figures depicted by Amoako Boafo, and Otis Kwame Kye Quaicoe, for instance, offer nuanced consideration of "Africanness" as an innately cosmopolitan condition. In so doing, they advance the idea of the continent and its peoples as the inheritors of complex, hybrid identities that are, in the words of Cameroonian philosopher Achille Mbembe, "born out of overlapping genealogies, at the intersections of multiple encounters with multiple elsewheres." Artists such as Souleimane Barry and Christopher Myers conjure dreamlike scenes that merge the real and the imaginary to posit African cultures and myths as sites of endlessly rich narrative possibilities. In the powerful work of Gastineau Massamba and Everlyn Nicodemus, the most senior artist represented in the exhibition whose highly regarded career spans over thirty years, we see paintings that set personal traumas against the backdrop and collective pain of Africa's often fraught political history.

In addressing a "new" African portraiture, the exhibition seeks to underscore two recent developments. Firstly, it highlights how a developing infrastructure of artist-run spaces and not-for-profit organizations in Africa is making

EINLEITUNG

The New African Portraiture ist eine Gruppenausstellung, die führende Vertreter:innen einer Generation spannender figurativer Künstler:innen afrikanischer Herkunft versammelt. Die ausstellenden Künstler:innen nehmen den afrikanischen Kontinent und die Diaspora in den Blick und setzen sich mit komplexen Fragen der Identität, Ästhetik und Kunstgeschichte auseinander. Als fesselnde Porträts laden ihre Arbeiten dazu ein, sich mit der oftmaligen Fehldarstellung oder dem Übergehen Schwarzer Menschen in der westlichen Maltradition zu befassen.

Die eleganten Figuren etwa von Amoako Boafo oder Otis Kwame Kye Quaicoe bieten eine nuancierte Betrachtung von „Africanness" (dt. etwa „Afrikanität") als einem immanent kosmopolitischen Zustand. Auf diese Weise befördern sie die Vorstellung vom Kontinent und seinen Völkern als Erben komplexer, hybrider Identitäten, die, mit den Worten des kamerunischen Philosophen Achille Mbembe, „geboren sind aus sich überschneidenden Genealogien, an den Kreuzungspunkten vielfältiger Begegnungen mit vielfältigen Anderswos." Künstler:innen wie Souleimane Barry und Christopher Myers beschwören traumartige Szenen herauf, die das Reale mit dem Imaginären verschmelzen, um afrikanische Kulturen und Mythen als Schauplätze unendlich reicher narrativer Möglichkeiten herauszustellen. In den kraftvollen Arbeiten von Gastineau Massamba und Everlyn Nicodemus – der ältesten der in der Ausstellung vertretenen Künstler:innen, deren viel beachtete künstlerische Laufbahn 30 Jahre umfasst – sehen wir Malereien, die persönliche Traumata vor dem Hintergrund des kollektiven Schmerzes und der oft belasteten politischen Geschichte Afrikas darstellen.

up for a lack of state funding for the arts and establishing a new environment of support and opportunity within which artists are increasingly thriving. Secondly, the exhibition situates the emergence of a rising wave of African visual artists within the context of a wider flourishing of creative culture from the continent: a growing number of figures in related fields such as literature, cinema, architecture, photography, and popular music are also achieving unprecedented success on the international stage. The "new," therefore, does not come out of nowhere. It is the result of long-evolving social and cultural forces. And counted among these are the collective efforts of an emergent generation that insists on the visibility and voice of the African presence in contemporary culture.

Indem die Ausstellung eine als „neu" titulierte afrikanische Porträtkunst vorstellt, will sie zwei Entwicklungen der jüngsten Zeit hervorheben. Sie wirft erstens ein Schlaglicht darauf, wie eine sich entwickelnde Infrastruktur von künstlerbetriebenen Räumen und Non-Profit-Organisationen in Afrika einen Ausgleich für den Mangel an staatlicher Kunstfinanzierung und ein neues Umfeld der Unterstützung und Möglichkeiten schafft, in dem die Künstler:innen sich zunehmend entfalten. Zweitens stellt die Ausstellung den stetigen Zuwachs an afrikanischen bildenden Künstler:innen in den Kontext einer umfassenderen Blüte der kreativen Kultur des Kontinents: Eine wachsende Zahl von Künstler:innen aus verwandten Bereichen wie Literatur, Kino, Architektur, Fotografie und populärer Musik erzielt ebenfalls beispiellose Erfolge auf der internationalen Bühne. Das „Neue" kommt also nicht aus dem Nichts. Es ist das Ergebnis sozialer und kultureller Kräfte, die sich seit Langem entwickeln. Dazu zählen auch die kollektiven Anstrengungen einer aufstrebenden Generation, die darauf beharrt, dass die afrikanische Präsenz in der zeitgenössischen Kultur vermehrt sichtbar und hörbar wird.

NEW POSSIBILITIES IN AFRICAN PORTRAITURE

EKOW ESHUN

A LEGACY OF FIGURATION

In Africa, figurative painting never acquired the deeply unfashionable status it had in the West during the latter half of the twentieth century. During this period, thanks to the dominance of abstraction and conceptual art, figuration seemed to be a doomed, or at least fatally anachronistic, art form. Even today, when the likes of Kerry James Marshall, Peter Doig, and Luc Tuymans have revitalized the medium, a 2020 exhibition of new figuration at London's Whitechapel gallery talked of wanting to "breathe new life" into "a seemingly outmoded medium."[1] Not so in Africa, where for better and for worse figuration has retained a central role. For better, because the influence of artists such as Ben Enwonwu and Ablade Glover continues to set a high standard to which artists might aspire. For worse, because an emphasis on figuration has led to a lack of experimentation in art schools and galleries, and a tendency for artists to focus instead on making works for the tourist market.

blaxTARLINES, the Kumasi, Ghana-based contemporary art collective, has described how an aesthetic of bland figuration that took over the Ghanaian art sector is still felt in the twenty-first century. Their account could equally apply to circumstances across much of the African continent. "The default ethos of exhibition-making in Ghana was premised on...filling up commercial gallery interiors with painting décor and romantic Africanist souvenirs contrived for the tourist's eye, pocket, and luggage bag.... Ambitious works, which challenged established beaux-arts genres, media, styles, and formats, were simply inadmissible, stigmatized, or shamed. There was a reflection of this silent censorship in an artist's training in art school, too."[2]

NEUE MÖGLICHKEITEN DER AFRIKANISCHEN PORTRÄTKUNST

EIN FIGURATIVES ERBE

In Afrika erlangte die figurative Malerei niemals den Ruf, völlig unzeitgemäß zu sein, den sie in der zweiten Hälfte des 20. Jahrhunderts im Westen hatte. Angesichts der Dominanz von Abstraktion und Konzeptkunst erschien die Figuration in dieser Zeit als eine dem Untergang geweihte oder zumindest fatal anachronistische Kunstform. Selbst heutzutage, da Künstler wie Kerry James Marshall, Peter Doig und Luc Tuymans das Medium neu belebt haben, spricht eine Ausstellung neuer Figuration in der Londoner Whitechapel Gallery 2020 davon, einem „scheinbar überholten Medium neues Leben einhauchen"[1] zu wollen. Nicht so in Afrika, wo die Figuration eine zentrale Rolle beibehalten hat, im Guten wie im Schlechten. Im Guten, weil der Einfluss von Künstlern wie Ben Enwonwu und Ablade Glover weiterhin hohe Standards setzt, denen andere Künstler:innen nachstreben können. Im Schlechten, weil die Fokussierung auf das Figurative zu einem Mangel an Experimentierfreude in Kunstschulen und Galerien geführt hat und unter Künstler:innen zu der Tendenz, sich eher darauf zu konzentrieren, Werke für den Touristenmarkt anzufertigen.

blaxTARLINES, das in Kumasi, Ghana, ansässige Kollektiv für zeitgenössische Kunst, hat beschrieben, dass eine Ästhetik der faden Figuration, die sich im ghanaischen Kunstsektor breitgemacht hatte, im 21. Jahrhundert noch immer zu spüren ist. Ihre Schilderung gilt gleichermaßen für die Verhältnisse in weiten Teilen des afrikanischen Kontinents: „Die Standardhaltung des Ausstellungsmachens in Ghana bestand darin, […] die Räume kommerzieller Galerien mit gemalten Dekobildern und romantischen Afrikasouvenirs zu füllen, erdacht für die Augen,

Yet within the past decade a remarkable shift has taken place among African artists. Figuration remains central. But a commitment to boldness and the imaginative has increasingly come to dominate the approach of younger artists, eclipsing the ethos of conservatism that once prevailed. Artists who were born on the continent, such as Ghana's Amoako Boafo and Otis Kwame Kye Quaicoe, or Ethiopia's Tesfaye Urgessa, are bringing a thrilling urgency and breadth of possibility to figurative painting, while also winning international acclaim in the process. Boafo's vibrant and compelling portrait paintings have led to his particularly dizzying rise, from a little-known painter five years ago to being hailed as "the art market's biggest star," including collaborating with Dior and even sending a triptych of paintings into space on a Jeff Bezos-owned rocket ship.

The exhibition *The New African Portraiture*, showcasing works from the Amir and Shahrokh Shariat collections, brings a number of these younger artists together alongside more senior figures like UK-based Everlyn Nicodemus and Kimathi Donkor, and US-based artists Basil Kincaid, Christopher Myers, and Josie Love Roebuck. The exhibition seeks to mark the expansive and thrilling diversity of approaches now being brought to bear on the legacy of African figuration. But to fully address the ascent of this wave of artists in recent years, it is also necessary to explore the cultural context in which they are working. And, in addition, to ask how the exhibition understands terms like *Africa* and *New* that make up its title.

WHAT IS AFRICA?

Imagine a king. His skin is lustrous. His gaze is direct. His fingers are long and graceful. A brown coat flows about him like a robe, revealing beneath it a garment of brilliant orange. In Boafo's *Untitled* (2019, cat. p. 24), as with his other paintings in the exhibition, every man and every woman is of regal bearing, carrying with them a lineage of self-regard passed down from their ancestors. We might infer from his work, and that of many other artists in *The New African Portraiture* who conjure similar depictions of elegance, that to

Hosentaschen und Reisekoffer von Tourist:innen. [...] Ambitionierte Werke, die etablierte Kunstgenres, Medien, Stile und Formate infrage stellten, waren schlicht unzulässig, stigmatisiert, verpönt. Diese stillschweigende Zensur spiegelte sich auch in der Ausbildung an den Kunstschulen wider." [2]

Im vergangenen Jahrzehnt jedoch fand unter afrikanischen Künstler:innen ein bemerkenswerter Umschwung statt. Zwar bleibt das Figurale weiterhin zentral. Die Herangehensweise jüngerer Künstler:innen aber dominiert zunehmend ein Bekenntnis zu Kühnheit und zum Imaginativen und lässt das einst vorherrschende konservative Ethos verblassen. Auf dem Kontinent geborene Künstler:innen wie Amoako Boafo und Otis Kwame Kye Quaicoe aus Ghana oder Tesfaye Urgessa aus Äthiopien verleihen der figurativen Malerei fesselnde Dringlichkeit sowie eine große Bandbreite an Möglichkeiten und erlangen dabei auch internationale Anerkennung. Boafos lebendige und fesselnde Porträtbilder haben ihm einen besonders schwindelerregenden Aufstieg beschert: Vor fünf Jahren war er noch ein wenig bekannter Maler, heute wird er als „größter Star des Kunstmarkts" gefeiert, was eine Zusammenarbeit mit Dior ebenso miteinschloss wie den Weltraumflug eines Gemäldetriptychons von ihm in einem Jeff Bezos gehörenden Raketenschiff.

Die Ausstellung *The New African Portraiture*, die Werke aus den Sammlungen von Amir und Shahrokh Shariat zeigt, bringt eine Reihe dieser jüngeren Künstler:innen zusammen, Seite an Seite mit älteren Vertreter:innen wie Everlyn Nicodemus und Kimathi Donkor aus dem Vereinigten Königreich oder Basil Kincaid, Christopher Myers und Josie Love Roebuck aus den USA. Die Ausstellung will die breite und spannende Diversität der Zugänge aufzeigen, die Künstler:innen zu dem Erbe der afrikanischen Figuration gefunden haben. Um den Aufstieg dieser Künstler:innen in den letzten Jahren voll zu erfassen, ist es aber auch notwendig, den kulturellen Kontext zu betrachten, in dem sie arbeiten. Und zusätzlich die Frage zu stellen, wie die Ausstellung Begriffe wie *Afrika* und *neu*, die sie im Titel führt, versteht.

WAS IST AFRIKA?

Man stelle sich einen König vor. Seine Haut strahlend. Sein Blick direkt. Seine Finger lang und anmutig. Ein brauner Mantel umfließt ihn wie eine Robe und enthüllt darunter ein Gewand von leuchtendem Orange. Ob in Boafos *Untitled* (2019, Kat. S. 24) oder in seinen anderen Bildern in der Ausstellung, bei Boafo ist jeder Mann und jede Frau von königlichem Gebaren und trägt

share a connection with Africa is to be heir to a heritage of consummate sophistication. Look at the gorgeous couple lounging on a sofa of gold brocade in Matthew Eguavoen's *Conversations we must have* (2022); or the strength and composure of the woman in the orange dress staring out of Otis Kwame Kye Quaicoe's *Untitled* (2019, cat. p. 51). In these portraits the depicted figures hold a strikingly self-assured position in the world. Other works in the exhibition offer less assertive but no less powerfully resonant descriptions of African-originated being. Tesfaye Urgessa's "No Country for Young Men" series was inspired in part by the European migrant crisis of the 2010s, which peaked in 2015 when 1.3 million refugees from Syria, Nigeria, Eritrea, Afghanistan, and other nations requested asylum in Europe, the most in a single year since World War II. Urgessa's paintings show contorted figures squeezed into cramped spaces, the vivid corporeality of their naked bodies reminiscent of paintings by Lucian Freud. The title of Urgessa's series refers to the plight of the young men who made up the majority of the refugees, cast into stateless exile by war, climate change, and the economic depredations of globalization. Despite such precarious circumstances, Urgessa suggests the men retain autonomy over their lives. As figures on the move, "not bound by physical boundaries," he argues, they are able to build a new future for themselves "any place, where their dream is."[3] In Urgessa's paintings we glimpse the "new African migratory flows" identified by art historian Salah M. Hassan, in which, in the wake of colonialism, African peoples traverse the "migratory linkages between the colonial metropolis and former colonies" on their own terms as free agents.[4]

If there is a commonality to the works in *The New African Portraiture*, it has to do with the shared belief in an African cultural identity, birthed on the continent and defined in various ways across the diaspora, as an innately cosmopolitan condition. The confidence and agency with which the subjects in Boafo's, Quaicoe's, and even Urgessa's paintings carry themselves in the modern world offers a marked contrast to how Africans have been cast as primitive and undeveloped across the course of the Western imaginary. Consider, for instance,

eine von ihren Vorfahren überlieferte Tradition der Selbstachtung in sich. Aus seinem Werk und dem vieler anderer Künstler:innen in *The New African Portraiture*, die ähnliche Bilder von Eleganz beschwören, könnten wir den Schluss ziehen, dass eine Verbindung zu Afrika zu haben heißt, Erb:in eines Vermächtnisses vollendeter kultureller Finesse zu sein. Man betrachte das prachtvolle Paar auf dem Goldbrokatsofa in Matthew Eguavoens *Conversations we must have* (2022) oder die Stärke und Haltung der Frau im orangen Kleid, die einem aus Otis Kwame Kye Quaicoes *Untitled* (2019, Kat. S. 51) entgegenblickt. In diesen Porträts nehmen die dargestellten Figuren eine auffallend selbstbewusste Stellung in der Welt ein. Andere Arbeiten in der Ausstellung bieten weniger selbstgewisse, aber nicht weniger kraftvolle Beschreibungen der Existenz von Menschen afrikanischer Herkunft. Tesfaye Urgessas Serie „No Country for Young Men" wurde zum Teil von der europäischen Flüchtlingskrise der 2010er-Jahre inspiriert, die 2015 ihren Höhepunkt erreichte, als 1,3 Millionen Flüchtlinge aus Syrien, Nigeria, Eritrea, Afghanistan und anderen Ländern Asyl in Europa suchten, die höchste Anzahl innerhalb eines einzigen Jahres seit dem Zweiten Weltkrieg. Urgessas Bilder zeigen verrenkte Figuren, auf engstem Raum zusammengepfercht; die lebendige Körperlichkeit ihrer nackten Leiber erinnert an Gemälde von Lucian Freud. Der Titel der Serie von Urgessa bezieht sich auf die Zwangslage der jungen Männer, die die Mehrheit der Flüchtlinge stellten und durch Krieg, Klimawandel und die wirtschaftlichen Verwerfungen der Globalisierung in ein staatenloses Exil getrieben wurden. Trotz solch prekärer Umstände behalten sie, wie Urgessa andeutet, Kontrolle über ihr Leben. Als Menschen in Bewegung, „nicht gebunden an physische Grenzen", seien sie in der Lage, sich an „jedem Ort, wo ihr Traum ist"[3], eine neue Zukunft aufzubauen. Urgessas Bilder lassen uns einen Blick auf die „neuen afrikanischen Migrationsströme" werfen, die der Kunsthistoriker Salah M. Hassan beschrieben hat, bei denen afrikanische Völker im Gefolge des Kolonialismus die „migrantischen Verbindungswege zwischen der kolonialen Metropole und den vormaligen Kolonien" selbstbestimmt passieren, als freie Akteur:innen.[4]

Wenn die Arbeiten in *The New African Portraiture* etwas gemeinsam haben, dann ist es der Glaube an eine afrikanische kulturelle Identität – geboren auf dem Kontinent und auf verschiedene Weise in der Diaspora definiert – als ein kosmopolitischer Zustand. Das Selbstvertrauen und die Handlungs-

how the first Europeans arriving on the continent claimed that African people were so childlike that they mistook white travelers for gods. Or how Europe's leading thinkers dismissed the continent as the antithesis of modernity. Africa lay "'beyond' history...enveloped in the dark mantel of Night," declared the philosopher Georg Wilhelm Friedrich Hegel. Its people were representative of "natural man in his completely wild and untamed state." [5]

Writing in 1918, Sir Hugh Clifford, colonial governor of the Gold Coast (modern day Ghana), decried the backwardness of African culture and its "failure to develop any high form of civilization." "The West African Negro," he wrote "has never sculptured a statue, painted a picture, produced a literature, or even invented a mechanical contrivance worthy of the name." [6] Yet through the eyes of the artists in *The New African Portraiture* we understand the very opposite to be true. In the self-possession and sophistication on display in their paintings we see a continent and its peoples whose common experiences are forged out of the flows of commerce and migratory exchange, both forced and voluntary, that have shaped their continent over hundreds of years. To be African, argues the scholar Simon Gikandi, is "to be connected to knowable African communities, nations, and traditions; but it is also to live a life divided across cultures, language, and states. It is to embrace and celebrate a state of cultural hybridity—to be of Africa and of other worlds at the same time." [7]

WHAT IS THE NEW?

Beginning in the late 1950s a wave of independence and liberation movements in Africa sparked a political and social reordering across the continent. This was the era of self-determination movements like *Negritude*, *Pan-Africanism*, and *Arab Nationalism*; the period in which nation after nation won freedom from colonial rule; the years during which the long, hard liberation struggle in South Africa finally achieved success with the end of apartheid in 1994. The energy and optimism of the era was also the catalyst

macht, mit denen sich die Figuren in den Gemälden von Boafo, Quaicoe und auch Urgessa in der modernen Welt bewegen, steht in prononciertem Kontrast zur Darstellung afrikanischer Menschen als primitiv und unentwickelt, wie sie die westliche Bilderwelt durchzieht. Man denke nur daran, dass die ersten Europäer, die auf dem Kontinent ankamen, behaupteten, die Afrikaner:innen seien so kindlich, dass sie weiße Reisende für Götter hielten. Oder dass Europas führende Köpfe den Kontinent als Antithese der Modernität abtaten. Afrika liege „jenseits [...] der [...] Geschichte in die schwarze Farbe der Nacht gehüllt", erklärte der Philosoph Georg Wilhelm Friedrich Hegel. Seine Völker stellten den „natürlichen Menschen in seiner ganzen Wildheit und Unbändigkeit dar." [5]

1918 beklagte Sir Hugh Clifford, Kolonialgouverneur der Goldküste (des heutigen Ghana), die Rückständigkeit der afrikanischen Kultur und ihr „Unvermögen, irgendeine höhere Form von Zivilisation zu entwickeln." „Der westafrikanische Neger", schrieb er, „hat niemals eine Statue geformt, ein Bild gemalt, eine Literatur geschaffen oder auch nur einen mechanischen Apparat erfunden, der diese Bezeichnung verdient." [6] Doch mit den Augen der Künstler:innen in *The New African Portraiture* sehen wir, dass genau das Gegenteil zutrifft. In der Souveränität und Kultiviertheit, die ihre Bilder zeigen, sehen wir einen Kontinent und seine Völker, deren gemeinsame Erfahrungen aus den Handelsströmen und dem migrantischen Austausch, erzwungen wie freiwillig, entstanden sind, die den Kontinent über Hunderte von Jahren geprägt haben. Afrikanisch zu sein bedeutet, so der Literaturwissenschaftler Simon Gikandi, „mit afrikanischen Gemeinschaften, Nationen und Traditionen in Verbindung zu sein; es bedeutet aber auch, ein Leben zwischen Kulturen, Sprachen und Staaten zu führen. Es bedeutet, einen Zustand kultureller Hybridität anzunehmen und zu zelebrieren – aus Afrika und gleichzeitig aus anderen Welten zu sein." [7]

WAS IST DAS NEUE?

Ab den späten 1950er-Jahren löste eine Welle von Unabhängigkeits- und Befreiungsbewegungen eine politische und soziale Neuordnung auf dem gesamten Kontinent aus. Es war die Ära von Selbstbestimmungsbewegungen wie *Negritude*, *Panafrikanismus* und *arabischer Nationalismus*; eine Zeit, in der eine Nation nach der anderen Freiheit von kolonialer Herrschaft erlangte und auch der lange, harte Freiheitskampf in Südafrika mit dem Ende der Apartheid 1994 schließlich zum Erfolg führte.

for a tremendous blossoming of activity across the arts. Against the new terrain of self-rule an array of extraordinarily talented figures such as photographers Malick Sidibé and Samuel Fosso, writers Aimé Césaire and Chinua Achebe, and the musician Fela Kuti created works in which they grappled with "the complex drama of their postcolonial subjectivities." [8] In visual arts, painters and sculptors experimented with a variety of approaches, from Enwonwu's pursuit of figuration to Ernest Mancoba's embrace of abstraction, as they too tested the creative parameters of Africa's "short century." [9]

Today, as a further raft of prodigiously accomplished creative figures comes to the fore, another great era of African cultural flourishing appears to be taking shape.
Here we can cite the likes of global music stars Burna Boy, Davido, and Wizkid, actors and directors such as Lupita Nyong'o and Mati Diop, fashion designers Imane Ayissi and Thebe Magugu, and the lauded architects Sir David Adjaye OBE and Francis Kéré, winner of the 2022 Pritzker Architecture Prize. It is also relevant to note that in 2021, the world's three foremost literary awards, the Nobel Prize in Literature, the Booker Prize, and the Prix Goncourt, all went to African writers: Abdulrazak Gurnah, Damon Galgut, and Mohamed Mbougar Sarr. As the media network *TRACE Africa* recently proclaimed, "the African creative renaissance is NOW." It is within this milieu of stellar accomplishments that a generational wave of contemporary artists is rising to prominence. Their ascent has been aided by a developing infrastructure of exhibition platforms, biennials, residencies, and galleries taking shape on the continent. Outside of major new institutions, such as Togo's Palais de Lomé and Dakar's Museum of Black Civilizations, state support for visual art in Africa remains scant. As a consequence, it is non-for-profit organizations such as Accra's Nubuke Foundation; the Norval Foundation and A4 Arts Foundation in Cape Town; the Raw Material Company in Dakar; and the Centre for Contemporary Art, Lagos, founded by the late pioneering curator Bisi Silva, that are making much of the headway by offering space for contemporary artists to be inventive and experimental outside the boundaries

Energie und Optimismus dieser Ära wirkten auch als Katalysatoren für ein ungeheures Aufblühen der Aktivitäten in allen Künsten. Auf dem neuen Terrain der politischen Selbstbestimmung schufen außergewöhnlich talentierte Persönlichkeiten wie die Fotografen Malick Sidibé und Samuel Fosso, die Schriftsteller Aimé Césaire und Chinua Achebe und der Musiker Fela Kuti Werke, in denen sie sich mit dem „komplexen Drama ihrer postkolonialen Subjektivität" [8] auseinandersetzten. In den bildenden Künsten experimentierten Maler:innen und Bildhauer:innen mit einer Vielzahl von Ansätzen, von Enwonwus Beschäftigung mit der Figuration bis zu Ernest Mancobas Hinwendung zur Abstraktion, während auch sie die schöpferischen Parameter von Afrikas „kurzem Jahrhundert" [9] auf die Probe stellten.

Heute, da eine weitere Riege bereits erstaunlich vollendeter kreativer Persönlichkeiten in den Vordergrund tritt, scheint sich neuerlich eine Ära afrikanischer kultureller Blüte abzuzeichnen.
Hier lassen sich globale Musikstars wie Burna Boy, Davido und Wizkid ebenso nennen wie Schauspieler:innen und Regisseur:innen wie Lupita Nyong'o und Mati Diop, die Modedesigner Imane Ayissi and Thebe Magugu und die gefeierten Architekten Sir David Adjaye OBE und Francis Kéré, der Gewinner des Pritzker-Architekturpreises 2022. Erwähnenswert ist auch, dass die drei bedeutendsten Literaturpreise der Welt, der Nobelpreis für Literatur, der Booker-Preis und der Prix Goncourt, 2021 allesamt an afrikanische Schriftsteller gingen: Abdulrazak Gurnah, Damon Galgut und Mohamed Mbougar Sarr. Wie das Mediennetzwerk *TRACE Africa* unlängst proklamierte: „Afrikas kreative Renaissance ist JETZT!" In diesem Milieu fulminanter Leistungen steigt eine neue Generation zeitgenössischer Künstler:innen zu Bekanntheit auf. Ihr Aufstieg wurde unterstützt durch eine sich entwickelnde Infrastruktur von Ausstellungsplattformen, Biennalen, Residency-Programmen und Galerien, die auf dem afrikanischen Kontinent Gestalt annimmt. Abseits großer neuer Institutionen wie dem Palais de Lomé in Togo oder dem Musée des civilisations noires in Dakar bleibt die staatliche Unterstützung für bildende Künste in Afrika dürftig. Infolgedessen sind es Non-Profit-Organisationen wie die Nubuke Foundation in Accra, die Norval Foundation und die A4 Arts Foundation in Kapstadt, die Raw Material Company in Dakar sowie das von dem mittlerweile verstorbenen kuratorischen Pionier Bisi Silva gegründete Centre for Contemporary Art in Lagos, die Fortschritt möglich machen, indem sie zeitgenössischen Künstler:innen Räume für Innovation und Experimente außerhalb des kommerziellen Galeriebetriebes zur

of the commercial-gallery sector. The most notable development in recent years has been the opening of a number of new sites by leading artists from Africa and the diaspora. These include Kehinde Wiley's artist residency program Black Rock Senegal; Yinka Shonibare CBE's cultural center, Guest Artists Space Foundation, in Lagos; Michael Armitage's Kenya-based art space, Nairobi Contemporary Art Institute; and Ibrahim Mahama's ambitious network of buildings and projects spread across a vast acreage in Tamale, northern Ghana, including the Savannah Centre for Contemporary Art and the Red Clay studio complex.

The artists in *The New African Portraiture* are drawn primarily from East and West Africa, the UK, and the US. Bringing together such a diverse group under the designation of "the new" raises some questions: In which way are these artists breaking fresh ground? And by which criteria are they categorized as *new*?

In a 2021 column in *The Art Newspaper*, writer Chibundu Onuzo argues that "whenever a Black artist breaks through, their 'newness' is often highlighted. There's an emphasis on 'discovery' and the 'discoverer' is often from outside the community of said Black artist. The discoverer has never seen anything like it and so therefore, nothing like this has ever been created before."[10] Onuzo's observation returns us to the long strand of hostility towards African culture that runs through Western art history.

African masks and statues started to reach Europe from Africa in the 1870s and 1880s, congruent with the expansion of the colonial presence on the continent. Displayed in ethnographic museums without individual attribution to their makers, African works were treated as "vulgar curios justifying 'civilizing' colonial missions on the continent."[11] The disdain with which such objects were treated, and the decision to categorize them as the work of anonymous tribal craftspeople, had its origins in colonial ideology. The scholar Olu Oguibe states that it was the policy of colonial authorities in

Verfügung stellen. Die bemerkenswerteste Entwicklung der letzten Jahre aber war die Eröffnung einer Reihe neuer Orte für die Kunst durch führende Künstler:innen aus Afrika und der Diaspora. Dazu zählen das von Kehinde Wiley begründete Residency-Programm Black Rock Senegal, das von Yinka Shonibare CBE ins Leben gerufene Kulturzentrum Guest Artists Space Foundation in Lagos, das Nairobi Contemporary Art Institute, ein von Michael Armitage gegründetes Kunstzentrum in Kenia, sowie Ibrahim Mahamas ambitioniertes, über eine riesige Fläche in Tamale in Nordghana sich ausbreitendes Netzwerk von Gebäuden und Projekten, darunter das Savannah Centre for Contemporary Art und der Atelierkomplex Red Clay.

Die in *The New African Portraiture* gezeigten Künstler:innen kommen vor allem aus Ost- und Westafrika, aus dem Vereinigten Königreich und den USA. Eine derart heterogene Gruppe unter der Bezeichnung des „Neuen" zu versammeln, wirft einige Fragen auf: In welcher Hinsicht betreten diese Künstler:innen Neuland? Und anhand welcher Kriterien kann man sie überhaupt als *neu* bezeichnen?

In einer Kolumne in *The Art Newspaper* stellt die Schriftstellerin Chibundu Onuzo 2021 fest, dass, „wann immer Schwarze Künstler:innen den Durchbruch schaffen, meist ihre ‚Neuheit' hervorgehoben wird. Die Betonung liegt auf ‚Entdeckung', und die ‚Entdeckenden' sind häufig von außerhalb der Community besagter Schwarzer Künstler:innen. Die Entdeckenden haben so etwas noch nie zuvor gesehen, und also wurde so etwas auch noch nie zuvor geschaffen."[10] Onuzos Beobachtung führt uns zurück zu dem langen Strang der Feindseligkeit gegenüber der afrikanischen Kultur, der sich durch die die westliche Kunstgeschichte zieht.

Afrikanische Masken und Statuen gelangten ab den 1870er- und 1880er-Jahren von Afrika nach Europa, zeitgleich mit der Ausweitung der kolonialen Präsenz auf dem Kontinent. In völkerkundlichen Museen wurden Werke aus Afrika ohne Nennung ihrer Schöpfer:innen ausgestellt und als „volkstümliche Kuriosa" behandelt, die „‚zivilisierende' koloniale Missionen auf dem Kontinent rechtfertigten".[11] Die Geringschätzung, die diesen Objekten entgegengebracht wurde, und die Entscheidung, sie als das Werk anonymer „Stammes"-Handwerker:innen zu kategorisieren, hatte ihren Ursprung in der kolonialen Ideologie. Der Wissenschaftler Olu Oguibe konstatiert, dass es die Politik der Kolonialbehörden in Westafrika war, Kunst-

West Africa to discourage the teaching of art and to deprecate indigenous artistic traditions. In late nineteenth-century Ghana, locally created art objects were seized by the ton and destroyed in bonfires. "The deracination of material cultures among the colonized on the one hand, and the prohibition of access to Western art or schooling on the other, provided perfect conditions for the manufacture of the...utilitarian craftsman with no traditions of great art and no access to Imperial Enlightenment."[12]

The so-called discovery of African art at the turn of the century by Picasso and the Fauves did little to fundamentally alter perceptions. The cultural borrowings sparked by modernism's engagement with African art produced exhilarating works like *Les Demoiselles d'Avignon* (1907). But even as the European avant-garde thrilled at its encounter with l'art negre, its view of African culture remained rooted in colonial stereotype. For Picasso, African masks and statues were "magical things"—objects richer in supernatural mystery than artistic virtue. The modernists "embraced a deeply romanticized view of African culture (conflating many cultures into one) and considered Africa the embodiment of humankind in a pre-civilized state, preferring to mystify rather than to examine its presumed idol-worship and violent rituals."[13]

In 1901, the painter Aina Onabolu began producing highly skilled realist portraits of the city's cultural and political elites. He is generally regarded as the earliest artist in West Africa to draw and paint in a modern Western idiom. Initially working without formal training, Onabolu took inspiration from the realist traditions of court art from classical-era Ife, Nigeria. But his obvious facility as an artist was met with skepticism. Onabolu was "actively discouraged and on occasion subtly threatened" by British colonial administrators who refused to believe that an African with no art education could mount such an eloquent challenge to the notion of European cultural superiority.[14]

Despite their opposition, Onabolu prevailed and is hailed today as "the father of modern African art."[15] His ability to turn Ife art practice towards dramatic

unterricht zu unterbinden und einheimische Kunsttraditionen abzuwerten. Im Ghana des späten 19. Jahrhunderts wurden lokal erzeugte Kunstobjekte tonnenweise beschlagnahmt und verbrannt. „Die Ausrottung der materiellen Kulturen der Kolonisierten einerseits und das Verbot des Zugangs zu westlicher Kunst oder Ausbildung andererseits schufen perfekte Bedingungen für die Hervorbringung des [...] nützlichen Handwerkers bar jeder bedeutenden künstlerischen Tradition und ohne Zugang zur imperialen Aufklärung."[12]

Die sogenannte Entdeckung afrikanischer Kunst durch Picasso und die Fauvisten um die Jahrhundertwende trug wenig dazu bei, diese Sichtweise grundsätzlich zu verändern. Die kulturellen Anleihen, die aus der Auseinandersetzung des Modernismus mit der afrikanischen Kunst resultierten, führten zu anregenden Werken wie *Les Demoiselles d'Avignon* (1907). Doch auch wenn die europäische Avantgarde von ihrer Begegnung mit *l'art nègre* elektrisiert war, blieb ihre Sicht auf die afrikanische Kultur in kolonialen Stereotypen verwurzelt. Für Picasso waren afrikanische Masken und Statuen „magische Dinge" – Objekte, die eher von übernatürlichen Geheimnissen denn von künstlerischem Talent zeugten. Die Modernist:innen „machten sich eine zutiefst romantisierte Sicht der afrikanischen Kultur zu eigen (die viele Kulturen zu einer verschmolz) und betrachteten Afrika als Verkörperung der Menschheit in einem vorzivilisierten Zustand; sie zogen es vor, die angenommene Götzenanbetung und gewalttätigen Rituale zu mystifizieren statt zu erforschen."[13]

1901 begann der Maler Aina Onabolu überaus gekonnte realistische Porträts der kulturellen und politischen Eliten der Stadt anzufertigen. Er gilt allgemein als der erste Künstler in Westafrika, der in einem modernen westlichen Idiom zeichnete und malte. Onabulo, der anfänglich ohne formale Ausbildung arbeitete, bezog seine Inspiration aus den realistischen Traditionen der höfischen Kunst im Ile-Ife der klassischen Ära in Nigeria. Seine offensichtliche künstlerische Begabung stieß jedoch auf Skepsis. Onabulo wurde von britischen Kolonialbeamten „aktiv entmutigt und gelegentlich auch subtil bedroht"; diese weigerten sich zu glauben, dass ein Afrikaner ohne künstlerische Ausbildung die Vorstellung der europäischen kulturellen Überlegenheit so beredt infrage stellen könnte.[14]

Ungeachtet ihres Widerstandes setzte Onabolu sich durch und wird heute als „Vater der modernen afrikanischen Kunst"[15] gefeiert. Seine Fähigkeit, mit künstlerischen Praktiken von Ife

new ends is a striking reminder of how innovation does not necessarily emerge from a fundamental split with tradition. Following a similar logic, we may say that the *new* in *The New African Portraiture* does not imply a radical break with the past. Instead, its use invites recognition of the dazzling facility with which African contemporary artists are continually reinventing the continent's legacy of figuration.

Consider some of the different approaches to picture-making employed by the exhibition's artists. For example, paintings by Boluwatife Oyediran and Bouvy Enkobo offer a reckoning with the overlooked and under-regarded role of the Black figure in Western art history. Where the likes of Manet, Cézanne, and Géricault have featured Black people in their paintings they have done so while omitting their names and personal stories from the record, robbing them of agency and reducing them to an exotic "other." In riposte, Oyediran and Enkobo reimagine the art-historical canon to situate the Black figure at its center. Enkobo's *Mabele Mokonzi/Marat* (2022) depicts the assassination of Congolese president Laurent Kabila by way of David's *The Death of Marat* (1793). And Oyediran revisits Manet's *Olympia* (1863), foregrounding Black presence in contrast to the original painting, where the Black servant Laure occupies an "invisible, ignored" position in the picture.[16] Oyediran sets his now-centrally located female figure against a backdrop both sumptuous and strange, and has her attended to by a maid who looks disquietingly alien—a commentary perhaps on how Laure might have been regarded by Manet's audience in nineteenth-century Paris.

Other artists take portraiture in a different direction. Boafo and Eric Adjei Tawiah offer reflection on the nature of Black cultural identity by way of the non-naturalistic skin tones of the subjects in their paintings. Instead of using a brush, Boafo paints with his fingers conjuring figures out of a thick, swirling impasto of browns and blues. The non-realist, hyper-stylized approach to skin color taken by the artists prompts a reminder that the concept of "race" is itself an artificial conceit, albeit one that maintains a determining sway

neue dramatische Ergebnisse zu erzielen, ist eine eindrückliche Erinnerung daran, dass Innovation nicht notwendigerweise aus einer fundamentalen Abkehr von der Tradition entsteht. Einer ähnlichen Logik folgend, können wir sagen, dass das *Neue* in *The New African Portraiture* keinen radikalen Bruch mit der Vergangenheit impliziert. Stattdessen lädt die Wortwahl dazu ein, die verblüffende Leichtigkeit anzuerkennen, mit der zeitgenössische afrikanische Künstler:innen das figurative Erbe des Kontinents beständig neu erfinden.

Man denke nur an die unterschiedlichen Ansätze, die die Künstler:innen der Ausstellung in der Bilderstellung verfolgen. So ist die Malerei von Boluwatife Oyediran und Bouvy Enkobo eine Abrechnung mit der übersehenen und zu wenig beachteten Rolle der Schwarzen Figur in der westlichen Kunstgeschichte. Wo Künstler:innen wie Manet, Cézanne und Géricault in ihren Bildern People of Color darstellten, taten sie es unter Weglassung von deren Namen und persönlichen Geschichten, was sie ihrer Handlungsmacht beraubte und auf das exotische „Andere" reduzierte. Im Gegenzug denken Oyediran und Enkobo den kunstgeschichtlichen Kanon neu und rücken die Schwarze Figur in den Mittelpunkt. Enkobos *Mabele Mokonzi/Marat* (2022) stellt die Ermordung des kongolesischen Präsidenten Laurent Kabila in der Art von Davids *Tod des Marat* (1793) dar. Und Oyediran kehrt zu Manets *Olympia* (1863) zurück, stellt aber die Person of Color in den Vordergrund, im Gegensatz zum Originalgemälde, in dem die Schwarze Zofe Laure eine „unsichtbare, unbeachtete" Position einnimmt.[16] Oyediran stellt seine nunmehr ins Zentrum gerückte Frauenfigur vor einen Hintergrund, der zugleich luxuriös und ungewöhnlich ist, und zeigt, wie sie von einem Dienstmädchen bedient wird, das beunruhigend fremd wirkt – vielleicht ein Kommentar dazu, wie Laure von Manets Publikum im Paris des 19. Jahrhunderts möglicherweise gesehen wurde.

Andere Künstler:innen führen die Porträtkunst in eine andere Richtung. Boafo und Eric Adjei Tawiah bieten durch die nichtnaturalistischen Hauttöne der in ihren Bildern Dargestellten eine Reflexion über das Wesen Schwarzer kultureller Identität. Tawiahs Figuren sind beunruhigend blau. Anstatt mit dem Pinsel malt Boafo mit den Fingern und zaubert Figuren aus dicken pastosen Wirbeln von Braun- und Blautönen. Der nichtrealistische, hyperstilisierte Umgang dieser Künstler mit Hautfarbe ruft in Erinnerung, dass das Konzept „Race" an sich künstlich und eine Fiktion ist, wenn auch eine, die – insbesondere im englischsprachigen Raum – gängige Auffassungen

over popular perceptions of the world. Their paintings ask, how might the Black body be imagined if we surrender the notion that the term *Black* represents anything other than a socially constructed fiction? Or to put it another way, what might it mean to be African without a history of being othered? Without the history of the colonial gaze? What does it look like to be free?

The earliest works in *The New African Portraiture* are paintings by Everlyn Nicodemus, primarily from her "Wedding" series (1991/92). Here we see a further iteration of the possibilities of figuration—in this case as a forum to revisit, in intensely personal terms, the consequences of the West's caricaturing of Africa and its people as irredeemably primitive. The "Wedding" series depicts a female form, rendered in black with a blank face, in varying states of duress. One painting shows the figure struggling across a red floor, legs writhing and her arm reaching up forlornly for help that does not seem to be forthcoming. In another we see her with arms stretched out in a pose reminiscent of the crucifixion. *The Wedding No. 58* (1992, cat. p. 87), shows the figure posing for a portrait, dressed in colorful, patterned clothing and for once her facial features are visible. But her gaze is turned away from the viewer and her fingers are knitted together in what might be an indication of her anxiety. Nicodemus was born in Tanzania in 1954 and spent many years moving across Europe, living in Sweden, France, and Belgium, before eventually settling in Scotland in 2008. Her years of emigration were fraught. Arriving in Sweden in 1973, she encountered racism for the first time and to her shock was treated as though she was "savage and uncivilized."[17] In France, the decapitated carcass of a black cat was dumped on her doorstep. Local youths, their faces painted black, blew trumpets and banged drums outside her house. After years of harassment, she suffered a breakdown and came close to dying. Two years later she began the set of large-scale self-portraits that became the eighty-four works of the "Wedding" series. Centered on her own body, the paintings chart her pain, despair and "desperate fight" with death.[18] Despite the trauma it depicts, the series is also a testament to her hard-won recovery. It is figuration as a form of healing. As Nicodemus describes it, it is a "painted ballad" that honors her "return to the space of life and…restored Self."[19]

der Welt noch immer maßgeblich beeinflusst. Ihre Bilder fragen, wie der Schwarze Körper sich vorstellen ließe, wenn wir die Idee aufgeben, dass das der Begriff *Schwarz* für irgendetwas anderes steht als eine sozial konstruierte Fiktion. Oder, anders gefragt: Was könnte es bedeuten, afrikanisch zu sein ohne eine Geschichte der Andersheit? Ohne die Geschichte des kolonialen Blicks? Wie sieht es aus, frei zu sein?

Die frühesten Werke in *The New African Portraiture* sind Bilder von Everlyn Nicodemus, hauptsächlich aus ihrer Serie „Wedding" (1991/92). Hier sehen wir eine weitere Spielart der Möglichkeiten der Figuration – in diesem Fall als ein Schau-Platz, um auf sehr persönliche Weise die Konsequenzen der westlichen Karikatur Afrikas und seiner Bevölkerung als hoffnungslos primitiv zu reflektieren. Die „Wedding"-Serie zeigt eine in Schwarz und mit leerem Gesicht wiedergegebene weibliche Gestalt in verschiedenen Zwangslagen. Eine Bild zeigt die Figur, wie sie sich über einen roten Boden vorankämpft, die Beine verkrümmt, die Arme verzweifelt nach Hilfe ausgestreckt, die nicht zu kommen scheint. Ein andermal sehen wir sie mit ausgebreiteten Armen in einer Pose, die an eine Kreuzigung erinnert. *The Wedding No. 58* (1992, Kat. S. 87) zeigt die Figur für ein Porträt posierend, in bunten gemusterten Kleidern, und erstmals sind auch ihre Gesichtszüge auszumachen. Ihr Blick ist jedoch von den Betrachter:innen abgewandt, und ihre Finger sind ineinander verknotet, was ein Hinweis auf ihre Ängste sein könnte. Nicodemus wurde 1954 in Tansania geboren und zog viele Jahre lang durch Europa, lebte in Schweden, Frankreich und Belgien, ehe sie sich 2008 in Schottland niederließ. Die Jahre in der Emigration waren belastend. Als sie 1973 in Schweden eintraf, begegnete sie zum ersten Mal Rassismus und wurde, ein Schock für sie, behandelt, als wäre sie „eine unzivilisierte Wilde".[17] In Frankreich wurde ihr der enthauptete Kadaver eine schwarze Katze vor die Tür gelegt. Jugendliche aus der Gegend randalierten mit schwarz bemalten Gesichtern mit Tröten und Trommeln vor ihrem Haus. Nach Jahren der Schikanen erlitt sie einen Zusammenbruch und war dem Tode nahe. Zwei Jahre später begann sie eine Reihe großformatiger Selbstporträts, aus denen die 84 Werke der „Wedding"-Serie wurden. Auf ihren eigenen Körper zentriert, erfassen die Bilder ihren Schmerz und ihren „verzweifelten Kampf" mit dem Tod.[18] Trotz des Traumas, das sie zu Bild bringt, ist die Serie auch ein Zeugnis ihrer mühsam errungenen Genesung. Es ist Figuration als eine Form der Heilung. Es ist, wie Nicodemus es beschreibt, eine „gemalte Ballade" zu Ehren ihrer „Rückkehr in den Raum des Lebens und […] zu einem wiederhergestellten Selbst."[19]

Durch die Vielfalt der Ansätze, die in *The New African Portraiture* erkundet werden, sehen wir die gelebte Erfahrung

Through the range of approaches explored in *The New African Portraiture* we see the lived experience of African cultural identity on the continent and across the diaspora, as a tableau of possibilities. The *new* in this context doesn't connote novelty. But rather the capacity to imagine *anew* the hybrid complexity of the African condition. As the paintings in the exhibition remind us, to culturally belong to Africa is to be of peoples, and of places, and of the world, all at once, with all the myriad hope, wonder, struggle against adversity and capacity for beauty inherent to that proposition.

1 Exhibition guide to *Radical Figures: Painting in the New Millennium*, Whitechapel Gallery, February 6–August 30, 2020.
2 Edwin Bodjawah et al., "Transforming Art from Commodity to Gift: kąrî'kạchä seid'ou's Silent Revolution in the Kumasi College of Art," *African Arts* 54, no. 2 (2021): 22–35.
3 Tesfaye Urgessa, "No Country For Young Men 2", ArtsandCulture.Google.com, https://artsandculture.google.com/asset/no-country-for-young-men-2-tesfaye-urgessa/4QG7e_ziWxFVYQ?hl=en.
4 Salah M. Hassan, "African Modernism: Beyond Alternative Modernities Discourse," *South Atlantic Quarterly* 109, no. 3 (July 1, 2010): 451–73.
5 Ronald Kuykendall, "Hegel and Africa: An Evaluation of the Treatment of Africa in the Philosophy of History," *Journal of Black Studies* 23, no. 4 (1993): 571–81.
6 Hugh Clifford in Olu Oguibe, "Appropriation as Nationalism in Modern African Art," *Third Text* 16, no. 3 (2002): 243–59.
7 Salah M. Hassan, "Contemporary African Art as a Paradox: Is 'Afropolitan' the Answer?" *Nka*, no. 46 (May 1, 2020): 8–26.
8 Chika Okeke-Agulu, "Postcolonial Modernism: Art and Decolonization," in *Twentieth-Century Nigeria* (Duke University Press, 2015), 15.
9 This term was coined by curator Okwui Enwezor for his landmark survey exhibition *The Short Century: Independence and Liberation Movements in Africa 1945–1994*, which toured venues in Germany and the US between February 15, 2001 and May 5, 2002.
10 Chibundu Onuzo, "Why Black Contemporary Artists Shouldn't Just Be Shown Through a Western Lens," *The Art Newspaper*, November 12, 2021, https://www.theartnewspaper.com/2021/11/12/why-black-contemporary-artists-shouldnt-just-be-shown-through-a-western-lens.
11 Joshua I Cohen, *The Black Art Renaissance: African Sculpture and Modernism across Continents* (University of California Press, 2020), 4.
12 Olu Oguibe, "Appropriation."
13 Patricia Leighten, "The White Peril and L'Art Nègre: Picasso, Primitivism, and Anticolonialism," *The Art Bulletin* 72, no. 4 (1990): 609–30.
14 Olu Oguibe, "Appropriation."
15 Everlyn Nicodemus, "The Black Atlantic: And the Paradigm Shift to Modern Art in Africa," *Critical Interventions* 2, nos. 3–4 (2008): 7–20.
16 Hilarie M. Sheets, "New Attention for Figures in the Background," *New York Times*, October 28, 2018, F2.
17 Lanre Bakare, "'They told me I was a savage'—The Unstoppable Painter Everlyn Nicodemus," *The Guardian*, April 19, 2022, https://www.theguardian.com/artanddesign/2022/apr/19/savage-unstoppable-painter-everlyn-nicodemus-kilimanjaro-defiance-richard-saltoun.
18 Everlyn Nicodemus, "'Modernity as a Mad Dog': On Art and Trauma," in *Over Here: International Perspectives on Art and Culture*, eds. Jean Fisher and Gerardo Mosquera (Cambridge: MIT Press, 2004), 258–77.
19 Nicodemus, "'Modernity.'"

afrikanischer kultureller Identität auf dem Kontinent und in der Diaspora als ein Tableau von Möglichkeiten. Das *neu* bedeutet in diesem Kontext nicht Novität. Vielmehr die Fähigkeit, die hybride Komplexität des Afrikanischseins *neu* zu imaginieren. Wie die Bilder in der Ausstellung uns in Erinnerung rufen, heißt kulturelle Zugehörigkeit zu Afrika, zugleich Völkern, Orten und der Welt anzugehören, mit all den unzähligen Hoffnungen, dem Staunen, dem Kampf gegen Widrigkeiten und der Fähigkeit zu Schönheit, die diesem Gedanken innewohnen.

1 Ausstellungsführer zu *Radical Figures. Painting in the New Millennium*, Whitechapel Gallery, 06.02.–30.08.2020.
2 Edwin Bodjawah u. a., „Transforming Art from Commodity to Gift. kąrî'kạchä seid'ou's Silent Revolution in the Kumasi College of Art", in: *African Arts* 54, Nr. 2 (2021), S. 22–35.
3 Tesfaye Urgessa, „No Country For Young Men 2", in: ArtsandCulture.Google.com, https://artsandculture.google.com/asset/no-country-for-young-men-2-tesfaye-urgessa/4QG7e_ziWxFVYQ?hl=en.
4 Salah M. Hassan, „African Modernism: Beyond Alternative Modernities Discourse", in: *South Atlantic Quarterly* 109, Nr. 3 (01.07.2010), S. 451–473.
5 Georg Friedrich Wilhelm Hegel, *Vorlesungen über die Philosophie der Geschichte*, Frankfurt a. M. 1986, S. 120, 122.
6 Hugh Clifford zit. nach Olu Oguibe „Appropriation as Nationalism in Modern African Art", in: *Third Text* 16, Nr. 3 (2002), S. 243–259.
7 Salah M. Hassan, „Contemporary African Art as a Paradox. Is ‚Afropolitan' the Answer?", in: *Nka*, Nr. 46 (01. 05. 2020), S. 8–26.
8 Chika Okeke-Agulu, „Postcolonial Modernism. Art and Decolonization", in *Twentieth-Century Nigeria*, Durham, NC, 2015, S. 15.
9 Der Begriff wurde vom Kurator Okwui Enwezor für seine exemplarische Überblicksausstellung *The Short Century. Independence and Liberation Movements in Africa 1945–1994* geprägt, die zwischen 15. Februar 2001 und 5. Mai 2002 Stationen in Deutschland und den USA bereiste.
10 Chibundu Onuzo, „Why Black Contemporary Artists Shouldn't Just Be Shown Through a Western Lens", in: *The Art Newspaper* (12. 11. 2021), https://www.theartnewspaper.com/2021/11/12/why-black-contemporary-artists-shouldnt-just-be-shown-through-a-western-lens.
11 Joshua I. Cohen, *The Black Art Renaissance. African Sculpture and Modernism across Continents*, Berkeley, CA, 2020, S. 4.
12 Olu Oguibe, „Appropriation".
13 Patricia Leighten, „The White Peril and L'Art Nègre. Picasso, Primitivism, and Anticolonialism", in: *The Art Bulletin* 72, Nr. 4 (1990), S. 609–630.
14 Olu Oguibe, „Appropriation".
15 Everlyn Nicodemus, „The Black Atlantic. And the Paradigm Shift to Modern Art in Africa", in: *Critical Interventions* 2, Nr. 3–4 (2008), S. 7–20.
16 Hilarie M. Sheets, „New Attention for Figures in the Background", in: *New York Times* (28. 10 .2018), Section F, S. 2.
17 Lanre Bakare, „They told me I was a savage' – The Unstoppable Painter Everlyn Nicodemus", in: *The Guardian* (19. 04 .2022), https://www.theguardian.com/artanddesign/2022/apr/19/savage-unstoppable-painter-everlyn-nicodemus-kilimanjaro-defiance-richard-saltoun.
18 Everlyn Nicodemus, „‚Modernity as a Mad Dog'. On Art and Trauma", in: Jean Fisher/Gerardo Mosquera (Hg.), *Over Here. International Perspectives on Art and Culture*, Cambridge, MA, 2004, S. 258–277.
19 Nicodemus, „‚Modernity.'"

PORTRAITS

AMOAKO BOAFO

Artist Kennedy Yanko peers out of the painting (2021) with a distant look in her eyes. The red of her lips matches the lacrimal caruncles in the inner corners of her eyes, her head tilted slightly to one side against a white background. Her skin has been modeled by the painter's fingers, shaped by the artist's physique. In a manner recalling Yanko's own sculptures that are formed and pressed using her hands, the painter Amoako Boafo (b. 1984 in Accra, Ghana) recreates the sculptor on canvas with his fingers and hands.

Just as Alberto Giacometti created his faces from layers of accumulated paint and, in Jean-Paul Sartre's view, surrounded his painted figures with a void like a sculptor,[1] Boafo creates his three-dimensionally modeled figures like sculptures enveloped by space. Whereas Giacometti sought to reproduce closeness and distance in the tension between sculpture and painting, Boafo distinctly explores the physical proximity to his protagonists, literally feeling their faces and hands like a sculptor. Like a synthesis of Kazuo Shiraga's bodily actions and Jennifer Packer's color formations, Boafo uses his own physique in the form of his fingertips to apply and take away paint in forming facial and body structures. He always focuses on the face as a conveyor of expression and on the gestures of the hands as a means of communication. And comparable to Barkley L. Hendricks, Boafo places his subjects in a kind of neutral blue box, surrounded by the emptiness of a seemingly interchangeable background, with the focus always on the figure. Accordingly, there is something timeless about his portraits, as with *Kennedy*, who is modeled out of the white background like a bust, her likeness and shoulders seemingly emerging from the nothingness of the background. Boafo's figures also reference our time and its fashions through the posture of their bodies and heads as well as their clothing, as in *Untitled* from 2019, in which Boafo reveals a clothing style that is trendy today. His characters, acquaintances and friends, are cool and self-confident. In his most recent works, the artist has expanded his repertoire by copying wallpaper ornaments onto canvas, transforming the body covered in garments into pure, flat land. With his unique artistic technique, Boafo creates contemporary portraits combining the present with an eye toward the future.

1 See Jean-Paul Sartre, "Die Gemälde Giacomettis" (1954), in Sartre, *Die Suche nach dem Absoluten. Texte zur bildenden Kunst* (Reinbek bei Hamburg, 1999), 28.

Mit fernem Blick schaut die Künstlerin Kennedy Yanko aus dem Gemälde (2021). Das Rot ihrer Lippen ist mit den Tränenkarunkeln in den inneren Augenwinkeln farblich verklammert, ihr Kopf vor weißem Hintergrund leicht zur Seite geneigt. Ihre Haut ist mit den Fingern des Malers modelliert, mit der Physis des Künstlers geformt. Vergleichbar mit Yankos eigenen, mit Händen geformten und gequetschten Plastiken, lässt der Maler Amoako Boafo (geb. 1984, Accra, Ghana) die Bildhauerin mit seinen Fingern und Händen auf der Leinwand neu erstehen.

So wie Alberto Giacometti seine Gesichter mit geradezu angehäuften Farblagen gebildet und laut Jean-Paul Sartre seine gemalten Figuren wie ein Bildhauer mit einer Leere umgeben hat,[1] formt Boafo seine plastisch modellierten Figuren gleich einer Skulptur im umgebenden Raum. Doch während Giacometti Nähe und Distanz im Spannungsfeld zwischen Plastik und Malerei wiederzugeben suchte, ergründet Boafo eindeutig die physische Nähe zu seinen Protagonist:innen, erspürt buchstäblich wie ein Bildhauer deren Gesichter und Hände. Gleichsam zur Synthese von Kazuo Shiragas Körpereinsatz und Jennifer Packers Farbkörperbildungen dient Boafo die eigene Physis in Gestalt seiner Fingerkuppen dem Auf- und Abtragen des Farbmaterials zur Bildung von Gesichts- und Körperstrukturen. Dabei fokussiert er stets auf das Gesicht als Ausdrucksträger und auf die Gesten der Hände als Kommunikationsmittel. Und vergleichbar Barkley L. Hendricks stellt Boafo seine Dargestellten in eine Art neutrale Bluebox, die Leere eines scheinbar austauschbaren Hintergrunds, den Fokus stets auf die Figur gerichtet. Dadurch haftet seinen Porträts etwas Zeitloses an, wie bei *Kennedy*, die wie eine Büste aus dem weißen Hintergrund herausmodelliert ist und deren Konterfei und Schultern scheinbar aus dem Nichts des Hintergrunds auftauchen. Auch verweisen Boafos Gestalten sowohl durch ihre Körper- und Kopfhaltung als auch ihre Kleidung auf unsere Zeit und deren Moden, wie in *Untitled* von 2019, wo Boafo einen heute trendigen Kleidungsstil erkennen lässt. Seine Charaktere, Bekannte und Freund:innen, sind cool und selbstbewusst. In neuesten Werken hat der Künstler sein Repertoire durch Abklatsch von Tapetenornamenten auf die Leinwand erweitert, womit er den von Kleidungsstücken bedeckten Körper ins reine Flächenland transformiert. So kreiert Boafo mit seiner einzigartigen künstlerischen Technik zeitgenössische Porträts, in denen er das Heute mit einem Ausblick auf die Zukunft verbindet.

1 Vgl. Jean-Paul Sartre, „Die Gemälde Giacomettis" (1954), in: Ders., *Die Suche nach dem Absoluten. Texte zur bildenden Kunst*, Reinbek bei Hamburg 1999, S. 28.

DIETER BUCHHART

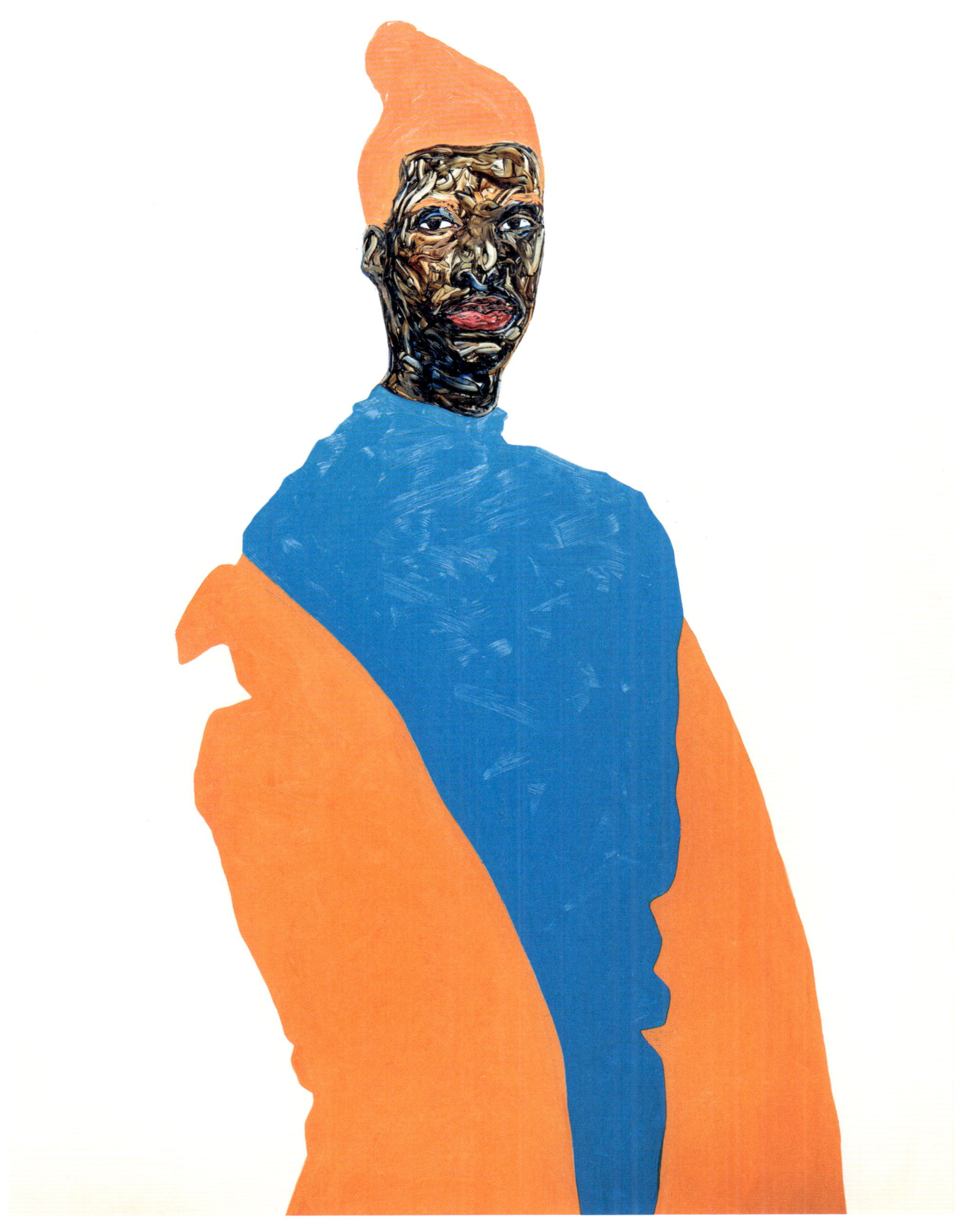

AMOAKO BOAFO
Untitled, 2019
Oil on canvas / Öl auf Leinwand, 206,5 × 155 cm

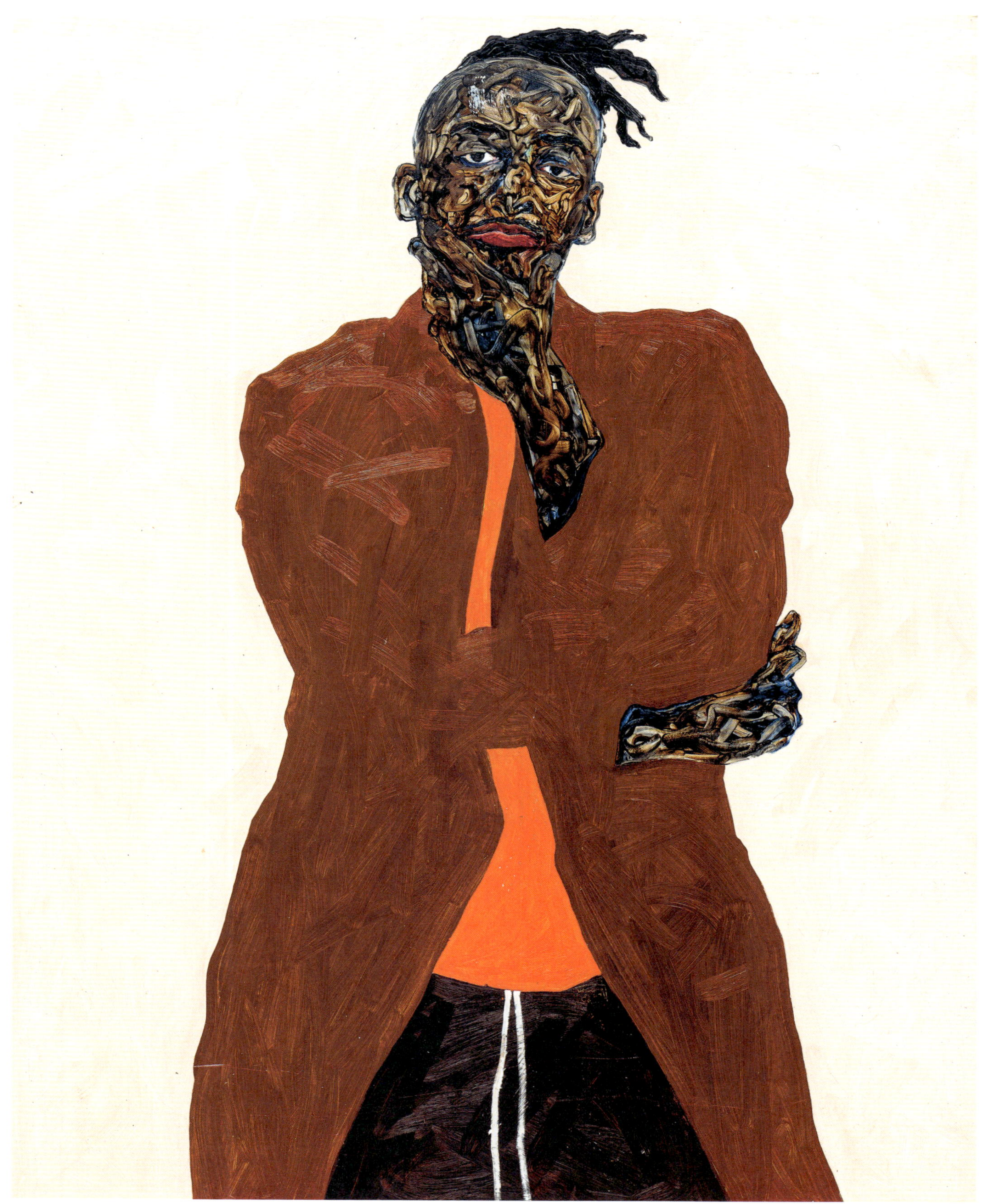

AMOAKO BOAFO
Untitled, 2019
Oil on canvas / Öl auf Leinwand, 195 × 155 cm

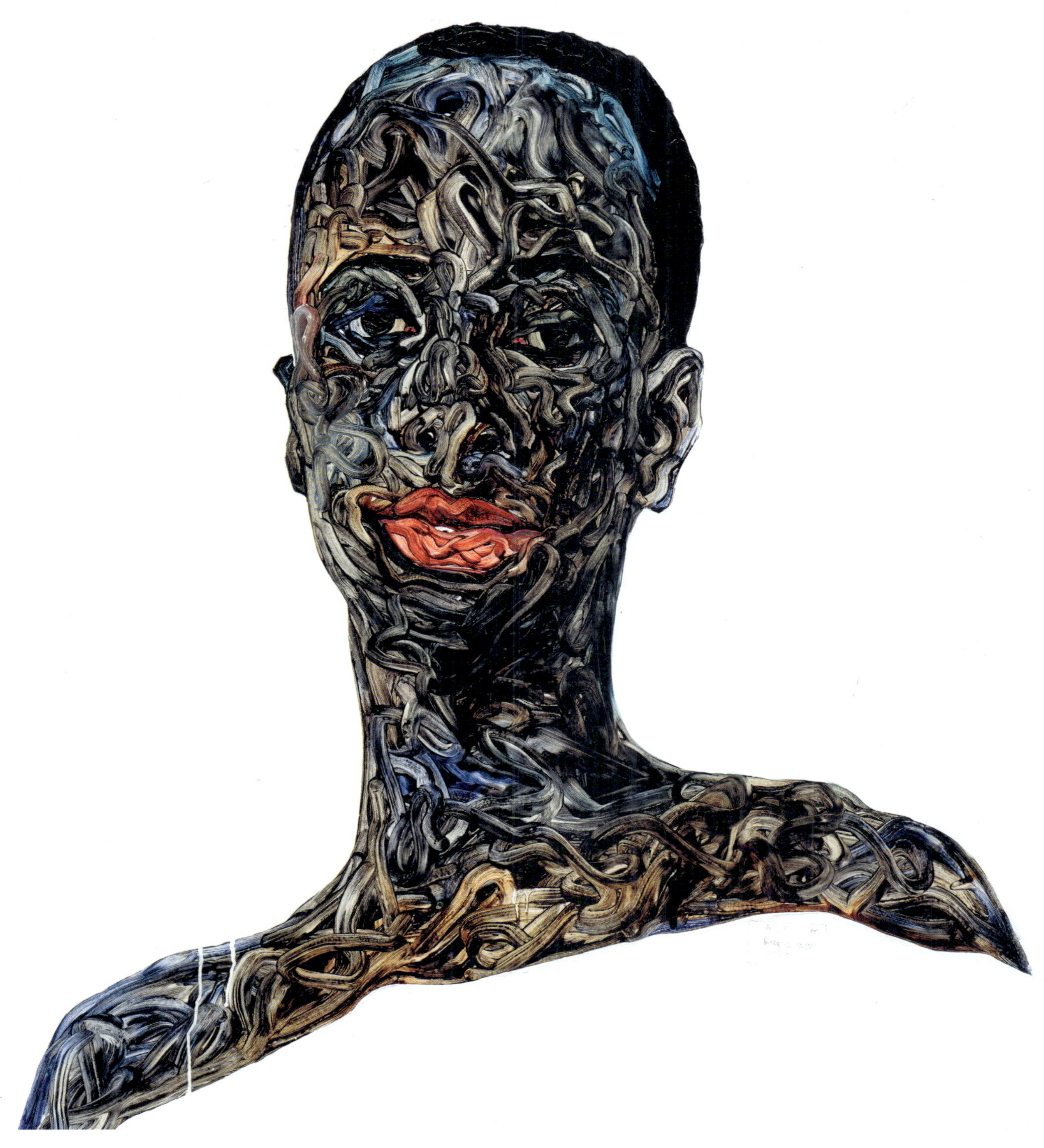

AMOAKO BOAFO
Kennedy, 2021
Oil on canvas / Öl auf Leinwand, 116,6 × 100,5 cm

AMOAKO BOAFO
Windbreaker, 2021
Oil on canvas / Öl auf Leinwand, 161,4 × 116,6 cm

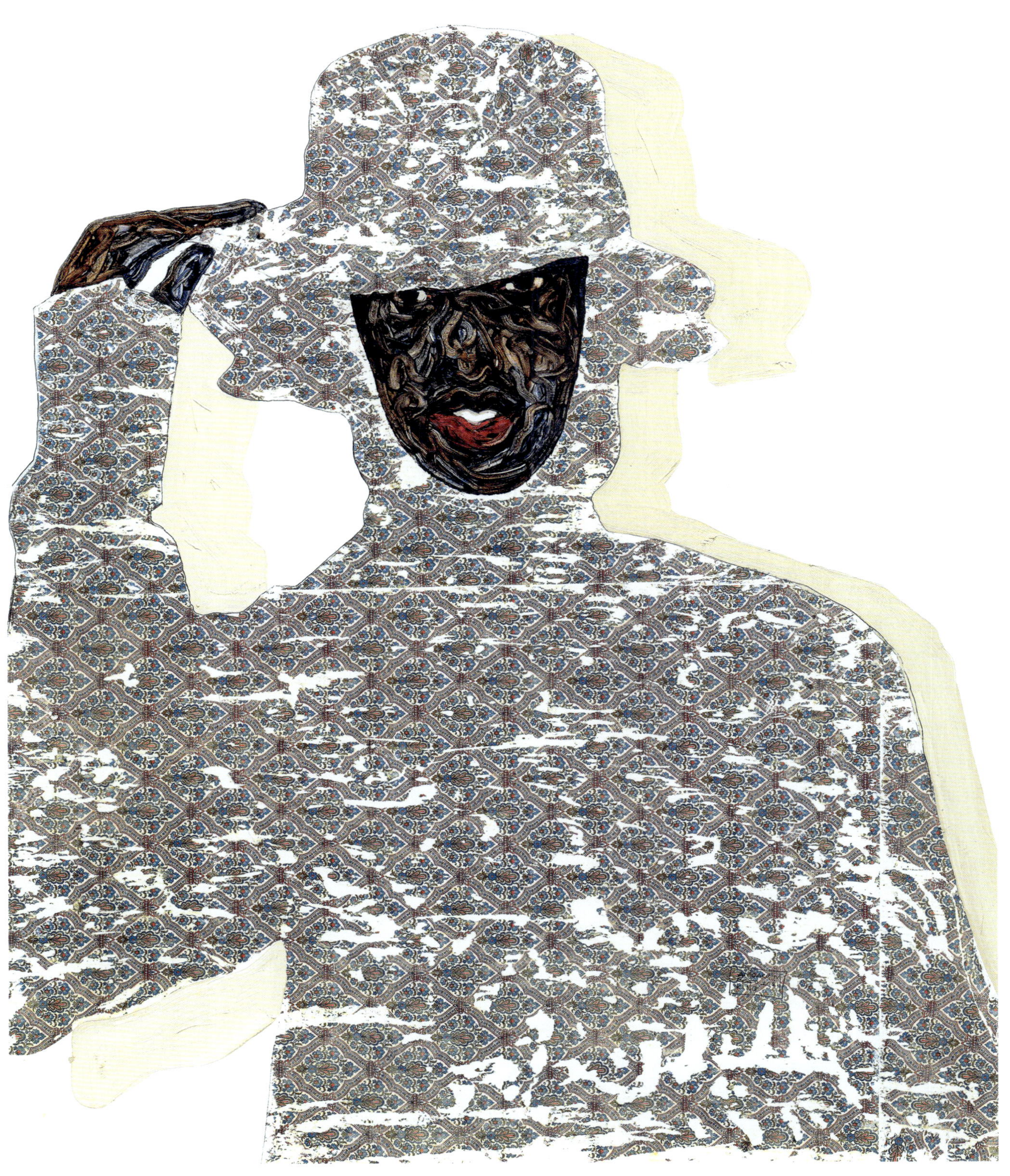

27

APLERH-DOKU BORLABI

Aplerh-Doku Borlabi (b. 1987 in Ghana) was born and raised in the CoCo Beach neighborhood of Accra, immersed in a world of ripe fruit and sparkling beaches. While his early paintings were academic in nature, founded in the compositions he studied at the Ghanatta College of Art and Design, eventually the artist returned to his roots: exploring the culture of his youth, sketching beside the ocean, depicting beach toys and even incorporating the coconut into his mixed-media work.

Seven years into his career, Borlabi has found his voice in works composed of oil paint and coconut husk on canvas. The coconut, by nature, is multifaceted and delicately layered. Its long hairs and varied shades of brown instill his subjects' skin with rich tones rendering the flesh and the muscles with hints of natural light. It is remarkable the effects the artist can achieve from a piece of fruit—leveraging different parts of the ingredient into his works, achieving a captivating effect from a distance and so much texture up close that one cannot help but linger on the large-scale canvas.

In *Red Nike* (2021), a work of coconut sheath and oil paint on canvas, Borlabi captures a female subject sitting comfortably in a bright pink chair, wearing a white bracelet and matching earrings with checkered pants, a floral blouse, and the star of the show: a pair of Nike sneakers that practically jump out of the foreground. The work displays remarkable color density, blending smooth, sleek tones with texturally complex renditions of skin. The woman seated on the chair is elegant and comfortable, multidimensional and proud of her statement Nikes. *Pink Jump Suit* (2021) is similar. Although the female subject gazes off into the distance, resting her head in her hand in contemplation, here again the subject wears colorful clothes: a striped shirt, a checkered hat, and bright pink statement pants that tie the piece together. A deep purple floor and lavender backdrop highlight the artist's use of lively pastel hues to contrast with his subjects' rich brown complexion.

A master of the medium, Borlabi captures the nuances of skin in the majority of his work. *Summer Is Here* (2021), for instance, offers a striking application of the coconut—a catalyst for depicting every pore, line, and detail of the human body. Perhaps most importantly, he finds purpose in an item about which few think twice. Using the coconut sheath, the artist captures the joy and power of Black people in Ghana and around the world.

CHARLES MOORE

Aplerh-Doku Borlabi (geb. 1987, Ghana) ist im Viertel Coco Beach in Accra aufgewachsen, inmitten einer Welt aus reifen Früchten und glitzernden Stränden. Während seine frühen Gemälde in ihrer Art noch akademisch waren und auf Kompositionen basierten, die er am Ghanatta College of Art and Design studiert hatte, kehrte er schließlich zu seinen Wurzeln zurück: Er erkundete die Kultur seiner Jugend, machte Skizzen am Meer, zeichnete Strandspielzeuge und bezog sogar die Kokosnuss in seine Mixed-Media-Arbeiten mit ein.

Nach sieben Jahren fand Borlabi seine Stimme als Künstler mit Kompositionen aus Ölfarben und Kokosnussschalen. Die Kokosnuss ist von Natur aus facettenreich und fein geschichtet. Ihre langen Fäden und unterschiedlichen Braunschattierungen verleihen der Haut der Porträtierten satte Farbtöne und geben Körperlichkeit und Muskeln mit einem Hauch von natürlichem Licht wieder. Die Effekte, die der Künstler mit dieser Frucht erzielen kann, sind bemerkenswert – er verwendet verschiedene Bestandteile und erzielt damit eine fesselnde Fernwirkung und eine derart starke Textur in Nahsicht, dass man sich von der großformatigen Leinwand kaum abwenden mag.

In *Red Nike* (2021), einer Arbeit aus Kokosschale und Ölfarbe auf Leinwand, stellt Borlabi eine Frau dar, die bequem auf einem leuchtend rosa Stuhl sitzt; sie trägt ein weißes Armband mit passenden Ohrringen, eine karierte Hose, eine geblümte Bluse und, der Blickfang der Darbietung, ein Paar Nike-Sneaker, die aus dem Bildvordergrund praktisch herausspringen. Die Arbeit zeigt eine bemerkenswerte Farbdichte, bei der sich sanfte glatte Töne mit komplex strukturierten Hautdarstellungen mischen. Die sitzende Frau wirkt elegant und entspannt, ist facettenreich und stolz auf ihr Statement-Piece. Ganz ähnlich ist *Pink Jump Suit* (2021). Obwohl die dargestellte Frau in die Ferne blickt und den Kopf nachdenklich in die Hand stützt, trägt auch sie farbenfrohe Kleidung: Ein gestreiftes Oberteil, einen karierten Hut und eine hellrosa Statement-Hose, die das Bild vervollständigt. Ein tief violetter Boden und lavendelfarbener Hintergrund unterstreichen Borlabis Verwendung lebhafter Pastelltöne als Kontrast zum dunklen Teint seiner Figuren.

Als Meister des Mediums fängt Borlabi in den meisten seiner Werke die Nuancen von Hauttönen ein. So zeigt *Summer Is Here* (2021) eine eindrucksvolle Verwendung der Kokosnuss – als Katalysator zur Darstellung jeder Pore, Linie und jedes Details des menschlichen Körpers. Vor allem aber findet er einen praktischen Nutzen für einen Gegenstand, an den nur wenige einen Gedanken verschwenden. Mithilfe der Kokosschale fängt der Künstler die Lebensfreude und Kraft Schwarzer Menschen ein, in Ghana und auf der ganzen Welt.

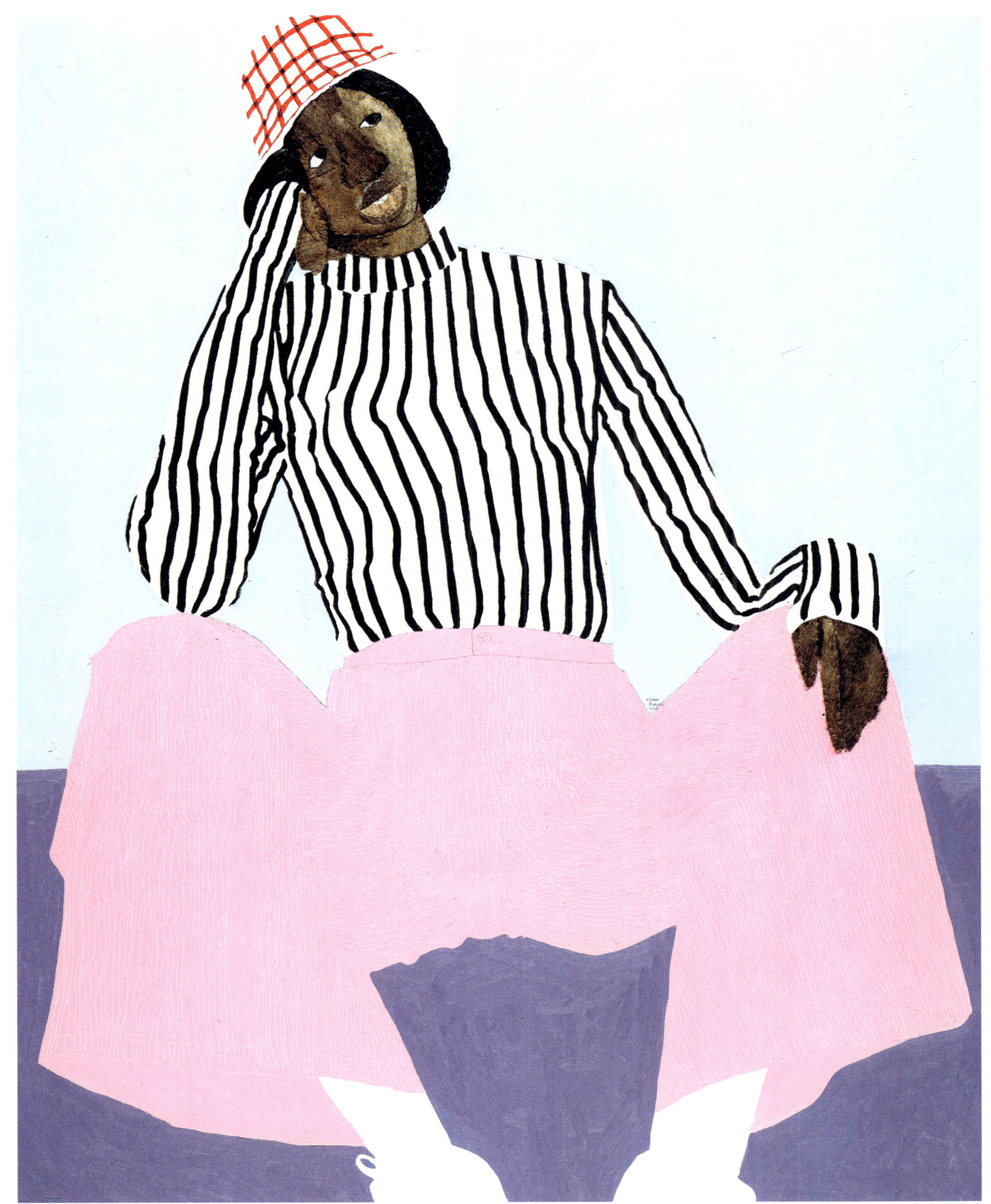

APLERH-DOKU BORLABI
Pink Jump Suit, 2021, Coconut sheath and oil on canvas /
Kokosnussschale und Öl auf Leinwand, 206 × 163 cm

APLERH-DOKU BORLABI
Red Nike, 2021, Coconut sheath and oil on canvas /
Kokosnussschale und Öl auf Leinwand, 206 × 152 cm

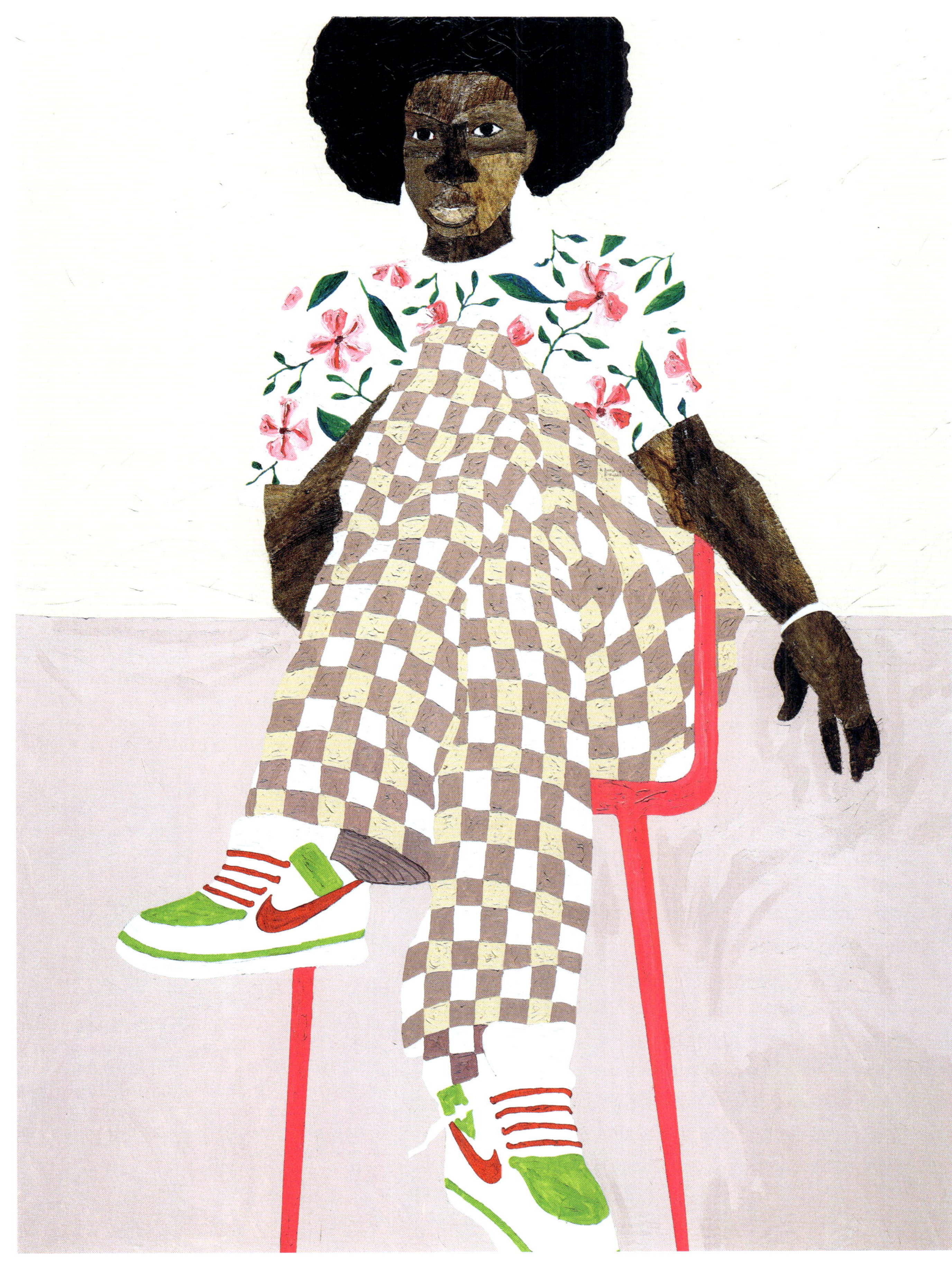

MILLICENT AKWELEY

Mixed-media artist Millicent Akweley (b. 2000), who paints under the name Akweley Ricco, celebrates her Ghanian heritage with vibrant life-size canvases. Her work is imbued with a sense of patchwork, each painting resembling a quilted surface with blended colors and diverse patterns that offer a nuanced take on the person, or people, depicted.

In *FYP (For You Page)* (2021), named after TikTok's discover feature, a lone male subject poses for a portrait in front of a mirror or window. The scene is confined to a large brown circle; the remainder of the off-white background creates an intimate, near-voyeuristic feel. The subject wears a purple hat and red pants, rich colors with connotations of royalty, and sits atop a multicolored sofa. The pink of his mouth is identical in hue to the neon splashes adorning his dress shirt. The subject's face, a blend of dark and light brown, features a collage of shapes and shades that highlight the complexity of skin.

***Tulsi* (2021) is named after holy basil, a medicinal herb known in many cultures and used to treat illness. A potted plant of the work's namesake sits on a table to one side, its leaves in full bloom beside the subjects, who are situated in close proximity to a striking pink wall. A young man faces the viewer. He is dressed in patterned slacks and a bright yellow shirt with a Mickey Mouse silhouette and his hand rests on the shoulder of a second subject who gazes off into the distance. Covered in a robe and a patterned blanket, this second subject is the likely recipient of the tulsi—and therefore in need of healing.**

In *I Have Finesse*, an azure background frames a woman lounging on an outdoor chaise lounge, hair wrapped in a towel and large red sunglasses masking her face. She raises a glass of some refreshing summer drink as she relaxes. The work is in the artist's signature style, and it speaks volumes about what it means to be comfortable in one's skin, and, in turn, to exist in the world when we think no one is watching.

***Aboagye Kwame Justice* acknowledges what might happen when we know the world *is* watching. The subject poses on a simple chair wearing a puzzle-like collaged outfit. A real-life zipper is applied to the striped slacks; colors and polka-dots adorn the canvas in such a complex way that the individual's face nearly—and intentionally—falls flat in comparison, featureless aside from the eyes, which are barely visible behind pink glasses. In every piece, Akweley leverages vast planes of color to convey the subject's identity.**

Die Mixed-Media-Künstlerin Millicent Akweley (geb. 2000), die als Malerin unter dem Namen Akweley Ricco arbeitet, feiert ihr ghanaisches Erbe mit kraftvollen, lebensgroßen Gemälden. Ihr Werk ist von Patchwork inspiriert, jede Arbeit ähnelt einer gesteppten Fläche mit kombinierten Farben und verschiedenen Mustern und bietet eine nuancierte Sicht der abgebildeten Personen.

In *FYP (For You Page)* (2021), benannt nach der Entdecken-Funktion bei TikTok, posiert eine einzelne männliche Gestalt vor einem Spiegel. Die Szene wird durch einen großen braunen Kreis beschränkt; der umgebende gebrochen weiße Hintergrund lässt eine intime, beinahe voyeuristische Atmosphäre entstehen. Der Porträtierte trägt einen purpurnen Hut und rote Hosen, satte Farben mit einer royalen Konnotation, und sitzt auf einem bunten Sofa. Das Pink seines Mundes hat den gleichen Farbton wie die neonfarbenen Spritzer, die sein Hemd zieren. Das Gesicht des Mannes ist in dunklem und hellem Braun wiedergegeben – eine Collage aus Formen und Schattierungen, die die Komplexität der Haut hervorheben.

Tulsi (2021) hat seinen Namen vom Heiligen Basilikum, einem in vielen Kulturen bekanntes Heilkraut zur Behandlung von Krankheiten. Ein eingetopfter Stock dieser namensgebenden Pflanze steht, die Blätter in voller Blüte, auf einem Tisch an der Seite, neben den Personen, die sich in unmittelbarer Nähe einer schreiend pinken Wand befinden. Ein junger Mann blickt den Betrachtenden entgegen. Er trägt eine gemusterte Hose und ein leuchtend gelbes Hemd mit einer Micky Maus darauf, seine Hand ruht auf der Schulter einer zweiten Person, die in die Ferne blickt. In einen Bademantel und eine gemusterte Decke gehüllt, ist diese zweite Person wohl Empfänger des Tulsis – bedarf also der Heilung.

In *I Have Finesse* umrahmt ein himmelblauer Hintergrund eine Frau, die sich auf einer Liege entspannt, das Haar in ein Handtuch gewickelt, eine große rote Sonnenbrille verdeckt ihr Gesicht. Sie hebt ein Glas mit einem erfrischenden Sommerdrink, während sie relaxt. Das Werk ist in dem für die Künstlerin typischen Stil gehalten und spricht Bände darüber, was es heißt, sich in seiner Haut wohlzufühlen, und was In-der-Welt-Sein bedeutet, wenn wir uns unbeobachtet fühlen.

Aboagye Kwame Justice führt vor, was passieren kann, wenn wir wissen, dass die Welt zusieht. Das Modell posiert auf einem einfachen Stuhl in einem puzzleartig zusammengesetzten Outfit. Die gestreifte Hose ist mit einem echten Reißverschluss versehen; Farben und Tupfen zieren die Leinwand auf so komplexe Weise, dass das Gesicht der Person beinahe – und absichtlich – flach wirkt, ohne prägende Züge mit Ausnahme der Augen, die hinter der pinken Brille kaum sichtbar sind. Akweley setzt in jeder Arbeit große Farbflächen ein, um die Identität der Person zu vermitteln.

CHARLES MOORE

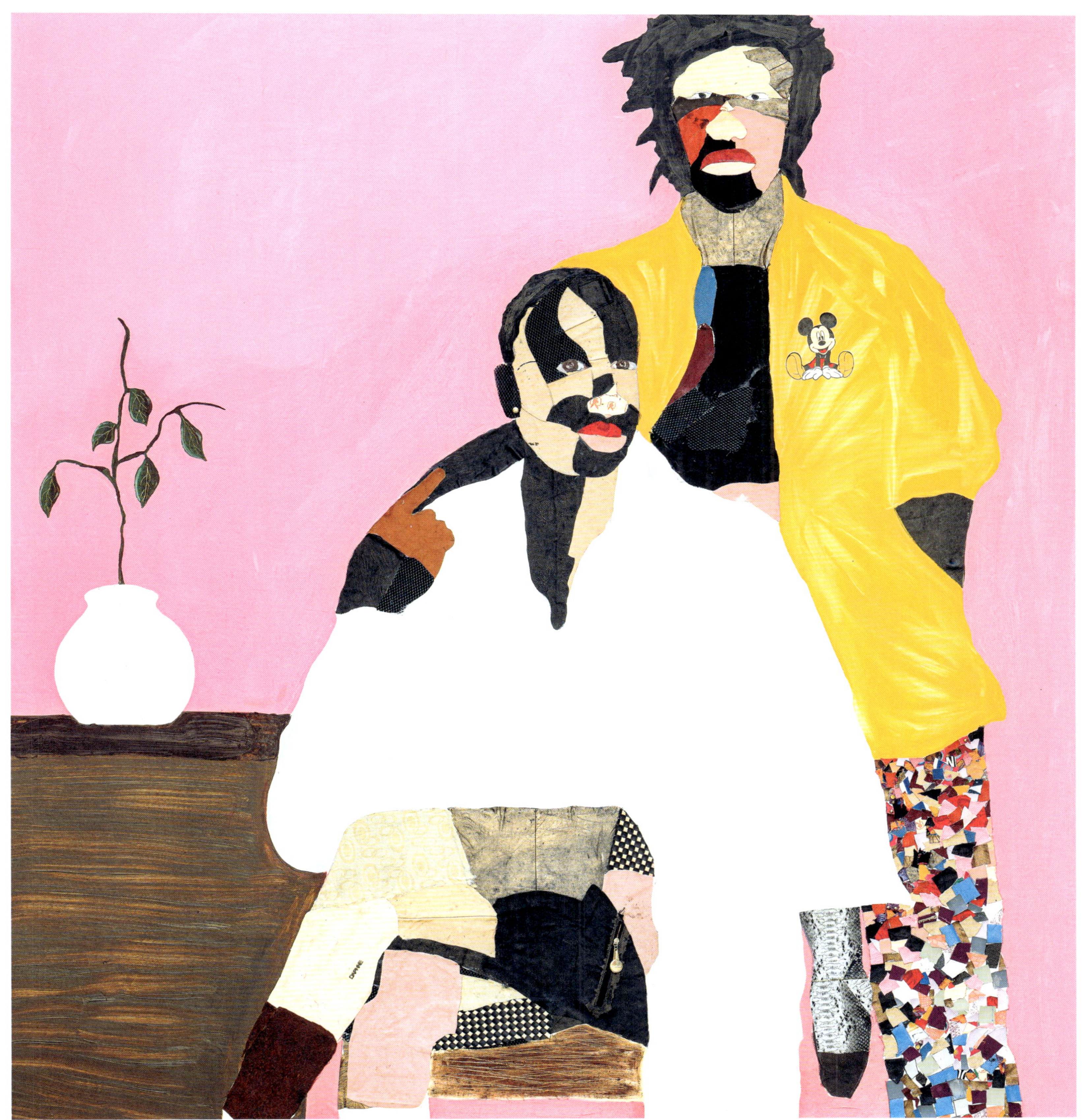

MILLICENT AKWELEY
Tulsi, 2021, Mixed media on canvas /
Mischtechnik auf Leinwand, 211 × 207 cm

MILLICENT AKWELEY
FYP (For You Page), 2021, Mixed media on canvas /
Mischtechnik auf Leinwand, 208 × 177 cm

35

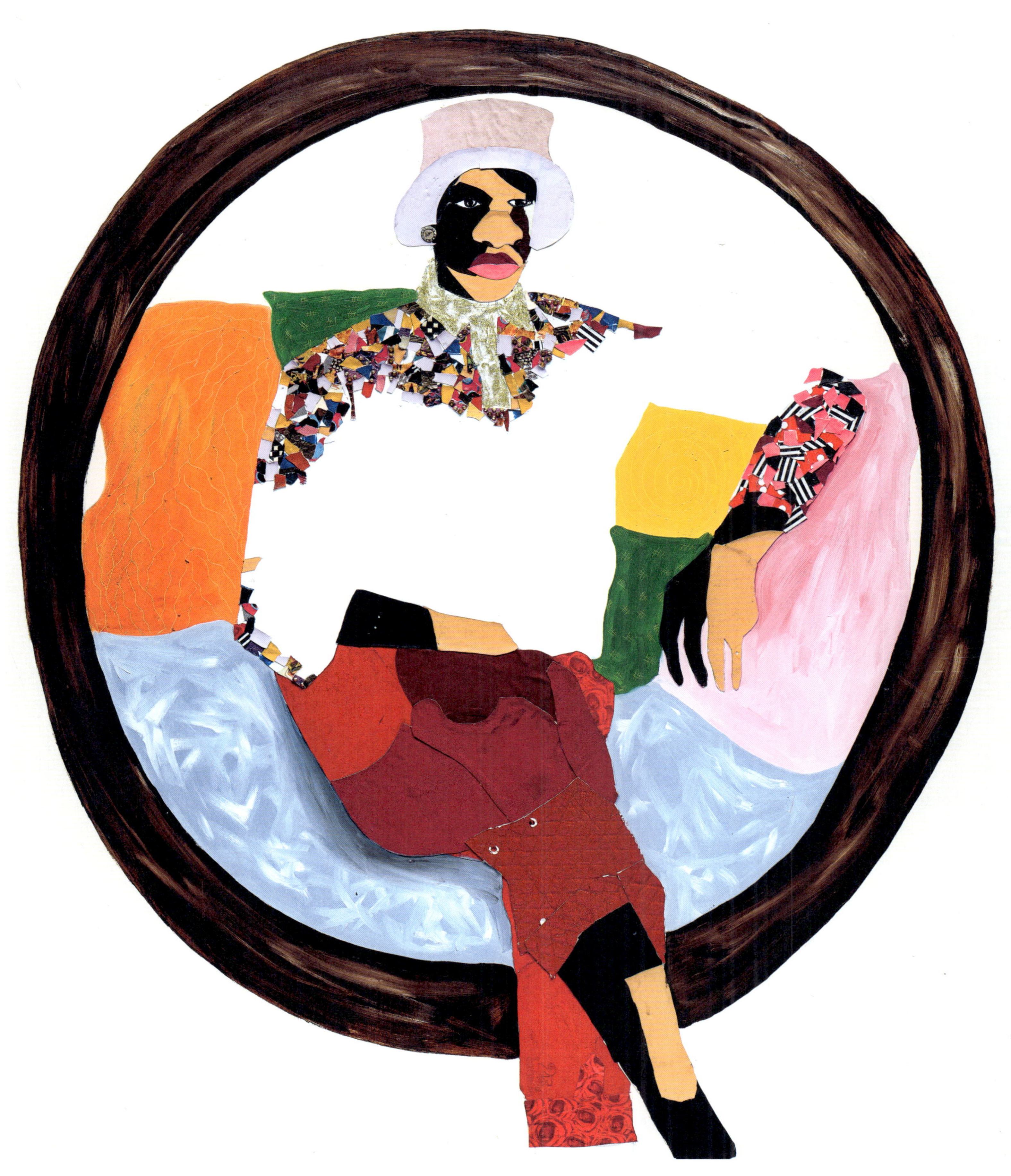

ERIC ADJEI TAWIAH

Ghanian artist Eric Adjei Tawiah (b. 1987) graduated from the renowned Ghanatta College of Art and Design, where he developed a unique approach to figurative painting that involved the use of a nylon sponge to enliven his subjects. Aptly named "sponge martial," the technique was inspired by Tawiah's witnessing of the washing of his mother's corpse, which he has since compared to the act of cleansing oneself from negative thought patterns. The artist weaves this same notion of cleansing into his work to craft unique pieces that depict moments of joy, or release, following dark times. Tawiah uses bright colors to represent these experiences, painting his subjects' skin a deep and vibrant blue that is simultaneously delicate and joyous, designed to reflect the presence of the moon. Colorful, stylish clothing and sensual flowers (reminiscent of those placed atop Tawiah's mother's grave) capture the artist's mind and spirit in a celebration of human kinship.

Many of his recent works showcase two Ghanian men, who are real-life friends practicing art and studying in Kumasi, Ghana. In *Synergy* (2022), the shirtless duo wear nice slacks and the taller man sports a warm-hued jacket that matches the nearby tangerine wall. A vine of some sort snakes across the background, from which green leaves sprout in a symbol of rebirth. In *Hued Up* (2022), the same pair stand together outside, one facing the camera and the other turned away. The friends are surrounded by greenery and wear vibrant pink and yellow shorts—a powerful contrast to the blue tones of their skin. The viewer can't help but be taken in by the subjects' dynamism, their lived experience seemingly on the precipice of mourning and solace. In the artist's paintings, each individual is strong yet vulnerable, eager to follow the glow of the moonlight forward.

By depicting flowers, mesh textures, and fashionable attire, Tawiah has fine-tuned his artistic voice in recent years to curate a body of work designed to inspire viewers during trying times and in everyday life. His compositions reveal a blend of male and female subjects, of public figures and personal friends, each work originating in a photograph before Tawiah sketches its iterations. Often, the artist will leave the background of the final canvas white, keeping the scene open to interpretation.

Tawiah recently completed a solo exhibition entitled *Threads of Past and Present* at Gallery 1957 in London. He lives and works in Accra, where he finds comfort in his community and culture.

CHARLES MOORE

Der ghanaische Künstler Eric Adjei Tawiah (geb. 1987) absolvierte das renommierte Ghanatta College of Art and Design, wo er einen einzigartigen Zugang zur figurativen Malerei entwickelte; dazu gehört die Verwendung eines Nylonschwamms zur Belebung seiner Motive. Die Entwicklung dieser Technik, die er treffend „sponge martial" nennt, geht auf die Erfahrung der Waschung der Leiche seiner Mutter zurück, was er mit einem Akt der Selbstreinigung von negativen Denkmustern vergleicht. Der Künstler verwebt diesen Gedanken der Reinigung in seine Arbeiten und gestaltet so einzigartige Werke, die Momente der Freude oder Erleichterung nach dunklen Zeiten einfangen. Tawiah verwendet leuchtende Farben, um diese Erfahrungen darzustellen, und malt die Haut seiner Figuren in tiefem und lebendigem Blau, das zugleich zart und fröhlich ist und die Gegenwart des Mondes widerspiegeln soll. Farbenfrohe, modische Kleidung und sinnliche Blumen (die an jene auf dem Grab von Tawiahs Mutter erinnern) geben das Denken und Fühlen des Künstlers in einer Feier menschlicher Verwandtschaft wieder.

Viele seiner jüngeren Arbeiten präsentieren zwei ghanaische Männer, die im wirklichen Leben Freunde sind, in Kumasi, Ghana, studieren und künstlerisch tätig sind. In *Synergy* (2022) trägt das hemdlose Duo schicke Hosen, der größere Mann eine Jacke in warmen Farben, die gut zur nahen ockerfarbenen Wand passen. Im Hintergrund schlängelt sich eine Art Ranke, aus der grüne Blätter als Symbol der Wiedergeburt sprießen. In *Hued Up* (2022) steht dasselbe Paar draußen im Grünen, der eine mit dem Gesicht zur Kamera, der andere abgewandt. Die Freunde tragen leuchtend pinke und gelbe Shorts – ein kraftvoller Kontrast zu den Blautönen ihrer Haut. Betrachter:innen können sich der Dynamik der Figuren nicht entziehen, deren gelebte Erfahrung am Grat zwischen Trauer und Trost situiert scheint. In den Bildern des Künstlers ist jedes Individuum stark, aber verwundbar, begierig, dem Leuchten des Mondes zu folgen.

Durch die Darstellung von Blumen, Netztexturen und modischer Kleidung hat Tawiah in den letzten Jahren seine künstlerische Stimme verfeinert und ein Werk geschaffen, das die Betrachter:innen in schwierigen Zeiten und im alltäglichen Leben zu inspirieren sucht. Seine Kompositionen zeigen männliche und weibliche Figuren, Persönlichkeiten des öffentlichen Lebens und Freunde; jede Arbeit basiert auf einem Foto, von dem ausgehend Tawiah Skizzen anfertigt. Oft lässt der Künstler den Hintergrund der Leinwand weiß und hält so die Szene für Interpretationen offen.

Tawiah, der kürzlich eine Einzelausstellung mit dem Titel *Threads of Past and Present* in der Gallery 1957 in London hatte, lebt und arbeitet in Accra, wo er Halt in seiner Gemeinschaft und Kultur findet.

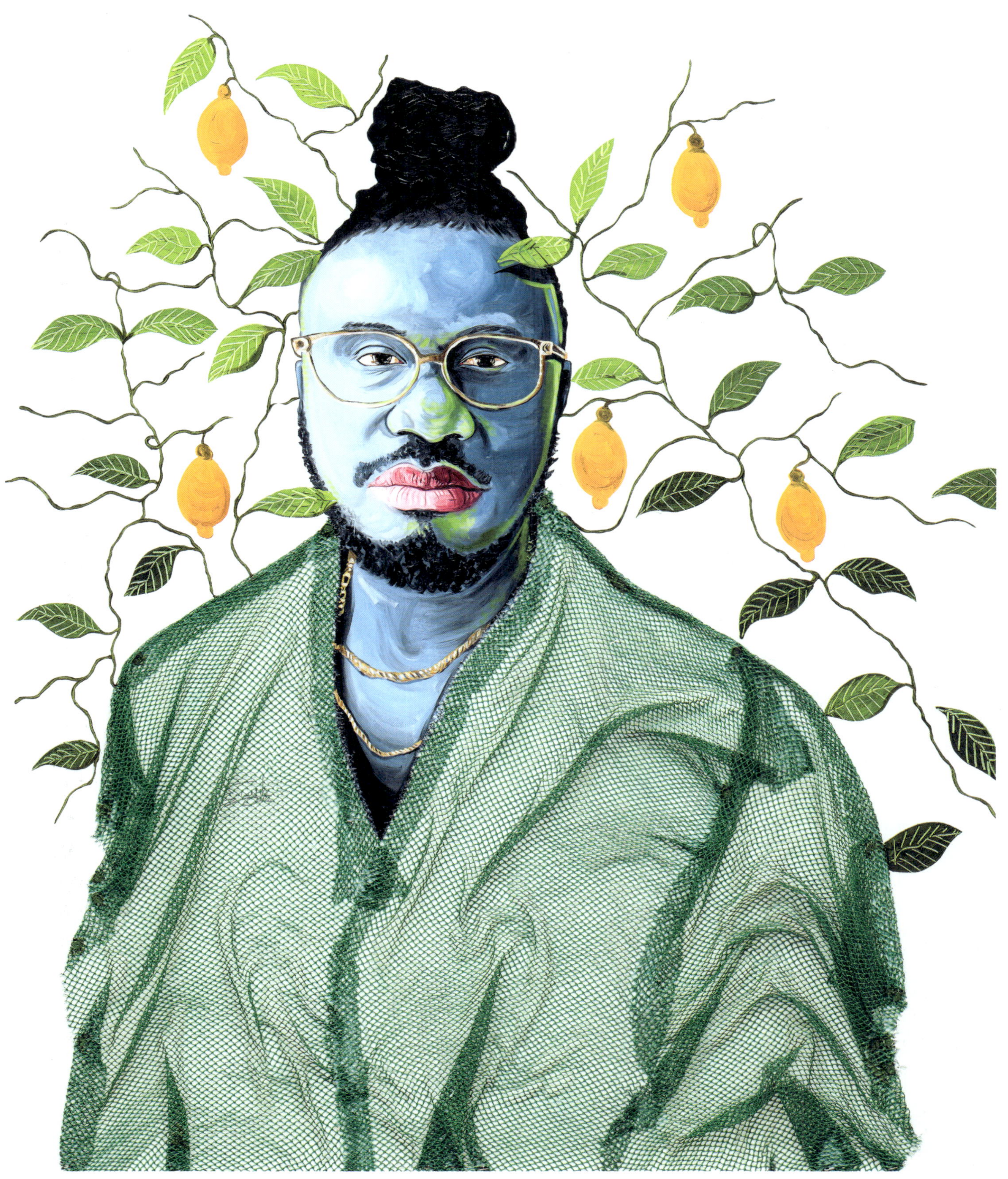

ERIC ADJEI TAWIAH
Otis, 2022, Sponge and oil on canvas /
Schwamm und Öl auf Leinwand, 120 × 100 cm

ERIC ADJEI TAWIAH
Adjei, 2021, Sponge and oil on canvas /
Schwamm und Öl auf Leinwand, 140 × 100 cm

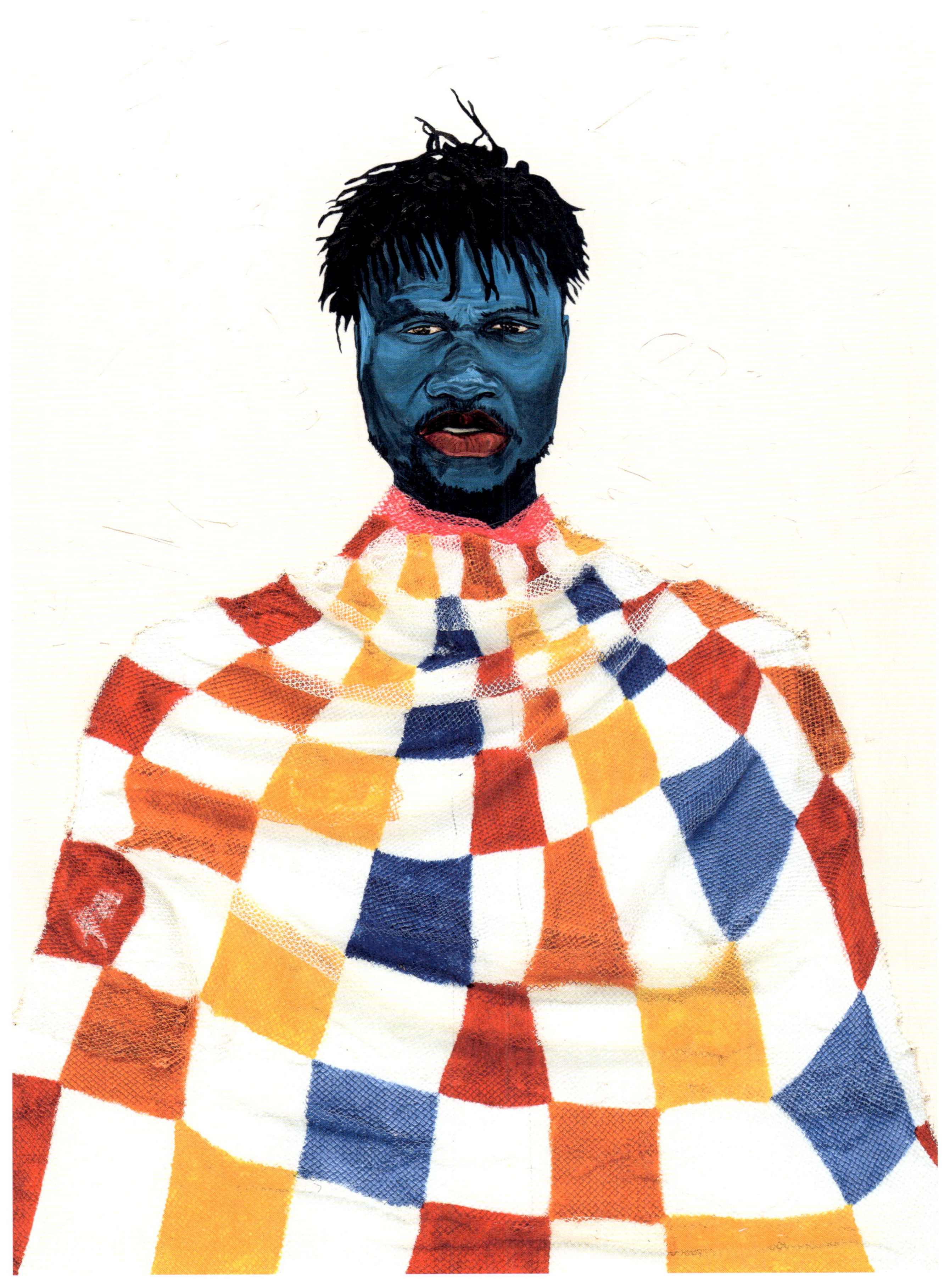

JAMES MISHIO

James Mishio (b. 1997, Ghana) is a mixed-media artist active in the contemporary Ghanaian art scene; he works and lives in Korle-Bu, Accra. His experimentation with various forms of media and materials and his sensitive exploration of his subjects' humanity fuels his work. Employing an impasto technique, he applies oil and fabric to canvas with a palette knife to create his works. His use of oil paint to render his subjects' complexion brings out the richness, wealth, and history of African heritage.

James found inspiration for his current "Identity Series" from Ahmad Cissé, the artist's freedom of expression, and the fact that he has not allowed his hairstyle to limit him from reaching the top of his professional career. As a fellow creative with deep connections to his Senegalese culture, Ahmad has always broken boundaries in his fields of practice, which includes, among others, modeling and photography.

Given the identity and limitations forced on him because of his own hairstyle, Mishio sought out other individuals who could inspire him to live a self-determined life in Accra without being held back by homophobic comments or branded as a criminal, a drug dealer, someone denied acceptance into jobs and professions, or looked down upon.

After getting to know and speaking with his inspiration Ahmad, James became interested in portraying his own expression in his photographs, his postures and body poses, in order to convey the freedom of his identity. A way of telling the world to accept him for who he is—a man proud of his dreadlocks. This prompted Mishio to paint his "Identity Series" based on strong Black male figures who, regardless of their hairstyles, defy every stereotype and societal view thrust upon them to become the best version of themselves.

His works have found their way into private collections and galleries and have been shown in notable exhibitions such as *Birds of a Feather*, a collaboration between Artemartis and the London auction house Phillips, as well as Coningsby Gallery, also based in London. With over six years of painting and maturing as an artist, Mishio focuses on communication and understanding among people, emphasizing the eyes of his subjects and redefining ways through which people communicate, taking inspiration from his mother and how she communicates effectively with him and his family through eye contact alone.

James Mishio (geb. 1997, Ghana) ist ein Mixed-Media-Künstler, der in der zeitgenössischen ghanaischen Kunstszene aktiv ist; er lebt und arbeitet im Stadtteil Korle-Bu in Accra. Das Experimentieren mit verschiedensten Medien und Materialien und seine sensible Erkundung des menschlichen Wesens seiner Modelle sind Triebfedern seiner Arbeit. Ölfarbe und textile Elemente bringt er in Impastotechnik mit der Spachtel auf die Leinwand auf. Die Art der Verwendung von Ölfarbe zur Wiedergabe der Haut seiner Modelle bringt die Fülle, den Reichtum und die Geschichte des afrikanischen Erbes zum Ausdruck.

Mishios aktuelle Werkreihe „Identity Series" ist inspiriert von Ahmad Cissé, seiner Freiheit im künstlerischen Ausdruck und der Tatsache, dass er nicht zuließ, dass seine Frisur ihn davon abhielte, den Gipfel seiner beruflichen Karriere zu erreichen. Als Künstlerkollege mit tiefer Verbundenheit zur senegalesischen Kultur hat Cissé in seinen Tätigkeitsfeldern, zu denen unter anderem die Arbeit als Model und das Fotografieren gehören, immer wieder Grenzen durchbrochen.

Angesichts der ihm wegen seiner Frisur aufgezwungenen Identität und Einschränkungen machte Mishio sich auf die Suche nach Menschen, die ihn zu einem selbstbestimmten Leben in Accra ermutigen konnten – ohne sich von homophoben Kommentaren abhalten, als Krimineller, Drogendealer, als jemand, dem Zugang zu Jobs oder Berufen verweigert wurde, abstempeln oder auf sich herabsehen zu lassen.

Nachdem er sein Vorbild Cissé kennengelernt und sich mit ihm ausgetauscht hatte, fing Mishio an, in seinen Fotos den eigenen Ausdruck, seine Körperhaltungen und Posen zu porträtieren, um die Freiheit seiner Identität zu vermitteln. Ein Weg, der Welt zu sagen, sie solle ihn als das akzeptieren, was er ist – ein Mann, der stolz auf seine Dreadlocks ist. Das wiederum veranlasste ihn, seine „Identity Series" zu malen, die starke männliche Schwarze Charaktere zeigt, die sich ungeachtet ihrer Frisur jedem Stereotyp und gesellschaftlicher Positionierung widersetzen, um zur bestmöglichen Version ihrer selbst zu werden.

Seine Werke haben ihren Weg in Privatsammlungen und Galerien gefunden und wurden in viel beachteten Ausstellungen gezeigt, etwa in *Birds of a Feather*, einer Zusammenarbeit von Artemartis und dem Londoner Auktionshaus Phillips, oder in der ebenfalls in London ansässigen Coningsby Gallery. Mit mehr als sechs Jahren Erfahrung als Maler und als Künstler gereift, konzentriert sich Mishio auf die zwischenmenschliche Kommunikation und Verständigung; er betont die Augen seiner Modelle und definiert die Art und Weise, wie Menschen kommunizieren, neu, wobei er sich von seiner Mutter inspirieren ließ, die allein durch Blickkontakt sehr wirkungsvoll mit ihm und der Familie kommuniziert.

SELASIE GOMADO

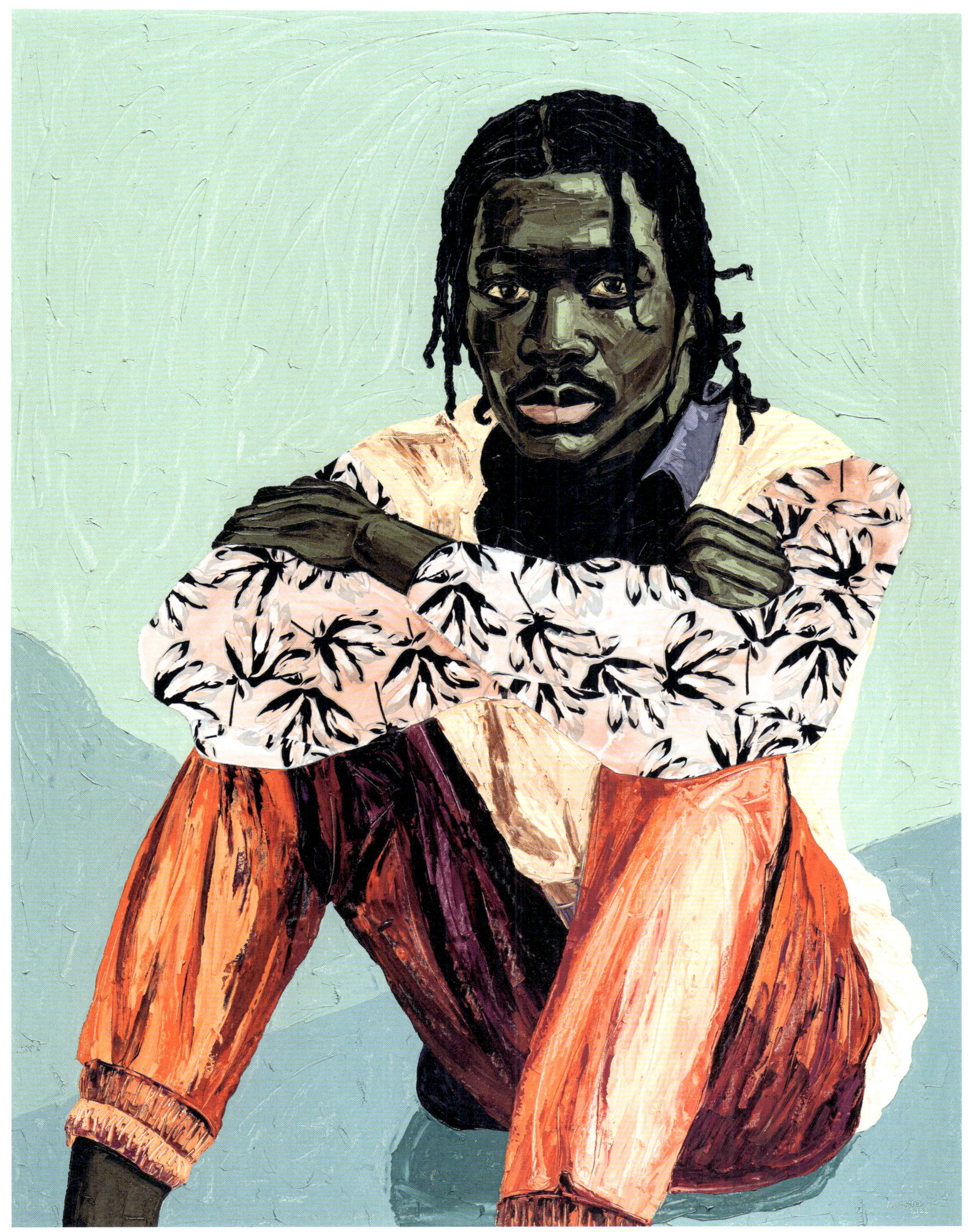

JAMES MISHIO
Look Into My Eyes I, 2022, Acrylic, oil and fabric on canvas /
Acryl, Öl und Stoff auf Leinwand, 170 × 130 cm

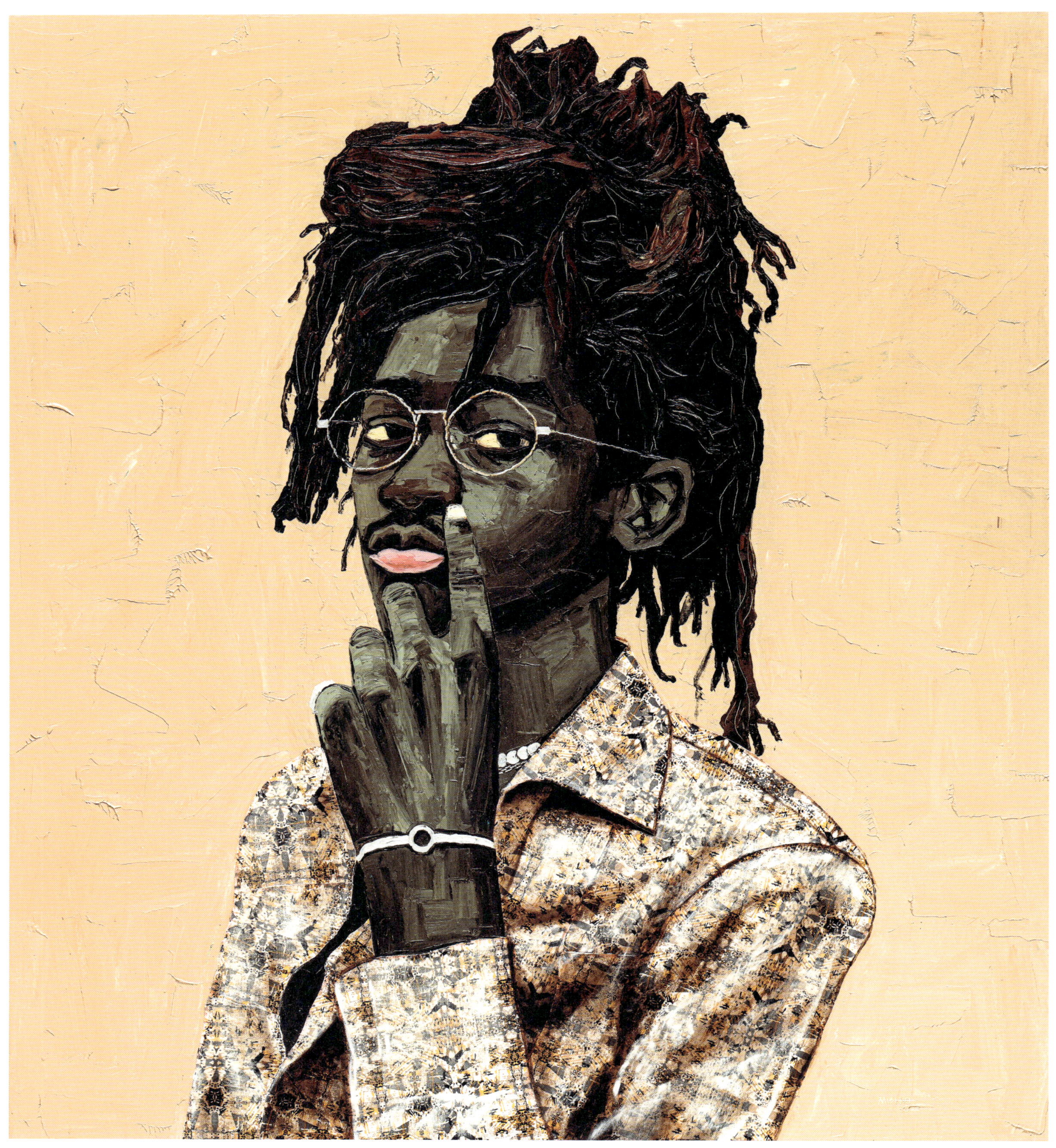

JAMES MISHIO
Second Lense II, 2022, Acrylic, oil and fabric on canvas /
Acryl, Öl und Stoff auf Leinwand, 114,3 × 127 cm

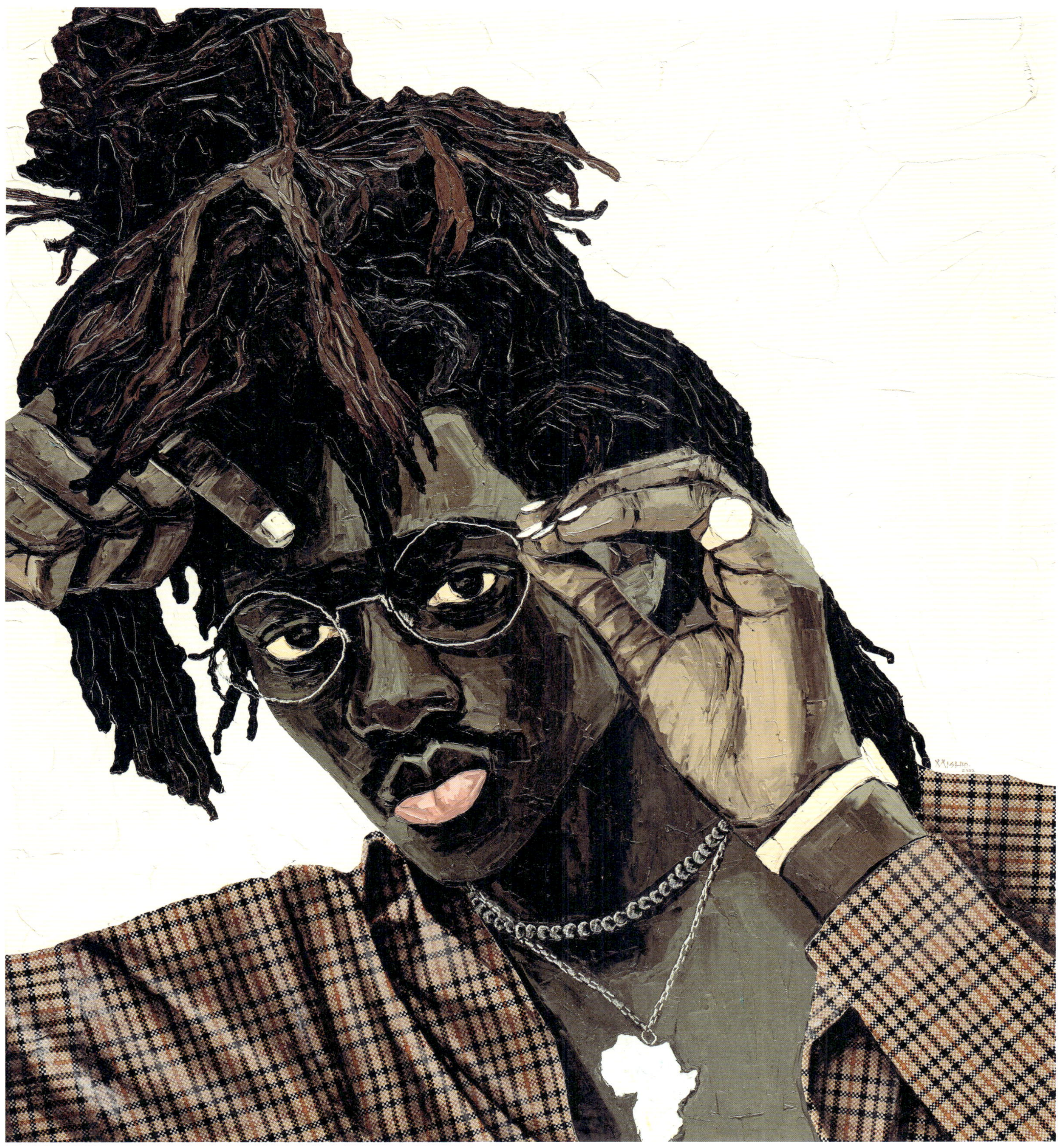

JAMES MISHIO
Second Lense I, 2022, Acrylic, oil and fabric on canvas /
Acryl, Öl und Stoff auf Leinwand, 114,3 × 127 cm

CRYSTAL YAYRA ANTHONY

Ghanaian multidisciplinary artist Crystal Yayra Anthony (b. 1997) writes, "I am a storyteller. I tell stories of misfits." The self-taught painter lives and works in Accra, and it was not until the onset of the pandemic, during her final year of university, that she decided to pursue a career in the arts. Anthony works in a studio located in Amoako Boafo's studio, learning from him as she researched the role of African art techniques in the international scene. She reveled in applying the traditions of her ancestors—among them, finger painting—to a contemporary world. Paying homage to her heritage, the artist's paintings break down gender stereotypes while telling the stories of everyday people.

It is a compelling narrative. Each work depicts a subject (generally a woman, though the artist does feature the occasional male subject in her figurative portraiture) in a real-life situation, nude yet approachable in a celebration of femininity and the human body. *What are you looking at?* (2021) shows a female subject standing naked within the confines of her fenced yard, peering over her shoulder as if to demand, per the title of the work, "What are you looking at?" A garden hose lies atop the lush emerald grass; sheets and clothes hang on a clothesline in the distance. The woman, her skin beautifully textured, merely goes about her daily tasks—so what if she's nude? In an era of simultaneous body positivism and social media censorship, the work is a remarkable assertion of women's power to *not* cover up.

Anthony's true-to-form presentation of women is one of the many things critics find striking about her work. In *I Wish Abby Selflove* (2021), a female subject sits on a bench inside her home, making direct eye contact with the viewer as though she's looking in the mirror. The vibrant green of houseplants brings the space to life and Abby's brown skin and piercing light eyes connect with the viewer with haunting immediacy. The subject's entire body is on display, stretch marks decorating her arms, lines, and curves adorning her stomach—the result is powerful. The work challenges viewers' biases, unraveling preconceived notions of beauty and sexuality. In every painting, the artist reveals that subjects are most beautiful when they are at ease, naked and vulnerable, yet confident.

Die multidisziplinäre ghanaische Künstlerin Crystal Yayra Anthony (geb. 1997) schreibt: „Ich bin eine Geschichtenerzählerin. Ich erzähle Geschichten von Außenseiter:innen." Die autodidaktische Malerin lebt und arbeitet in Accra; erst bei Ausbruch der Pandemie, während ihres letzten Jahres an der Universität, beschloss sie, eine künstlerische Laufbahn einzuschlagen. Anthony arbeitet in einem Atelier, das in jenem von Amoako Boafo untergebracht ist, und lernt so von ihm während sie die Rolle afrikanischer Kunsttechniken in der internationalen Szene erforscht. Es macht ihr Freude, die Traditionen ihrer Vorfahren – darunter die Fingermalerei – in die heutige Welt zu übertragen. Die Bilder der Künstlerin sind eine Hommage an ihr kulturelles Erbe; sie brechen Geschlechterstereotype auf und erzählen Geschichten von gewöhnlichen Menschen.

Es ist eine fesselnde Erzählung. Jedes Werk zeigt eine Person (in der Regel eine Frau, obwohl die Künstlerin in ihren figurativen Porträts gelegentlich auch Männer darstellt) in einer lebensechten Situation, nackt und doch nahbar, eine Feier der Weiblichkeit und des menschlichen Körpers. *What are you looking at?* (2021) zeigt eine weibliche Figur, die nackt in ihrem eingezäunten Garten steht und über die Schulter blickt, als wolle sie, wie der Werktitel besagt, fragen: „Was gibt's hier zu sehen?" Im üppigen, smaragdgrünen Gras liegt ein Gartenschlauch; im Hintergrund hängen Laken und Kleider auf einer Wäscheleine. Die Frau, deren Haut wunderschön wiedergegeben ist, geht lediglich ihren täglichen Tätigkeiten nach – wen kümmerts, wenn sie nackt ist? In einer Zeit von Body Positivity und gleichzeitiger Zensur in den sozialen Medien ist die Arbeit ein bemerkenswertes Bekenntnis zur Macht der Frauen, sich *nicht* zu bedecken.

Anthonys wirklichkeitsnahe Darstellung von Frauen ist einer der vielen Aspekte, die Kritiker:innen an ihrem Werk bemerkenswert finden. In *I Wish Abby Selflove* (2021) sitzt eine Frau auf einer Bank in ihrem Haus; sie nimmt direkten Blickkontakt mit den Betrachter:innen auf, als würde sie in den Spiegel schauen. Das kräftige Grün der Zimmerpflanzen erweckt den Raum zum Leben, und Abbys dunkle Haut und ihre durchdringenden hellen Augen treten mit eindrücklicher Direktheit mit den Betrachtenden in Verbindung. Der gesamte Körper der Protagonistin ist zu sehen, Dehnungsstreifen zieren ihre Arme, Falten und Kurven ihren Bauch – das Ergebnis ist beeindruckend. Das Werk stellt die Vorurteile der Betrachter:innen infrage und zerpflückt vorgefasste Vorstellungen von Schönheit und Sexualität. In jedem Gemälde zeigt die Künstlerin, dass Menschen am schönsten sind, wenn sie entspannt, nackt und verletzlich, aber gleichwohl selbstbewusst sind.

CHARLES MOORE

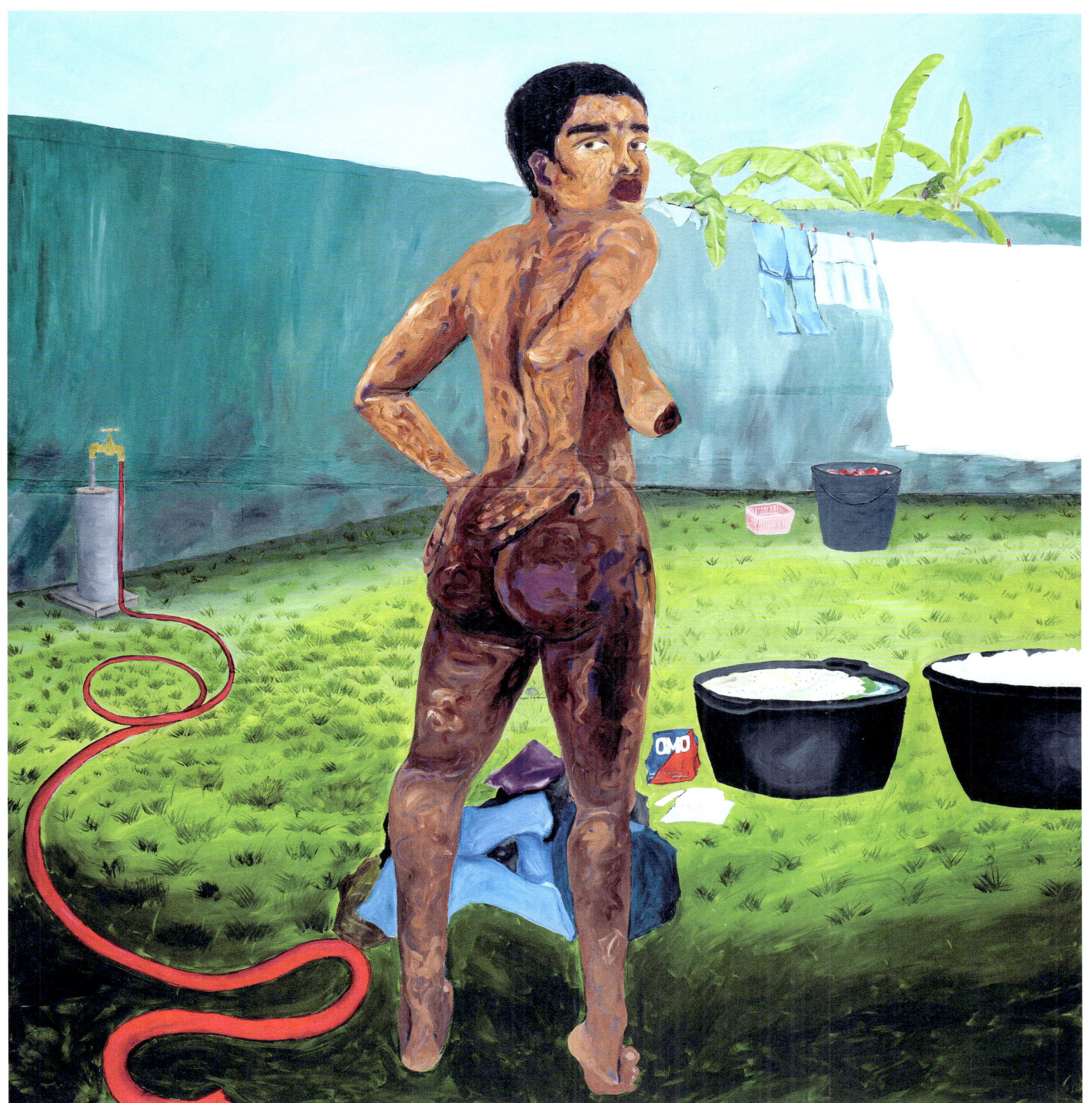

CRYSTAL YAYRA ANTHONY
What are you looking at?, 2021, Acrylic and oil on canvas / Acryl und Öl auf Leinwand, 211 × 201 cm

CRYSTAL YAYRA ANTHONY
I Wish Abby Selflove, 2021, Acrylic and oil on canvas /
Acryl und Öl auf Leinwand, 183 × 127 cm

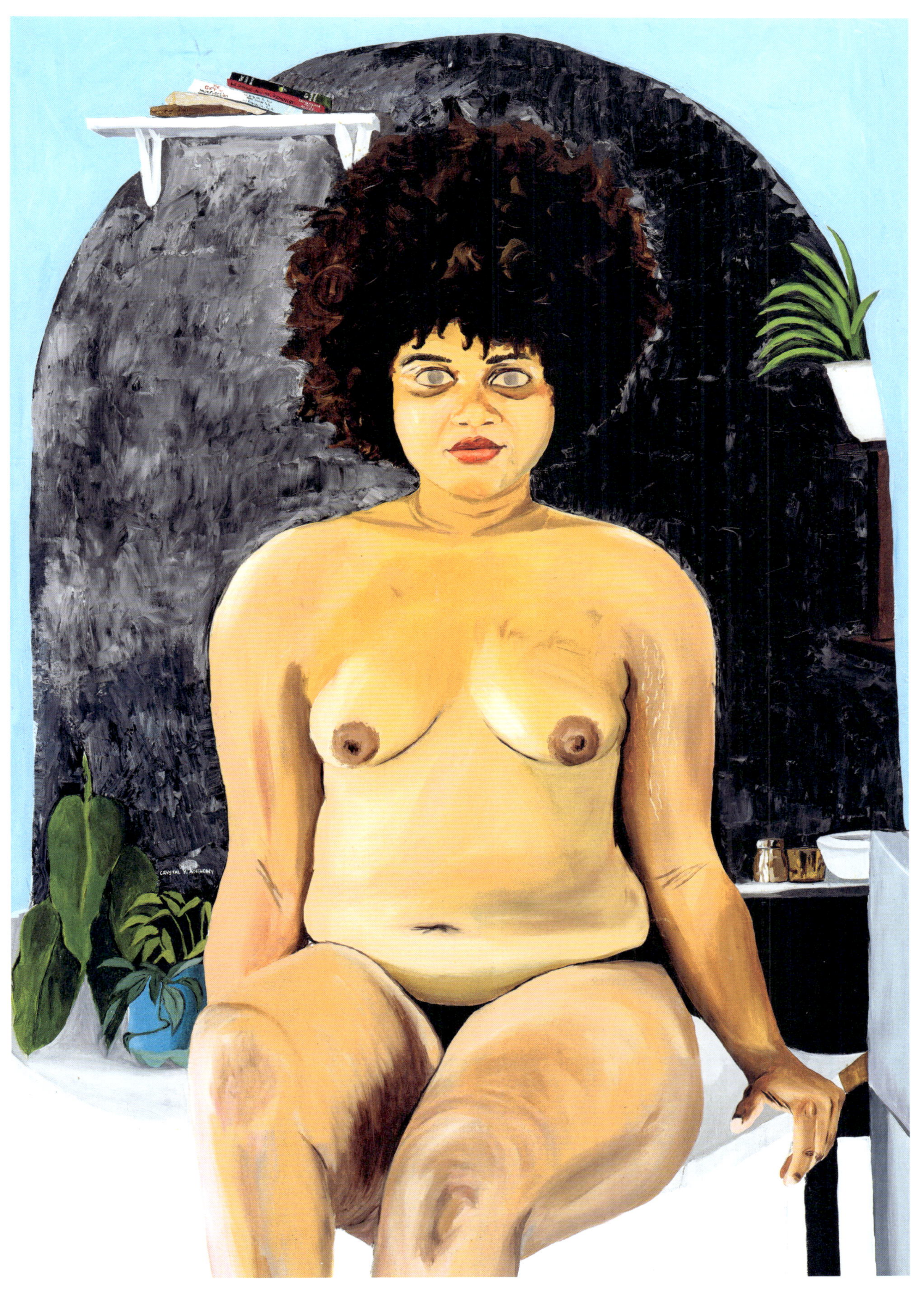
CRYSTAL Y. ANTHONY

OTIS KWAME KYE QUAICOE

Otis Kwame Kye Quaicoe (b. 1988 in Accra, Ghana, lives and works in Portland, US) paints vibrant, emblematic portraits that exude power and cultural pride. The portrayed individuals appear as strong characters, self-confident, and resilient. Positioned in the center of the painting, they occupy a spot long reserved for people of European descent. In Quaicoe's "Black portraits," the subjects tell about their personal histories in their social environments. "I'm a big fan of the old paintings; I learned a lot. I realized that these artists talked about what happened in *their time*. That is why it is very important that we do the same. Whatever goes on in my life, as a Black person, maybe in the US or wherever I find myself; what goes on and how I am received, I take all these things into consideration and put it on the canvas."[1]

The "Black Cowboy" series ranks among Quaicoe's most popular bodies of work. In these works, the artist seeks to rectify the myth of the "white cowboy" modeled after Gary Cooper and Clint Eastwood as prototypical Western heroes. In actuality, nearly a quarter of cowboys who drove herds of cattle across the prairie on horseback in the late nineteenth-century were people of color. The heroic figure of the white cowboy—the antipode of the "Indian"—only evolved later and is also partly a product of the Hollywood and Italian Spaghetti Western machinery. Quentin Tarantino, in reaction to this historically distorted cowboy image, starred a black cowboy in his film *Django Unchained*. Quaicoe's 2020 painting *Blue Mood* depicts a black cowboy in profile wearing a bandana, before a monochrome, blue background. The artist applied the impasto paint with a palette knife and brush, texturing the surface with a web of delicate, rippling dabs of color and brushwork. One is reminded of Vincent van Gogh's materially dense and gestural painting style, in particular his portrait backgrounds. In contrast to Quaicoe's genre paintings that include narrative and spatial elements, the backgrounds of the cowboy paintings are abstract.

1 Amah-Rose Abrams, "Kwesi Botchway and Otis Kwame Kye Quaicoe. Encounters," in *Elephant*, no. 45 (2021): 73.

Otis Kwame Kye Quaicoe (geb. 1988 in Accra, Ghana, lebt und arbeitet in Portland, USA) malt farbintensive repräsentative Porträts voller Kraft und kultureller Würde. Die gemalten Personen wirken charakterstark, selbstbewusst und resilient. Ins Bildzentrum gerückt, nehmen sie einen Platz ein, der lange Zeit Menschen europäischen Ursprungs vorbehalten war. In Quaicoes „Black Portraits" erzählen die Dargestellten ihre persönliche Geschichte in ihrem gesellschaftlichen Umfeld. „Ich bin ein großer Fan der alten Gemälde; ich habe eine Menge von diesen gelernt. Ich habe begriffen, dass diese Künstler davon sprechen, was in *ihrer Zeit* geschah. Deshalb ist es sehr wichtig, dass wir dasselbe tun. Was immer mir in meinem Leben als Schwarzer Mensch passiert, in den USA oder wo immer ich gerade bin, was also passiert und wie ich wahrgenommen werde, ich ziehe all das mit in Betracht und bringe es auf die Leinwand."[1]

Die „Black Cowboys" zählen zu den populärsten Werkgruppen von Quaicoes Œuvre. Der Künstler korrigiert mit ihnen den weißen Cowboy-Mythos, für den Gary Cooper und Clint Eastwood als Westernhelden prototypisch stehen. Tatsächlich waren etwa ein Viertel der Cowboys, die im ausgehenden 19. Jahrhundert die Rinderherden zu Pferd durch die Prärie trieben, People of Color. Der weiße Cowboy als heroische Figur, die dem „Indianer" gegenübersteht, entwickelte sich erst später und ist teils auch Produkt der Hollywood- und Italo-Western-Maschinerie. Quentin Tarantino reagierte in seinem Film *Django Unchained* mit einem Schwarzen Cowboy in der Hauptrolle auf dieses historisch verfälschte Cowboy-Image. In *Blue Mood* aus dem Jahr 2020 stellt Quaicoe den Schwarzen Cowboy in Profilansicht mit Mundtuch vor einen monochromen blauen Bildgrund. Die Farbe trug der Künstler pastos mit Spachtel und Pinsel auf und strukturierte die Ebene mit einem Gewebe aus delikaten sich kräuselnden Farbklecksen und Pinselstrichen. Man fühlt sich an Vincent van Goghs materiell-gestische Malspuren erinnert, insbesondere an die Hintergründe seiner Porträtbilder. Im Unterschied zu den Genrebildern Quaicoes mit narrativen und räumlichen Elementen ist der Bildgrund in den Gemälden von Cowboys abstrakt behandelt.

1 Amah-Rose Abrams, „Kwesi Botchway and Otis Kwame Kye Quaicoe. Encounters", in: *Elephant*, Nr. 45 (2021), S. 73 (Übers. v. Michael Strand).

FLORIAN STEININGER

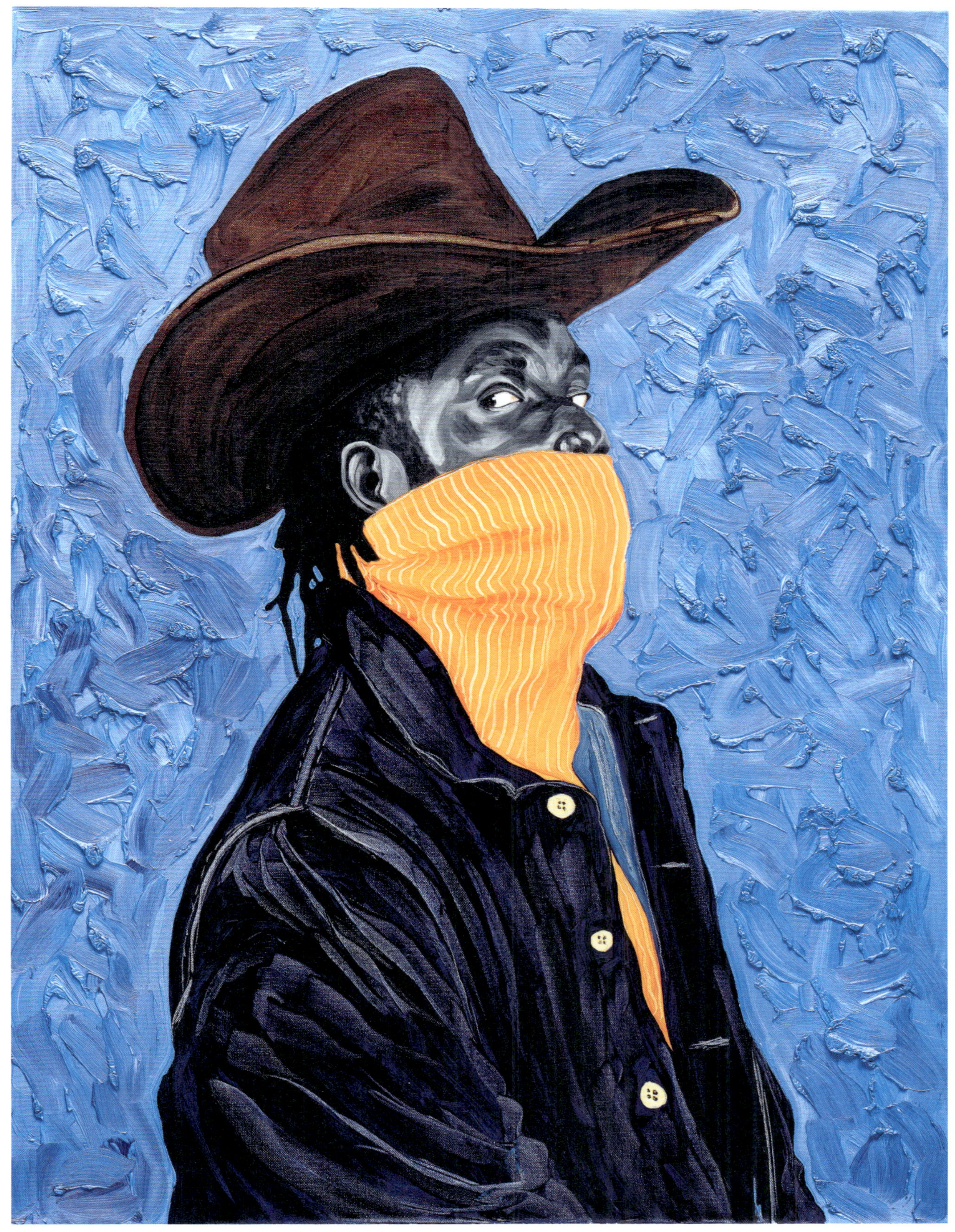

OTIS KWAME KYE QUAICOE
Blue Mood, 2020, Oil on canvas / Öl auf Leinwand, 101,6 × 76,2 cm
Collection Michael Ballack / Sammlung Michael Ballack

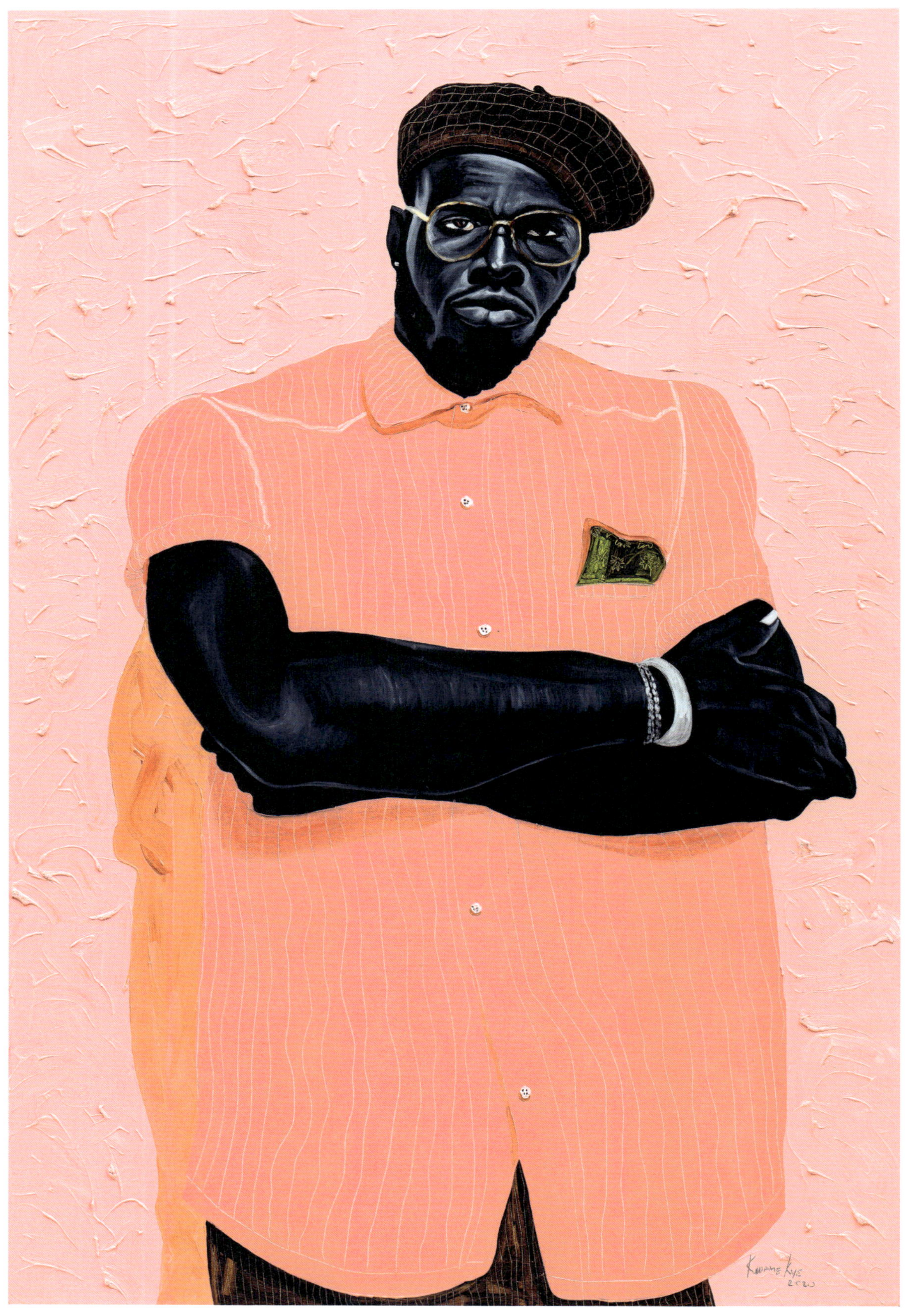

OTIS KWAME KYE QUAICOE
DJ Steelo, 2020, Oil on canvas /
Öl auf Leinwand, 152,4 × 101,6 cm

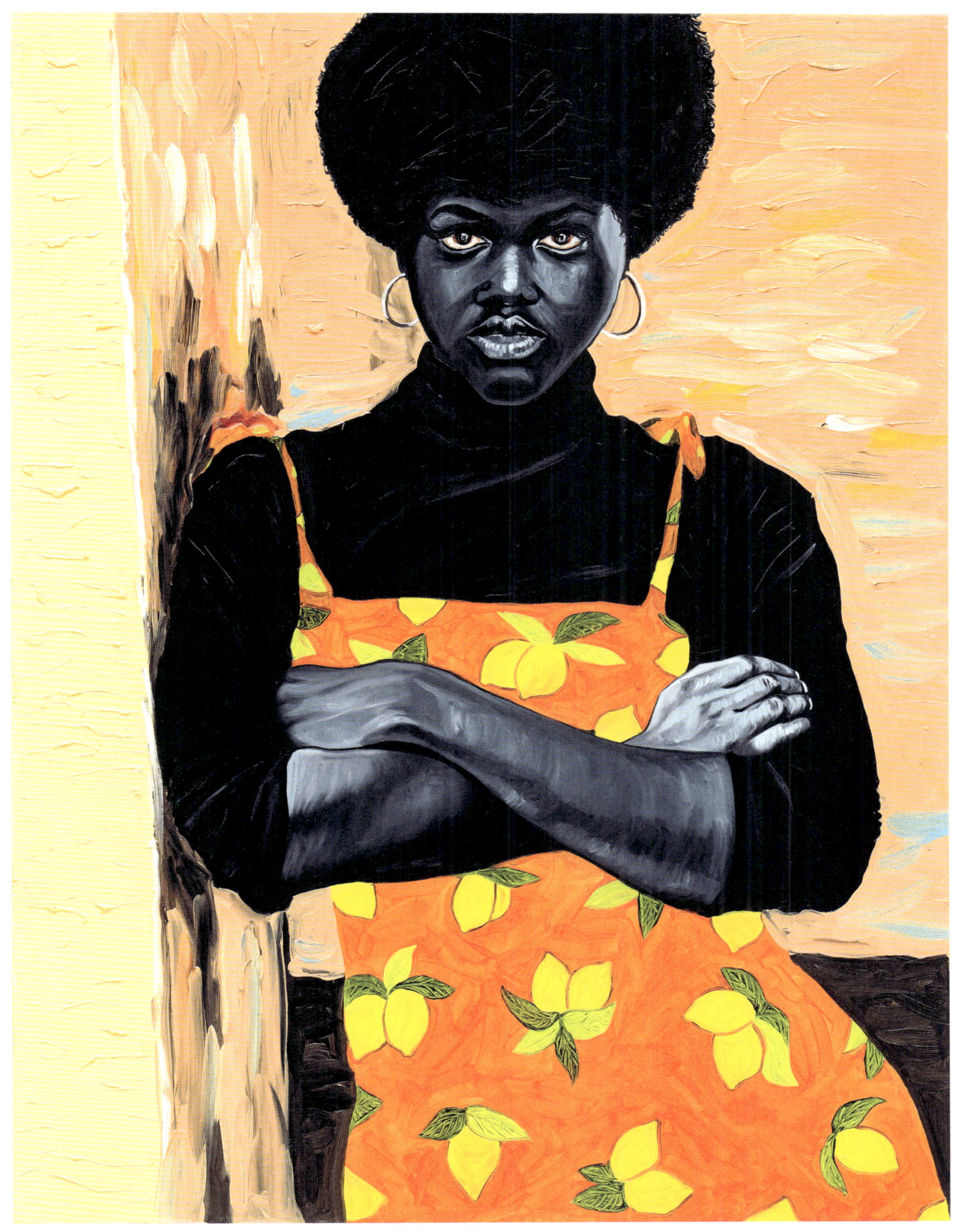

OTIS KWAME KYE QUAICOE
Untitled, 2019, Oil on canvas /
Öl auf Leinwand, 121,9 × 91,4 cm

OTIS KWAME KYE QUAICOE
Pink Seat, 2020, Oil on canvas /
Öl auf Leinwand, 209,1 × 132 cm

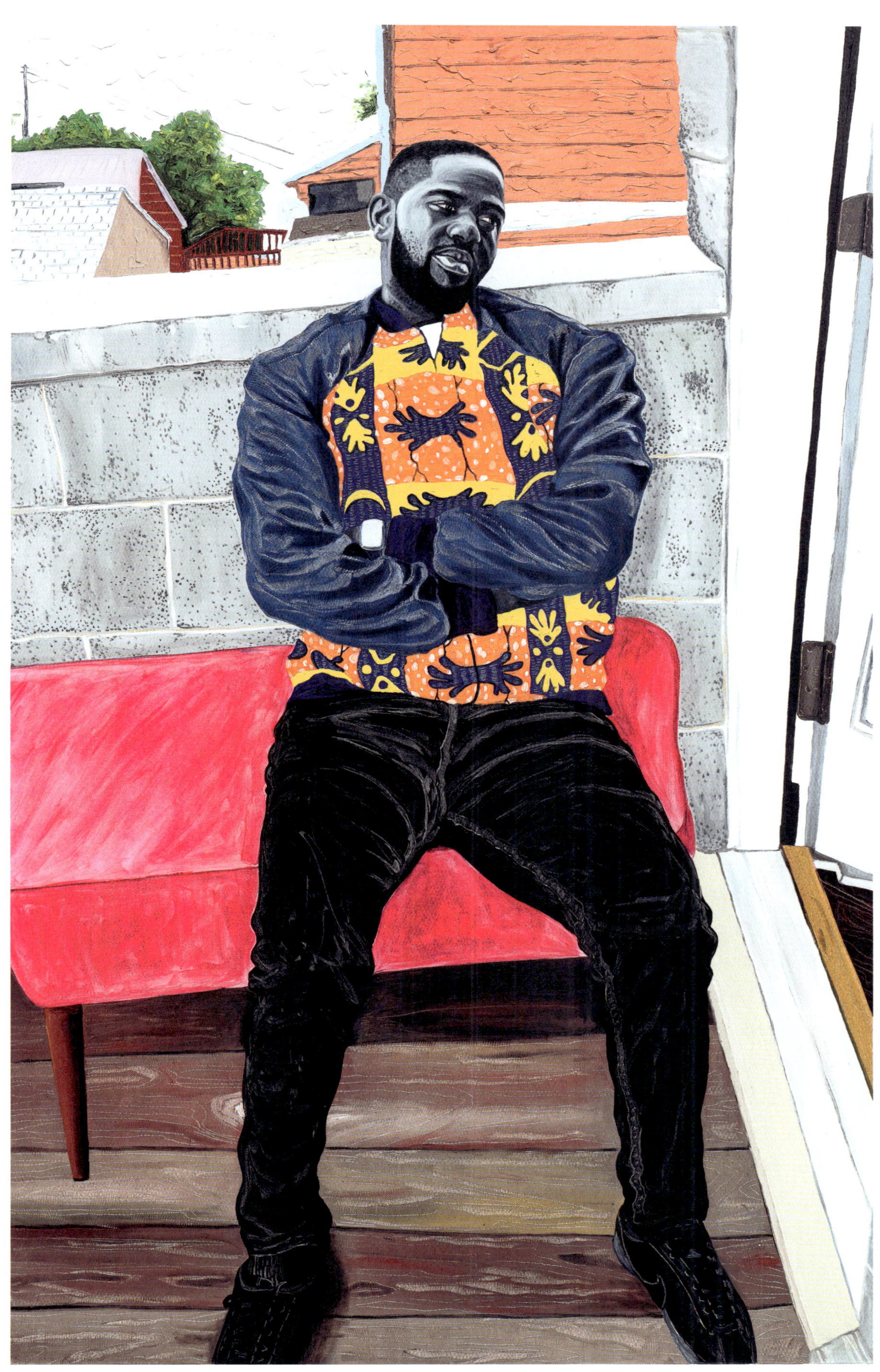

AFIA PREMPEH

Afia Prempeh (b. 1986 in Kumasi, Ghana) creates portraits of personalities, layered into complex painterly narratives. Each character forms the focus of and occupies a setting reminiscent of a still life painting: a rich and nuanced cultural context of artifacts, photographs, clothing, accessories, occupational references, color schemes, or designed interiors.

Drawing on her artistic origins as a landscape painter, Prempeh layers information into a detailed, painterly epistemology, in which characters are woven into tales on canvas. The two works included in the exhibition depict contemporary African women reigning over their spaces and sharing their respective stories as we follow them on a spiritual path of discovery. We are prompted to pay attention to nuance as Prempeh's works do not provide a definitive reading. Rather, we are witnesses to the women's seeking and searching for ways to take a seat at the table of life. The women may be self-sufficient, but are still confined by traditionally female gender roles. Do they own their female power (yet)? What impact are they making, or do they want to make? Are they merely dreaming of independence and self-sufficiency? How do we define the context for independence and gender roles? Whose cultural markers are we even considering for potential definitions? New African portraiture is often defined by agency, by the rewriting of history/ies, and a shift in perspective, and in Prempeh's paintings, her subjects could be red as synecdoches.

Prempeh finds grounding in a spirituality that informs not just her subjects' journeys, in constant flux and marked by unknowns. The mirrors and photographs appearing in Prempeh's paintings provide not only visual depth but offer an extended glimpse into the lives of the protagonists. Through the reflections created in them, we are invited to ponder and insert our own experiences. We are not confronted with "intentional fallacy" [the judging of a work based on the assumed intent of the creator]. The viewer is asked to engage and see beyond what is immediately perceptible. Even the drapes and walls suggest continuity. We may only see part of a room but know that something else lies beyond. Prempeh includes painted photographs in her works in order to allude to heritage and lineage. Her canvasses leave us to contemplate the future, in which we are open to explore our own spirituality, experiences, and notions of feminism and femininity.

HEIKE DEMPSTER

Afia Prempeh (geb. 1986 in Kumasi, Ghana) kreiert Porträts von Persönlichkeiten und bettet sie in komplexe malerische Erzählungen ein. Die dargestellten Personen stehen im Fokus der Gemälde und nehmen Räume ein, die an Stillleben erinnern: ein reichhaltiger, nuancierter kultureller Kontext, bestehend aus Artefakten, Fotografien, Kleidung, Accessoires, Verweisen auf die berufliche Tätigkeit, aus Farbschemata oder gestalteten Innenräumen.

Gestützt auf ihre künstlerischen Anfänge als Landschaftsmalerin entwirft Prempeh durch das Schichten von Informationen detaillierte malerische Epistemologien, gestaltet in Erzählungen verwobene Figuren. Die in der Ausstellung präsentierten Werke zeigen zeitgenössische afrikanische Frauen, die über ihre Umgebung herrschen und ihre Geschichten erzählen, während wir ihnen auf ihrem spirituellen Erkenntnisweg folgen. Wir werden aufgefordert, auf Nuancen zu achten, da Prempehs Werke keine endgültige Lesart vorgeben. Vielmehr werden wir Zeugen ihres Strebens und ihrer Suche nach einem sprichwörtlichen Platz am Tisch. Die Frauen scheinen selbstständig, sind jedoch weiterhin durch traditionelle Geschlechterrollen eingeschränkt. Verfügen sie (schon) über ihre weibliche Macht? Welchen Einfluss haben sie oder wollen sie haben? Träumen sie lediglich von Unabhängigkeit und Selbstständigkeit? Und wie definieren wir den Kontext für Unabhängigkeit und Geschlechterrollen? Welche Merkmale ziehen wir für eine Definition heran? Die neue afrikanische Porträtmalerei ist oft charakterisiert durch Aspekte wie Handlungsmacht, das Umschreiben von Geschichte und eine Verschiebung der Perspektive. In Prempehs Arbeiten sind die Porträtierten als Synekdochen zu verstehen.

Prempeh findet Halt in ihrer Spiritualität, die auch die sich ständig wandelnde und durch Ungewissheiten bestimmte Entwicklung ihrer Protagonist:innen beeinflusst. Die Spiegel und Fotografien in Prempehs Gemälden schaffen nicht nur visuelle Tiefe, sondern eröffnen einen Einblick in das Leben der Porträtierten. Die Spiegelungen laden zum Nachdenken ein und dazu, unsere eigenen Erfahrungen einzubringen. Wir werden nicht mit „intentionalen Fehlschlüssen" [die Beurteilung eines Werks auf Grundlage der angenommenen auktorialen Intention] konfrontiert. Die Betrachtenden werden aufgefordert, sich aktiv mit der Kunst zu befassen, über das unmittelbar Wahrnehmbare hinaus. Selbst die Vorhänge und Wände suggerieren Kontinuität. Zwar sind nur Teile eines Raumes zu sehen, aber dahinter verbirgt sich mehr. Prempeh bezieht gemalte Fotografien ein, um auf das kulturelle Erbe und die Herkunft zu verweisen. Ihre Leinwände überlassen es uns Betrachter:innen, über eine Zukunft nachzudenken, in der wir unsere Spiritualität, unsere Erfahrungen und unsere Vorstellungen von Feminismus und Weiblichkeit erkunden können.

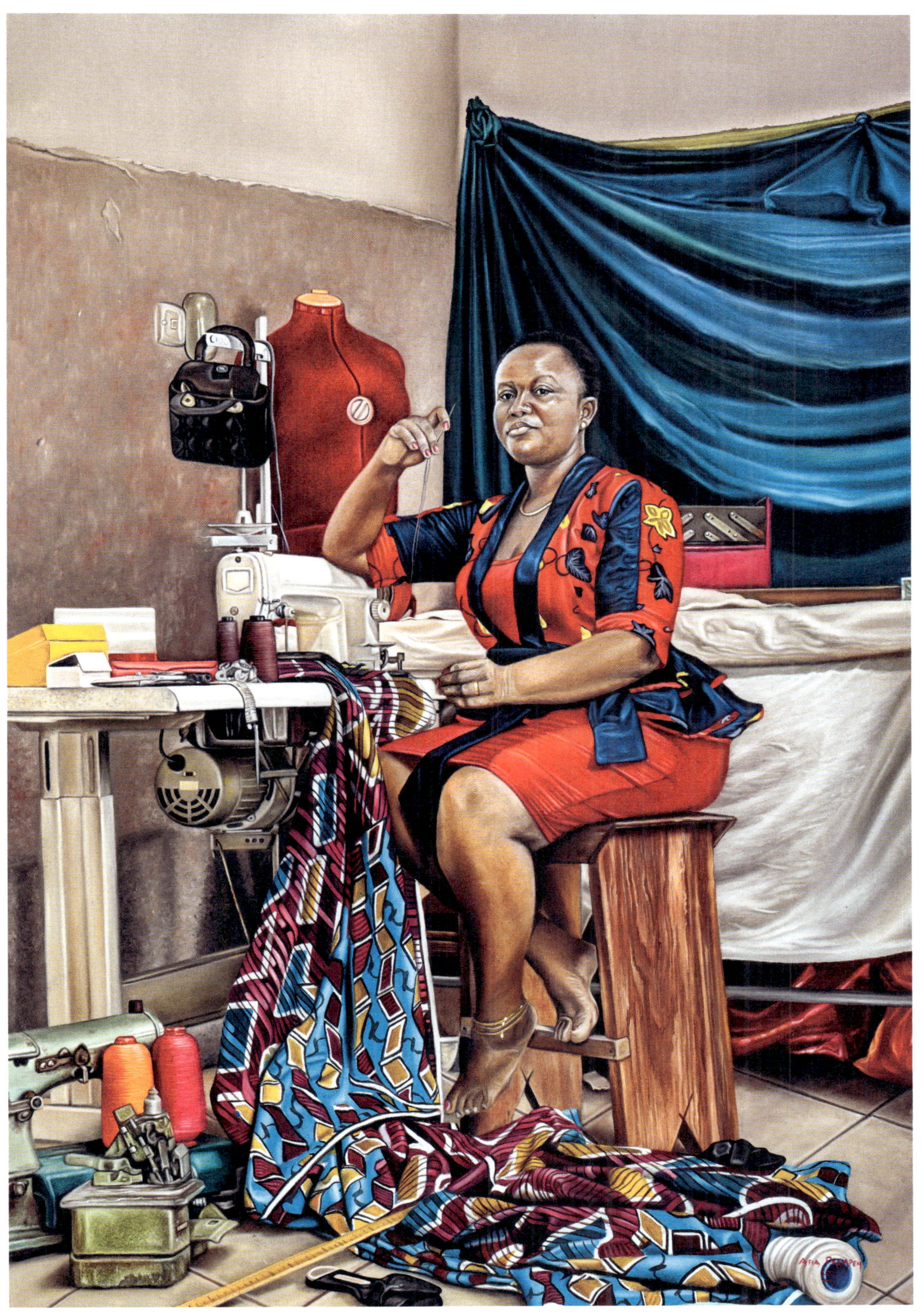

AFIA PREMPEH
Eno (Housewife Dreams), 2021
Oil on canvas / Öl auf Leinwand, 164 × 113 cm

AFIA PREMPEH
Samira (Dilemma of the Girl Child), 2021
Oil on canvas / Öl auf Leinwand, 150 × 120 cm

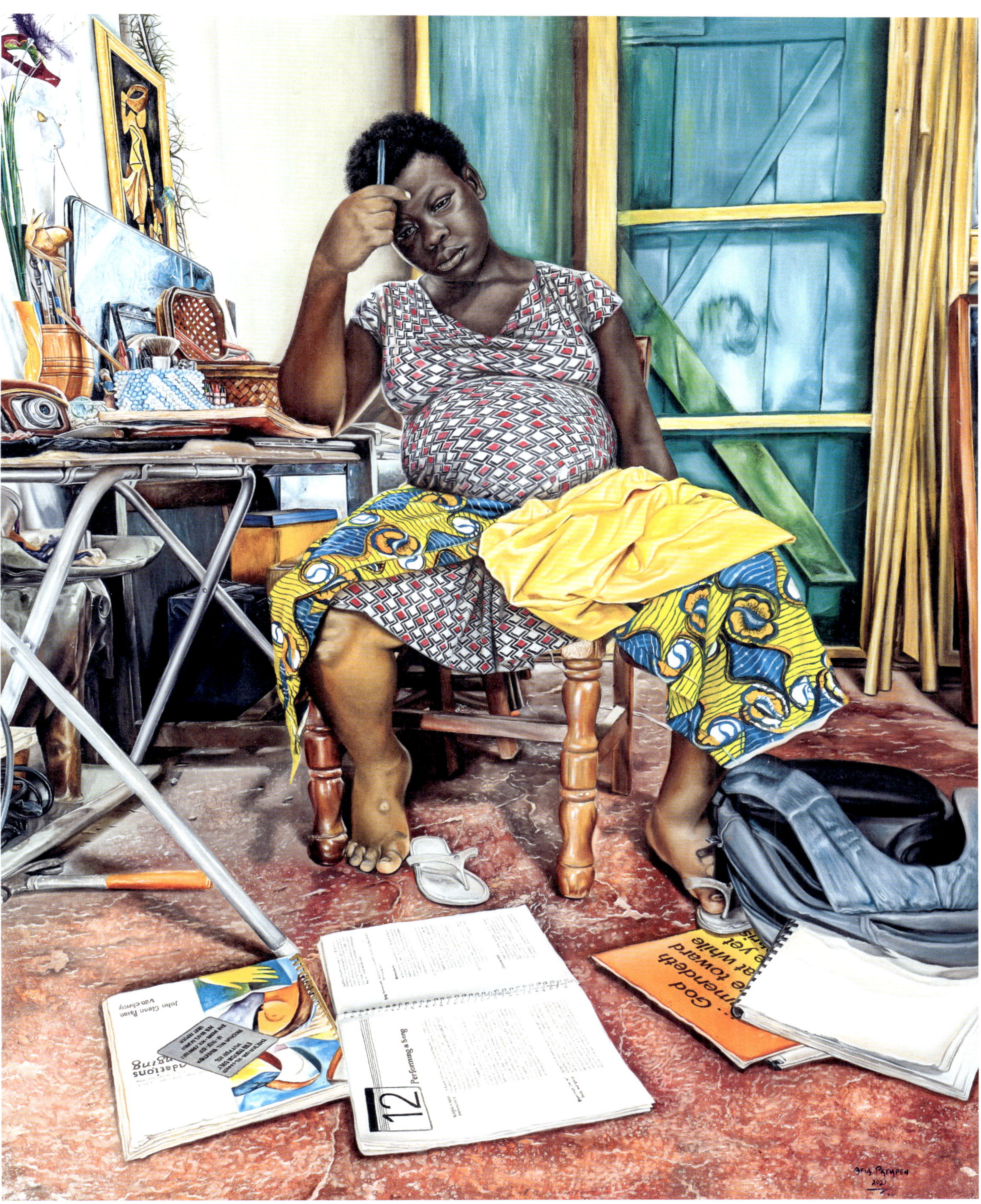
12
Performing a Song

CORNELIUS ANNOR

Cornelius Annor (b. 1990 in Mamobi, Ghana) is one of Ghana's most-compelling emerging artists. His evocative paintings provide temporal snapshots of quotidian Ghanaian life since independence. Using his own family's photo archive as a point of departure, Annor's mixed-media paintings captivate viewers with representations of Ghanaian domesticity and everyday life that feel both familiar and intimate. Meditating on history, culture, and identity, his works take a documentary-like form, offering glimpses of characteristically Ghanaian settings through their inclusion of textiles and fabrics from his own family. As the eye takes in his paintings, the ordinary becomes a vibrant, collaged composition of remembrance—a time capsule of Ghana's past that can be understood with a contemporary sensibility.

A Night with Osibisa **(2021), one of Annor's multimedia fabric collages, practically vibrates on the canvas. A sense of joy and connection is palpable not only in the way the figures embrace and are intertwined, but in the composition itself. The layering of a geometric tiled floor with a variety of authentically Ghanaian clothing coalesce in a scene exuding true celebration. Similarly,** ***Cabinet of Memories*** **(2022), on view at the Kunsthalle Krems, puts the past on display, transporting viewers to a distinct moment in Ghana's evolving post-colonial climate. A tapestry of fabrics, textiles, and painted artifacts of a bygone era—an old radio, a vintage cable TV box, and a VHS cassette player—evoke a sense of nostalgia and beauty within a uniquely Ghanaian setting.**

Annor's body of works provides a re-telling or a new lens through which to understand Ghanaian life. Out of his mining of archival materials, a beautiful synthesis of elements emerges shedding new light on pre-colonial and post-independence Ghana through to the present day.

Cornelius Annor (geb. 1990, Mamobi, Ghana) ist einer der beeindruckendsten aufstrebenden Künstler:innen Ghanas. Seine evokativen Bilder liefern Momentaufnahmen des ghanaischen Alltagslebens seit der Unabhängigkeit. Annors Malereien in Mischtechnik, für die er das Fotoarchiv der eigenen Familie als Ausgangspunkt nimmt, fesseln die Betrachter:innen mit Darstellungen des ghanaischen Familien- und Alltagslebens, die sowohl vertraut als auch intim wirken. Seine Arbeiten, die sich mit Geschichte, Kultur und Identität auseinandersetzen, haben eine quasidokumentarische Form und geben durch die Einbeziehung von Textilien und Stoffen aus seiner eigenen Familie Einblicke in typisch ghanaische Lebenssituationen. Wenn das Auge die Bilder auf sich wirken lässt, wird das Gewöhnliche zu einer pulsierenden, collagierten Komposition der Erinnerung – eine Zeitkapsel aus der Vergangenheit Ghanas, die sich auch mit einem heutigen Empfinden verstehen lässt.

A Night with Osibisa (2021), eine von Annors Mixed-Media-Textilcollagen, vibriert förmlich auf der Leinwand. Ein Gefühl der Freude und Verbundenheit ist spürbar, nicht nur in der Art, wie die Figuren sich umarmen und miteinander verflochten scheinen, sondern auch in der Komposition selbst. Die Überlagerung eines geometrischen Fliesenbodens mit einer Vielzahl authentischer ghanaischer Textilien lässt eine Szene entstehen, die ein echtes Hochgefühl verströmt. Auf ähnliche Weise stellt *Cabinet of Memories* (2022), das in der Kunsthalle Krems zu sehen ist, die Vergangenheit zur Schau; es versetzt die Betrachter:innen zurück in einen bestimmten Moment des sich entwickelnden postkolonialen Klimas in Ghana. Ein Bildteppich aus Stoffen, Textilien und gemalten Artefakten einer vergangenen Zeit – ein altes Radio, ein altmodischer Kabel-Receiver, und ein VHS-Videoplayer – rufen in einem typischen ghanaischen Setting ein Gefühl von Nostalgie und Schönheit wach.

Annors Arbeiten bieten eine Neuerzählung oder eine neue Sichtweise des ghanaischen Lebens. Durch das Zusammentragen von archivalischen Materialien entsteht eine wunderschöne Synthese von Elementen, die ein neues Licht sowohl auf das vorkoloniale als auch auf das unabhängig gewordene Ghana bis zum heutigen Tag wirft.

SIR DAVID ADJAYE OBE

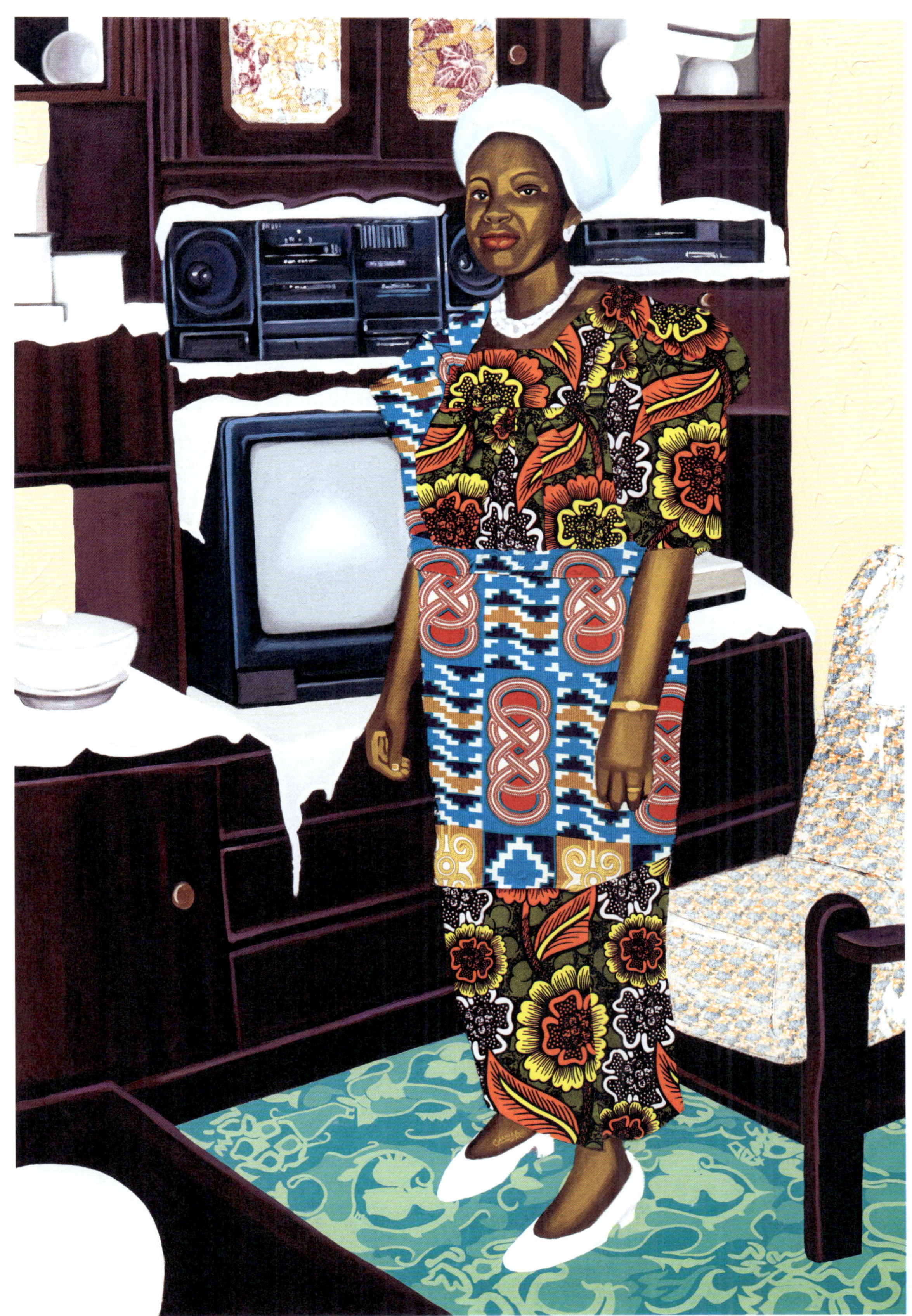

CORNELIUS ANNOR
Cabinet of Memories, 2022, Acrylic, fabric, and fabric transfer on canvas / Acryl, Stoff und Textiltransfer auf Leinwand, 182 × 121 cm

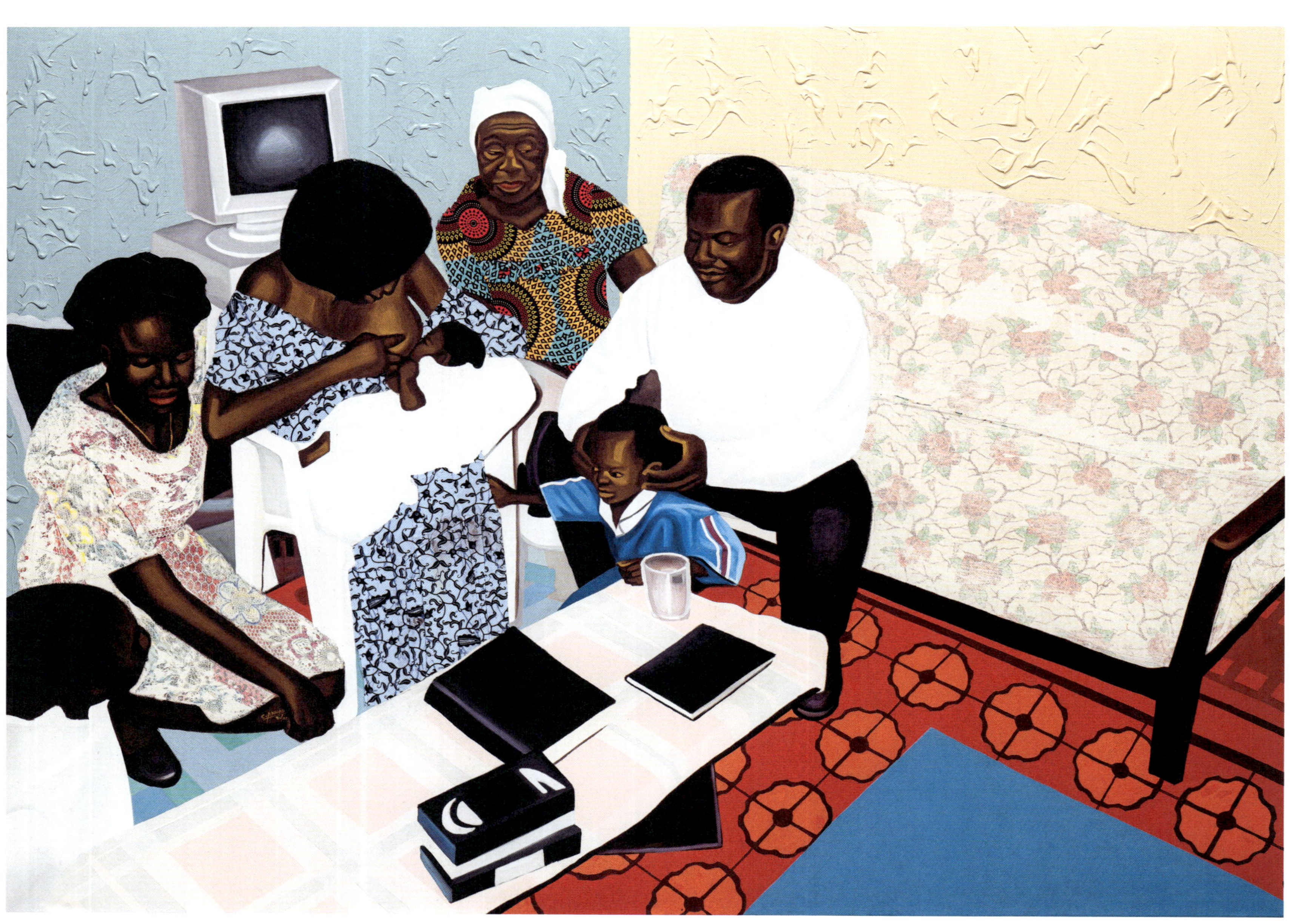

CORNELIUS ANNOR
Obaatan (Motherly Love), 2022, Acrylic, fabric and fabric transfer on canvas / Acryl, Stoff und Textiltransfer auf Leinwand, 152 × 212 cm

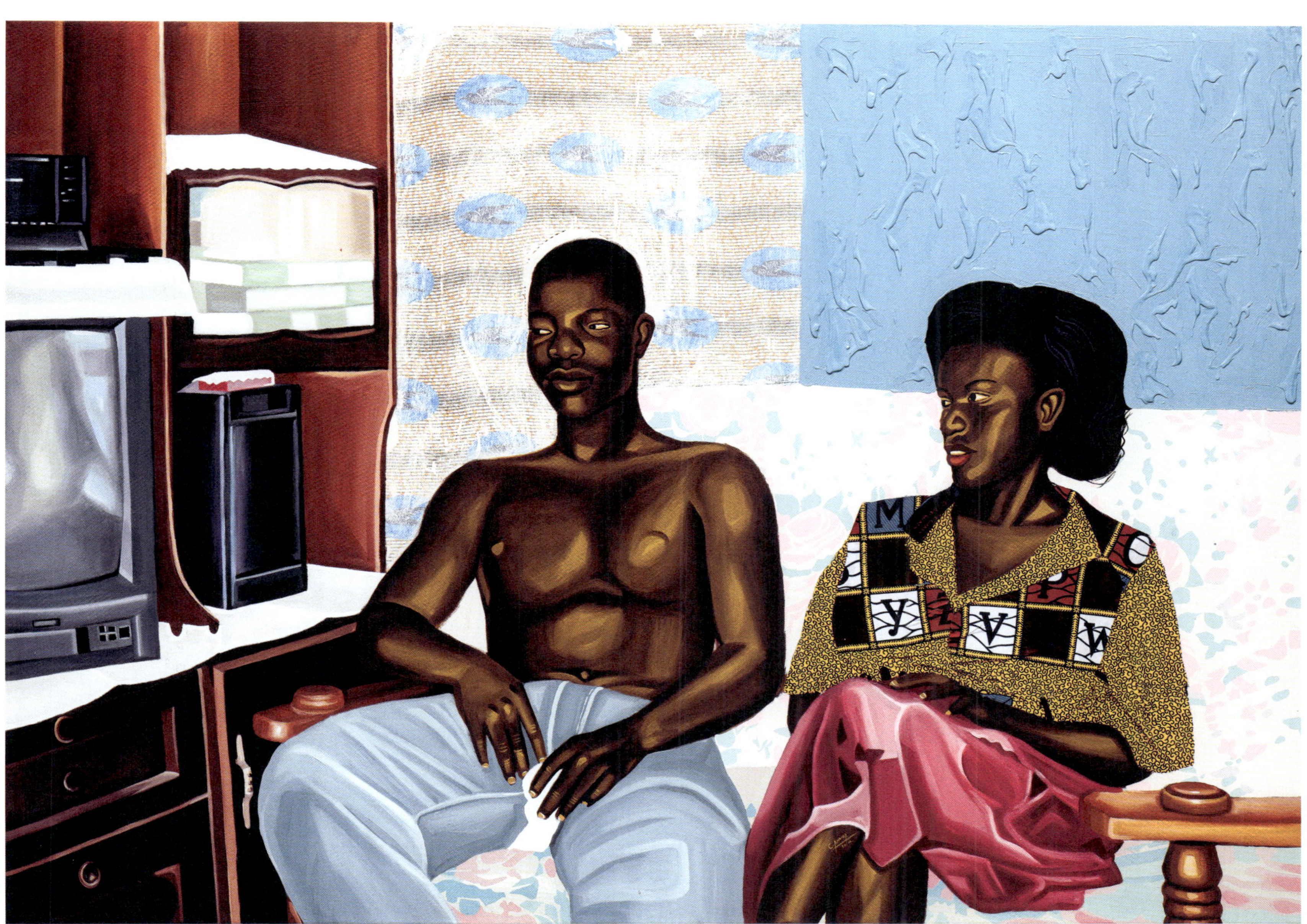

CORNELIUS ANNOR
Menua baa (My Sister), 2022, Acrylic, fabric, and fabric transfer on canvas / Acryl, Stoff und Texti transfer auf Leinwand, 152 × 212 cm

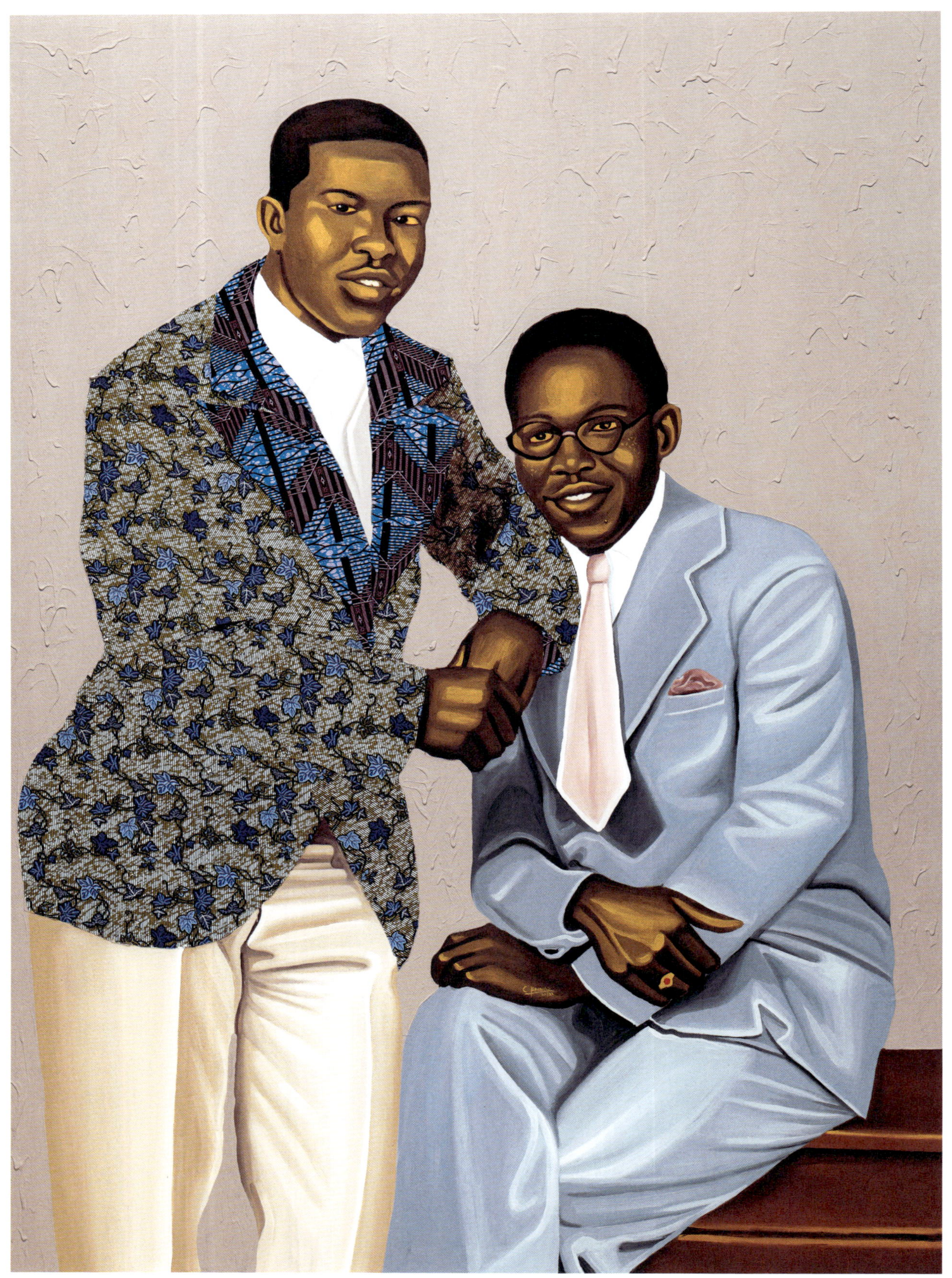

CORNELIUS ANNOR
Akonta M'adamf, 2022, Acrylic, fabric, and fabric transfer on canvas /
Acryl, Stoff und Textiltransfer auf Leinwand, 213 × 152 cm

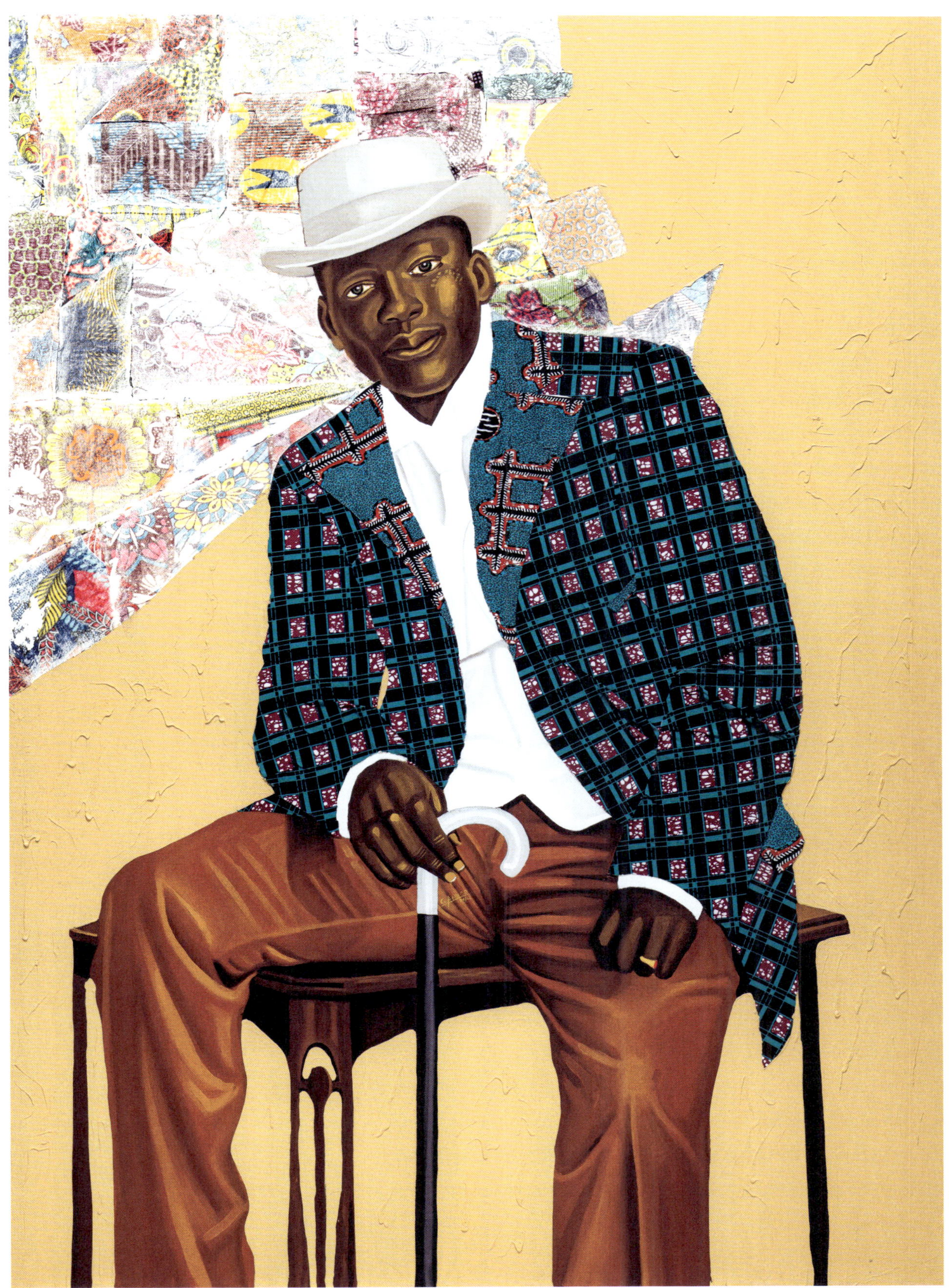

CORNELIUS ANNOR
Barima Katakyie (Great Man), 2022, Acrylic, fabric, and fabric transfer on canvas / Acryl, Stoff und Transfergewebe auf Leinwand, 213 × 152 cm

ATSOUPÉ

Born in Togo in 1986, Atsoupé lives and works in Paris. Her oeuvre features a myriad of faces, most of them female, that stare at the beholder with their lost yet insistent gazes. However, with heads frequently sutured and trimmed with a variety of wools or braids, these paintings bear no resemblance to what we would call the portrait genre. There is no interest in creating a likeness here! The painter does not have to worry about accuracy or beauty—something that prompted Matisse to say that "a portrait is a quarrel." Her aspiration lies elsewhere. Nothing is known of these faces that resemble anonymous figures floating bodilessly like ectoplasms, suspended between life and death. Perhaps they are disturbing memories that haunt the artist born from her early years spent in African countries ravaged by war.

While Atsoupé's paintings inevitably bear the mark of grief and trauma, they are also imbued with the magic of a childhood spent in contact with the landscapes of her native Africa. This has no doubt led to the mix of candor and muted violence that runs through the artist's work and gives the surface of the canvas—the substrate—the character of skin bearing traces of its past. While many of the heads are brutally riddled with holes or bear laceration marks as well as scars, occasionally evoking the destructive rage of Artaud's drawings, the artist also demonstrates a resilient form of artmaking, repairing her old paintings by patiently stitching them back up—performing a type of improvised *kintsugi* [the Japanese tradition of mending broken pottery with lacquer infused with the dust of precious metals] on her own paintings. This way of reappropriating her wounds through aesthetic transmutation lies at the heart of Atsoupé's artistic approach.

By using these humble materials found in her everyday environment, Atsoupé's artistic practice shows a clear kinship with outsider art; she's a successor to the Surrealists who wound their way through flea markets and back streets. But it also demonstrates her need to use these scraps to fulfil a more deeply rooted desire—to reassemble pieces of the past like the disjointed canvases she tirelessly repairs as if they were the pleats of a torn fabric, echoing her own fragmented childhood.

1986 in Togo geboren, lebt und arbeitet Atsoupé in Paris. Ihr Œuvre umfasst eine Vielzahl an meist weiblichen Gesichtern, die die Betrachtenden mit verlorenem, zugleich eindringlichem Blick fixieren.

Doch sind die Köpfe häufig vernäht sowie mit Wolle und Posamenten verziert und somit weit entfernt vom Genre der Porträtmalerei. Kein Gedanke an Abbildhaftigkeit! Die Malerin lässt sich nicht von Aspekten wie Genauigkeit oder Schönheit leiten, die Matisse veranlassten zu behaupten, ein Porträt sei eine Unstimmigkeit. Ihr Anliegen ist ein anderes. Über die Gesichter wissen wir nichts, sie wirken wie anonyme Figuren, die ohne Körper dahinschweben, wie Ektoplasmen, die in der Zwischenwelt von Leben und Tod umherirren. Vielleicht sind es Erinnerungen, die die Künstlerin heimsuchen und ihren ersten Lebensjahren in vom Krieg verwüsteten afrikanischen Ländern entspringen.

Atsoupés Malerei trägt die Spuren von Trauer und Trauma, ist zugleich aber durchdrungen vom Zauber einer Kindheit in den Landschaften ihrer afrikanischen Heimat. Daher rührt ohne Zweifel diese Mischung aus Offenheit und dumpfer Gewalt, die sich durch das Werk der Künstlerin zieht. Sie verleiht der Leinwandoberfläche, dem Untergrund, den Charakter einer Haut, die die Spuren der Vergangenheit trägt.

Während viele Köpfe wie wild durchlöchert oder von Rissen gezeichnet sind, wie Narben, die mitunter die zerstörerische Wut der Zeichnungen von Artaud evozieren, vertritt die Malerin zugleich eine Kunst der Widerstandsfähigkeit: Geduldig repariert und flickt sie ihre älteren Arbeiten und schafft so eine Form von *Kintsugi* [traditionelle japanische Reparaturmethode, bei der zerbrochene Keramiken mit einem mit Edelmetallen versetzten Lack gekittet werden] auf Grundlage ihrer eigenen Malereien. Diese Art der Wiederaneignung von Verletzungen durch eine regelrechte ästhetische Umwandlungsarbeit steht im Zentrum von Atsoupés künstlerischem Ansatz.

Ihr künstlerischer Zugang ist offensichtlich jenem der Outsider Art verwandt. Sie tritt das Erbe der Surrealist:innen an, die Trödelmärkte und Passagen zum Labyrinth ihrer Streifzüge machten. Zugleich zeugt er jedoch von dem Bedürfnis, solche Reste zu nutzen, um ein viel älteres Verlangen zu stillen: Fragmente der Vergangenheit wieder zusammenzusetzen – wie die aufgetrennten Leinwände, die sie unermüdlich flickt, wie die Falten eines zerrissenen Stoffes – ein Echo ihrer eigenen zerstreuten Kindheit.

PHILIPPE GODIN

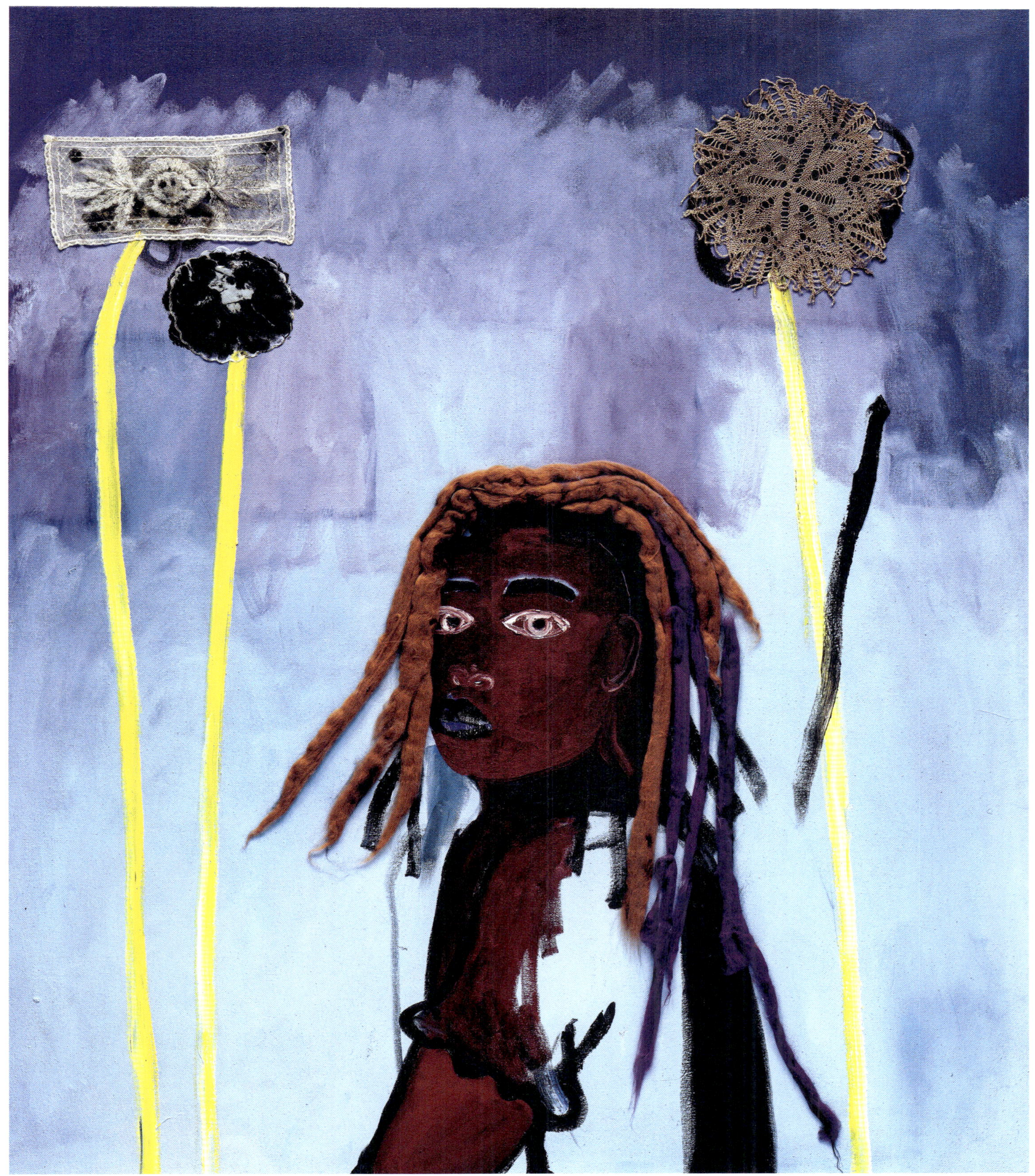

ATSOUPÉ
Fuite, 2021, Oil, wool, crochet and embroidery on canvas /
Öl, Wolle, Gehäkeltes und Stickerei auf Leinwand, 140 × 120 cm

ATSOUPÉ
Est-ce que tu vas bouger?, 2021, Oil and wool on canvas / Öl und Wolle auf Leinwand, 100 × 73 cm

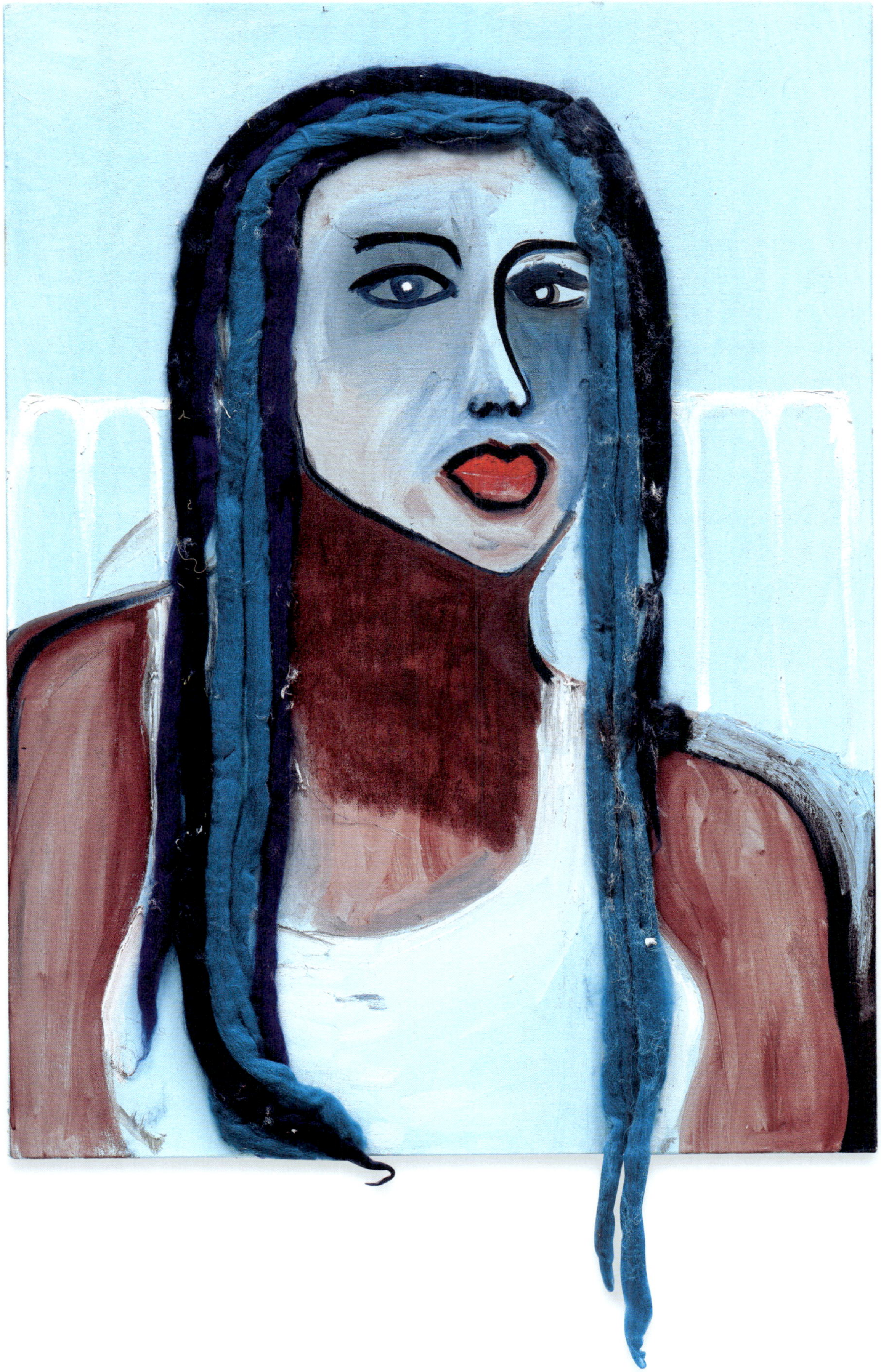

ALEXANDRE DIOP

Latex, metal cans, wood, textiles, paper, books, photos, animal fibers, fur, leather, cords, nails, plaster, burned elements, old car parts: Alexandre Diop (b. 1995, Paris) collects all these things on his forays through public space and abandoned houses. Such refuse, bearing traces of "*it was like this*" as a "certificate of presence,"[1] forms Diop's materials—along with glue, gouache, oil paint, pencil, varnish, and pastel—as well as the "colors," from which he constructs his complex assemblages. What is unnoticed and forgotten is brought together to form a disparate whole.

As with Jean-Michel Basquiat, everything resembles an explosion of energy and material. Diego Cortez describes this as an artistic strategy: "Fragments rather than the Cubist or post-Cubist way of building sections, hatching things together [...] a galaxy of reality that's been again exploded."[2] Diop shreds, cuts, stretches, tears, burns, glues, hammers, and staples his materials in such fashion. Fragmentation forms the premise and method of creating the new: an intertwining of explosion and reconstruction. In his *Autoportrait of the Young Black Diable at the Age of 25* and *Autoportrait qui baise la loi* (both 2021) Diop also "paints" with color and "refuse," which he selects, reshapes, and recontextualizes. Analogous to the process of production, the genders and social milieus of his figures, their faces and hands emphasized as conveyors of expression, are also held in a state of flux.

Diop also expands his painterly materials to include disregarded and discarded elements, providing them a stage for all the history and visible traces of the past they contain, and transforming his work into a phenomenon of our time with an eye toward what's to come. He opens up new spaces for thought without adhering to the limitations that are seemingly imposed on art discourse: a "galaxy of reality" as a fluid transition between music, dance, public space, the artist's studio, duration, the moment, and the "*it-was-like-this*," in which Diop destroys what has been saved and saves what has been destroyed, preserving the past and preparing fertile ground for something new.

1 Roland Barthes, *Camera Lucida* (New York: Hill and Wang, 1981), 87.
2 Diego Cortez, in Tamra Davis, *Jean-Michel Basquiat. The Radiant Child*, documentary film, with Jean-Michel Basquiat and others, Fortissimo Films, US 2010, timecode: 00:36:20–00:36:41.

Latex, Metalldosen, Holz, Textilien, Papier, Bücher, Fotos, tierische Fasern, Pelz, Leder, Schnüre, Nägel, Gips, verbrannte Elemente, alte Autoteile: all dies sammelt Alexandre Diop (geb. 1995, Paris) auf seinen Streifzügen durch den öffentlichen Raum und in verlassenen Häusern ein. Solcher Unrat, welcher die Spuren des „*Es-ist-so-gewesen*" als „Beglaubigung von Präsenz"[1] in sich trägt, bildet Diops Material und zusammen mit Klebstoff, Gouache, Ölfarbe, Bleistift, Firnis und Pastell auch die „Farben", aus denen er seine komplexen Assemblagen konstruiert. Unbeachtetes und Vergessenes werden zu einem disparaten Ganzen zusammengefügt.

Wie bei Jean-Michel Basquiat gleicht alles einer Explosion von Energie und Material. Als künstlerische Strategie beschreibt dies Diego Cortez: „Fragmente anstatt des kubistischen und postkubistischen Verfahrens, Ausschnitte zusammenzubauen, Dinge miteinander zu verhaken, [...] eine Galaxie von Wirklichkeit, die wieder in Stücke gesprengt wurde."[2] Derart zerfetzt, zerschneidet, dehnt, zerreißt, verbrennt, klebt, hämmert und klammert Diop seine Materialien. Die Fragmentierung bildet Voraussetzung und Methode der Neuschöpfung: ein Ineinander von Explosion und Wiederaufbau. Auch in seinem *Autoportrait of the Young Black Diable at the Age of 25* und *Autoportrait qui baise la loi* (beide 2021) „malt" Diop mit Farbe und „Müll", den er auswählt, entformt und neu kontextualisiert. Dabei sind seine Figuren mit ihren als Ausdrucksträgern betonten Gesichtern und Händen analog zum Herstellungsprozess auch hinsichtlich des Geschlechts und sozialen Gefüges im Fluss gehalten.

Diop erweitert das malerische Material hin zum Missachteten und Weggeworfenen, dem er eine Bühne gibt für all die darin gespeicherte Geschichte und sichtbaren Spuren der Vergangenheit, und transformiert es in ein Phänomen unserer Zeit mit der Perspektive auf das Kommende. Er eröffnet neue Denkräume, ohne sich an jene Grenzen zu halten, die dem Kunstdiskurs auferlegt scheinen: eine „galaxy of reality" als fließender Übergang zwischen Musik, Tanz, öffentlichem Raum, Künstleratelier, der Dauer, dem Moment und dem „*Es-ist-so-gewesen*", in der Diop Gerettetes zerstört und Zerstörtes rettet, die Vergangenheit konserviert und den Nährboden für etwas Neues bereitet.

1 Roland Barthes, *Die helle Kammer. Bemerkung zur Photographie*, Frankfurt a. M. 1985, S. 87 und 97.
2 Diego Cortez, in: Tamra Davis, *Jean-Michel Basquiat. The Radiant Child*, Dokumentarfilm, mit Jean-Michel Basquiat u. a., Fortissimo Films, USA 2010, Zeitcode: 00:36:20–00:36:41 (Übers. v. Michael Strand).

DIETER BUCHHART

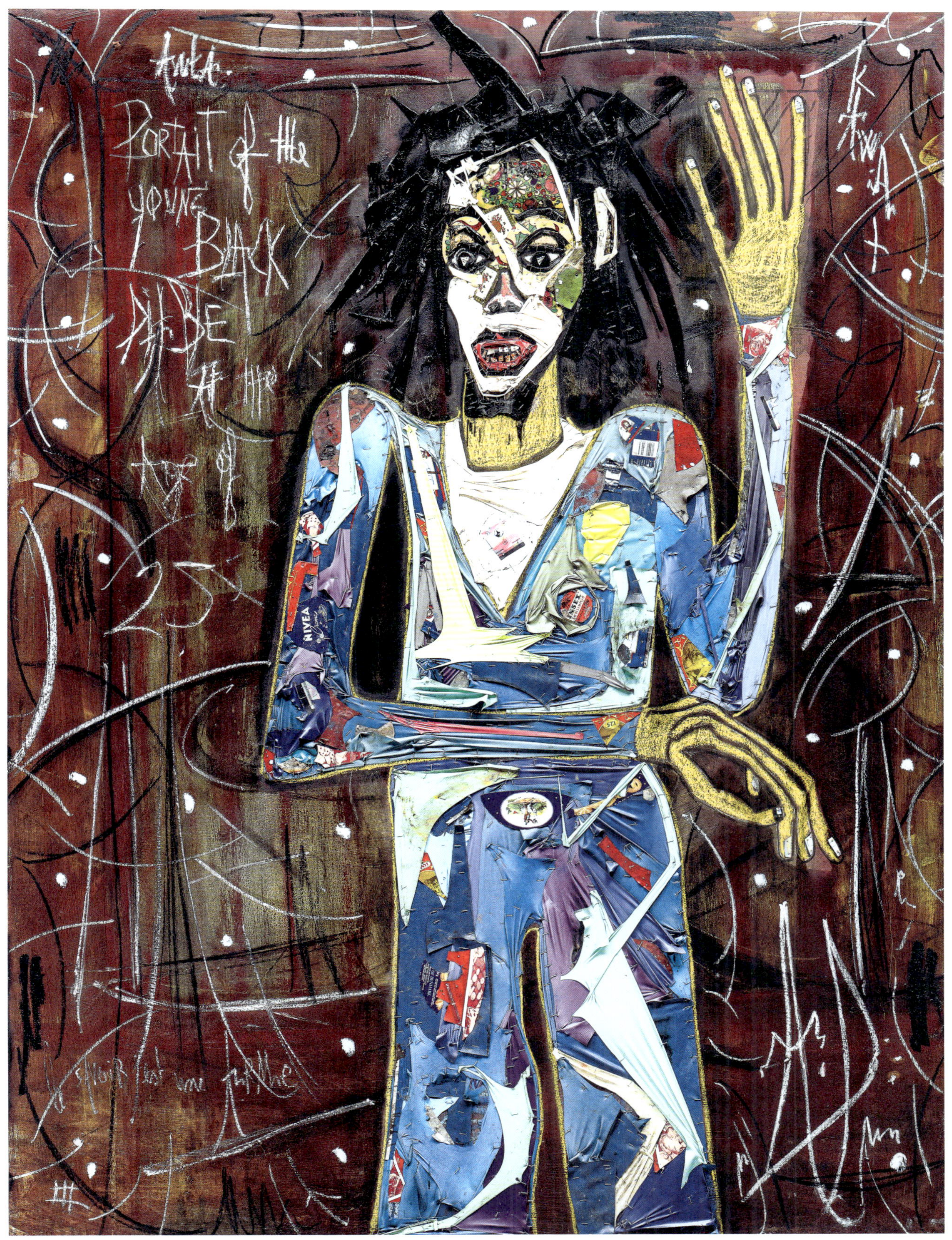

ALEXANDRE DIOP
Autoportrait of the Young Black Diable at the Age of 25, 2021
Mixed media on wood / Mischtechnik auf Holz, 215 × 160 cm

ALEXANDRE DIOP
Phillip Gintz Kill Bill, 2021
Mixed media on wood / Mischtechnik auf Holz, 189,5 × 130 cm

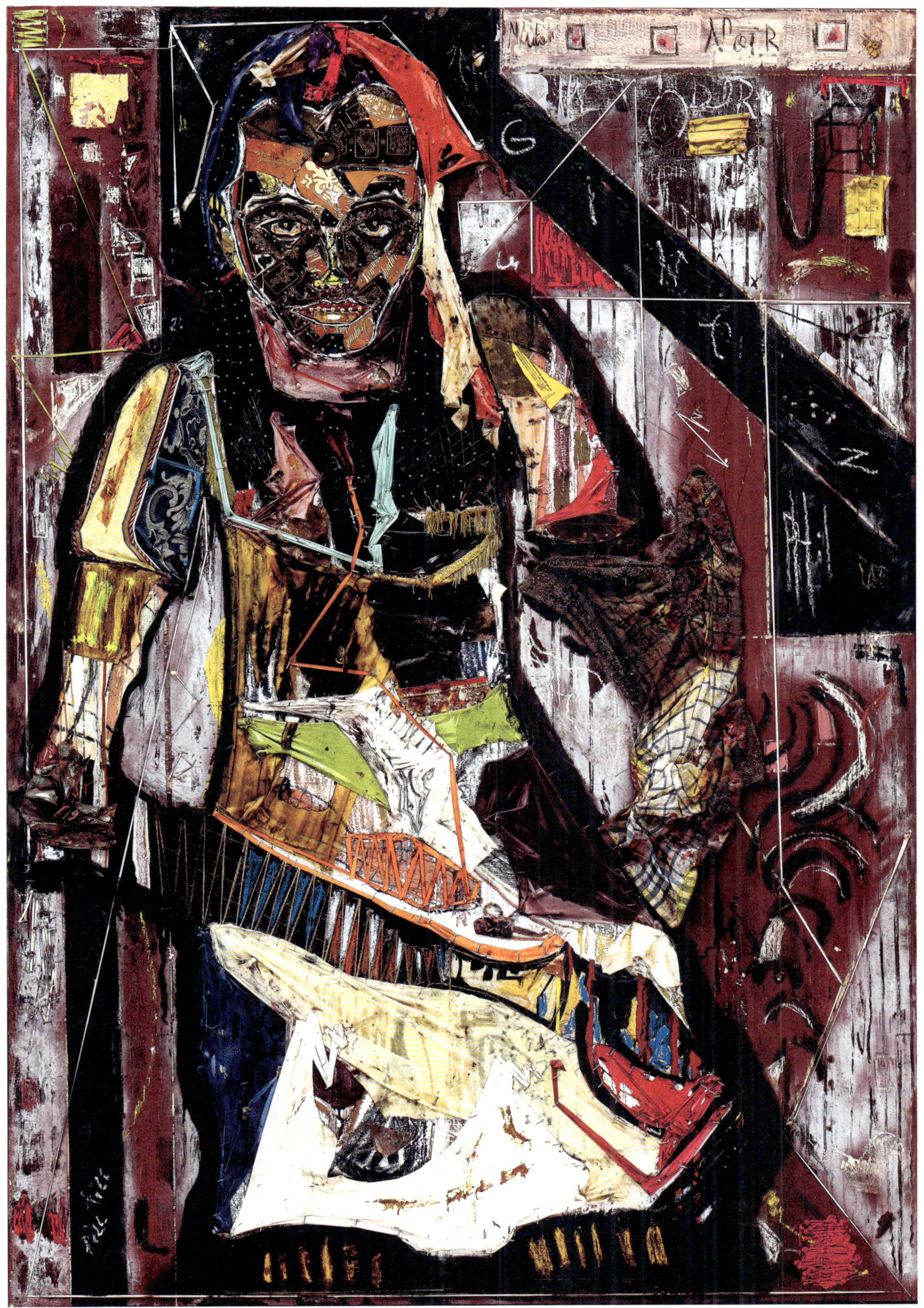

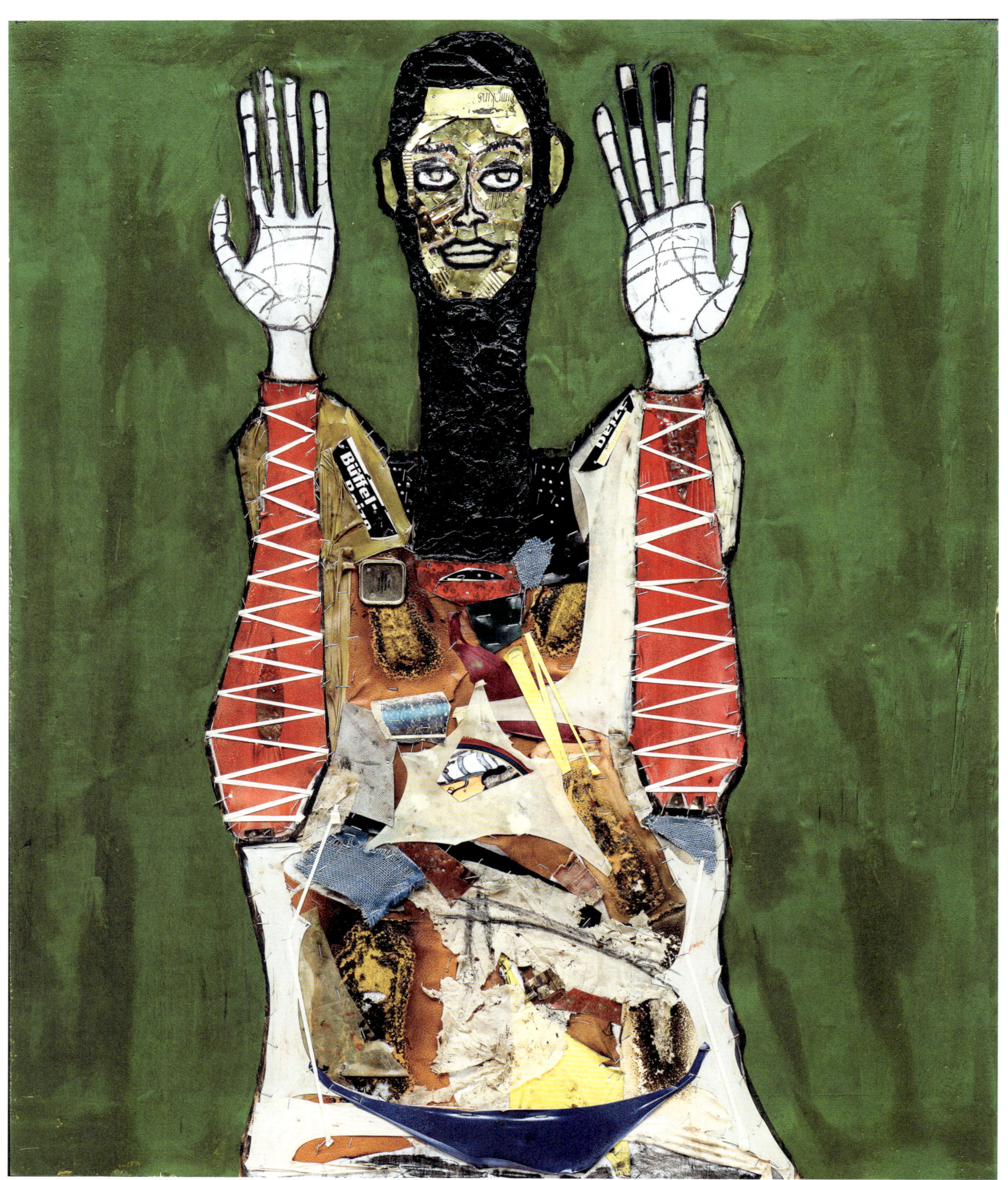

ALEXANDRE DIOP
Diplomat 06, 2021
Mixed media on wood / Mischtechnik auf Holz, 118 × 98 cm

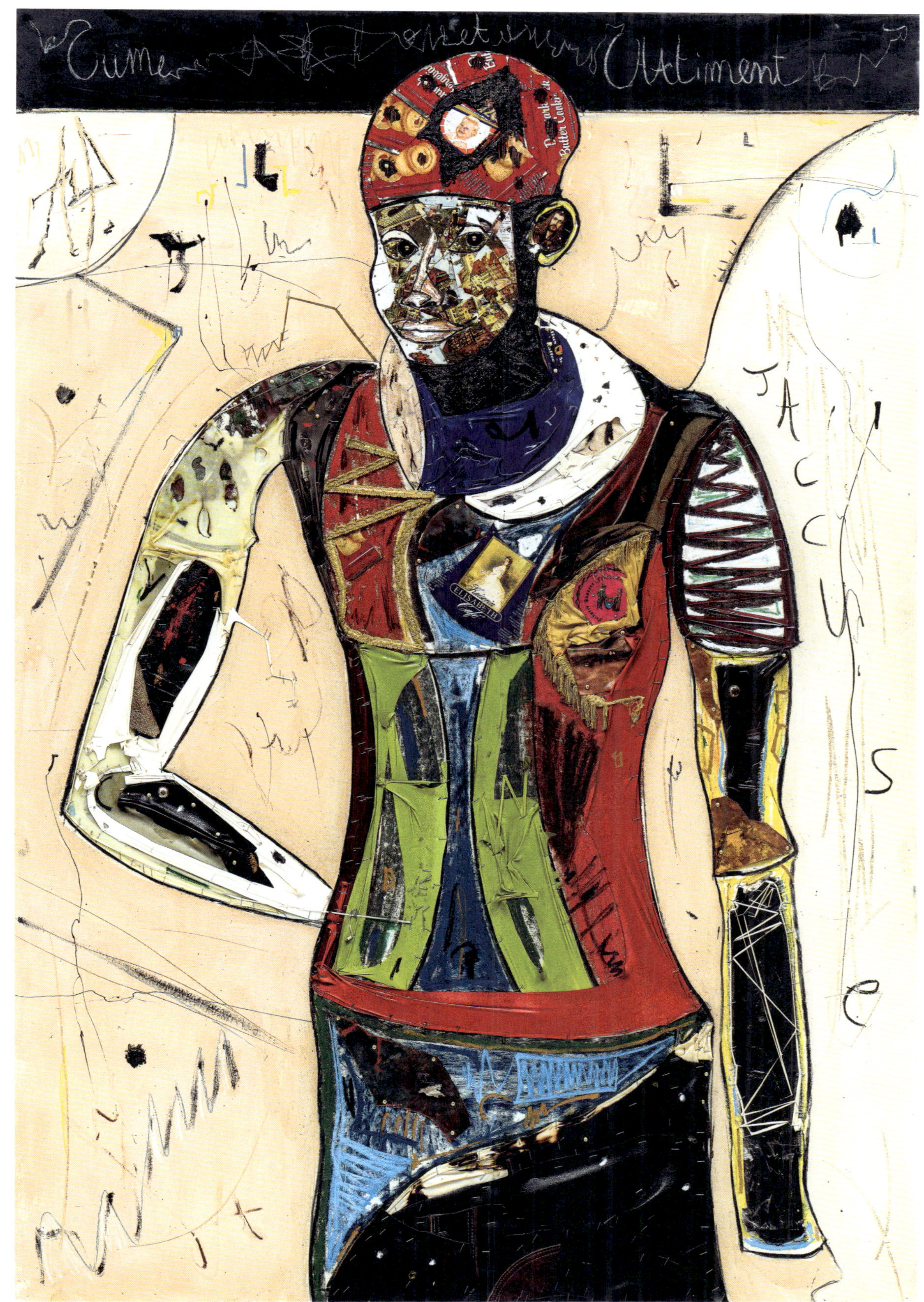

ALEXANDRE DIOP
Portrait de Mara Niang, 2021
Mixed media on wood / Mischtechnik auf Holz, 187,4 × 128,5 cm

ALEXANDRE DIOP
Autoportrait qui baise la loi / Showing the Authority the Middle Finger, 2021
Mixed media on wood / Mischtechnik auf Holz, 215 × 160 cm

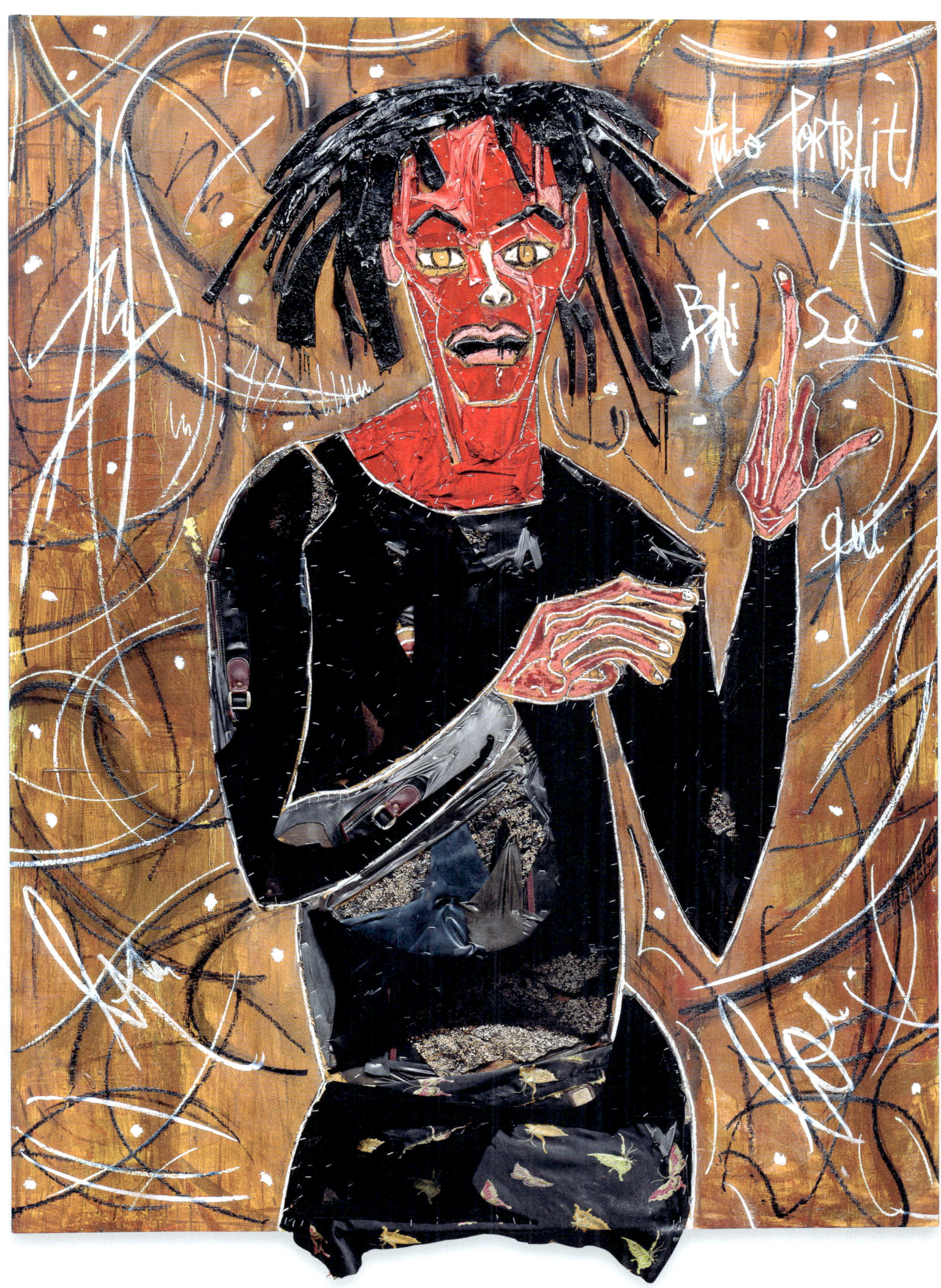
Auto Portrait

GASTINEAU MASSAMBA

Born in the Republic of Congo in 1973, Gastineau Massamba currently lives and works in Montreuil. Using acrylics and pastels helps him find the energy to vividly capture figures that he paints without drawing them first. The painter pays no heed to narration or elaboration; he gets straight to the point and tackles the design directly without preparing the canvas in advance. In good dramatic fashion, the artist's paintings go deeper than the flesh. The importance of restraint in this kind of painting with its black background is evident in the way the characters are isolated. An asceticism that virtually strips his canvases of all decor, reminiscent of the starkness of Beckett's theatre. Indeed, could it not be said that he creates overwhelming figures at the precise moment they exude fear itself? Is the ever-present cry not a form of resistance that philosopher Gilles Deleuze attributed to art; the only uplifting feature in a world devoid of transcendence? Is it not this ability to "stand firm" in the thick of the world and the most inhumane situations that the artist bears witness to in his own manner?
He shows us the fate of human beings fleeing political violence with no economic or social security—moving and migrating in search of better living conditions. The strength of this painting lies in its ability to make this silent cry visible and to make us perceive our own deafness to the suffering of others. Yet Gastineau Massamba's work is not a eulogy. A subtle mix of Expressionism and Mannerism runs through his style of painting, whose vitality allows us to reconcile the harshness of the subject and the exultation of the brushwork. His painting is a celebration despite the dramas playing out therein. Contrary to the pictorial tradition in which light is cast from above, the lighting here seemingly comes from the depths of the earth. Light from beyond the grave, perhaps? Rising up from the ground, it seems like a testament to our fruitful relationship with nature.

Gastineau Massamba, 1973 in der Republik Kongo geboren, lebt und arbeitet derzeit in Montreuil. Die Verwendung von Acryl und Pastell ermöglicht es ihm, die Energie zu finden, die es braucht, um die Figuren, die er ohne Vorzeichnung malt, lebhaft zu erfassen. Der Künstler verzichtet auf jegliche Narration oder Ausgestaltung. Er konzentriert sich auf das Wesentliche und nimmt das Motiv direkt in Angriff, ohne die Leinwand vorzubereiten. Als echter Dramatiker versteht es der Künstler, über das Fleischliche hinauszugehen. Wie wichtig die Zurückhaltung in dieser Malerei auf schwarzem Grund ist, zeigt sich in der Art und Weise, wie sie die Figuren isoliert. Eine Strenge, die seinen Gemälden jeglichen Dekor entzieht und die an die Nüchternheit des beckettschen Theaters erinnert. Könnte man nicht sogar sagen, dass er unbeugsame Figuren just in dem Moment zeigt, in dem sie das pure Entsetzen verkörpern? Ist der allgegenwärtige Schrei nicht Teil einer Form des Widerstandes, den der Philosoph Gilles Deleuze der Kunst als einzig erhebende Kraft in einer Welt ohne Transzendenz zuschreibt? Ist es nicht diese Fähigkeit, mitten in der Welt und in unmenschlichsten Situationen „durchzuhalten", der der Künstler auf seine Weise Ausdruck verleiht?
Er zeigt uns das Schicksal von Menschen, die vor politischer Gewalt fliehen, ohne wirtschaftliche oder soziale Sicherheit, die fort- und weiterziehen auf der Suche nach besseren Lebensbedingungen. Die Stärke dieser Malerei liegt darin, diesen stummen Schrei sichtbar zu machen und uns unsere eigene Taubheit gegenüber dem Leid anderer vor Augen zu führen. Dennoch hat die Kunst von Gastineau Massamba nichts von einer Trauerrede. Eine subtile Mischung aus Expressionismus und Manierismus durchzieht diese Malerei, deren Lebendigkeit es erlaubt, die Härte der Thematik mit dem Jubel des Pinselstriches in Einklang zu bringen. Die Malerei ist ein Fest, trotz all der Dramen, die sich in ihr abspielen. Entgegen einer darstellerischen Tradition, bei der das Licht von oben hinabfällt, scheint die Beleuchtung aus den Tiefen der Erde zu kommen. Ein Licht aus dem Totenreich? Es scheint aus der Erde aufzusteigen, als wolle es von der fruchtbaren Beziehung zeugen, die uns mit der Natur verbindet.

PHILIPPE GODIN

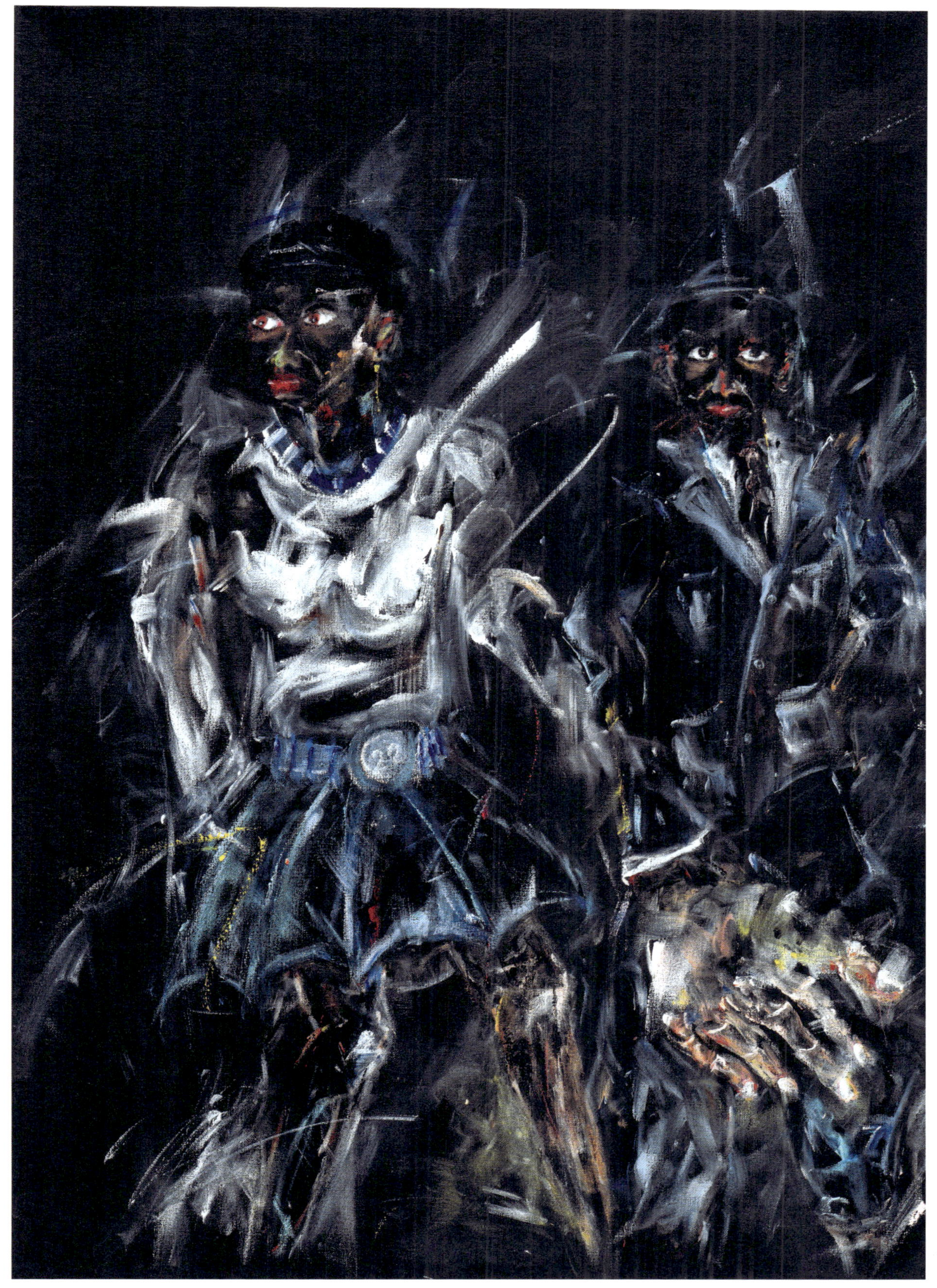

GASTINEAU MASSAMBA
LARI Family, 2021, Acrylic and pastel on black linen canvas / Acryl und Pastell auf schwarzer Leinwand, 100 × 70 cm

GASTINEAU MASSAMBA
RESILIENCE VI, 2021, Acrylic on black linen canvas /
Acryl auf schwarzer Leinwand, 124 × 96 cm

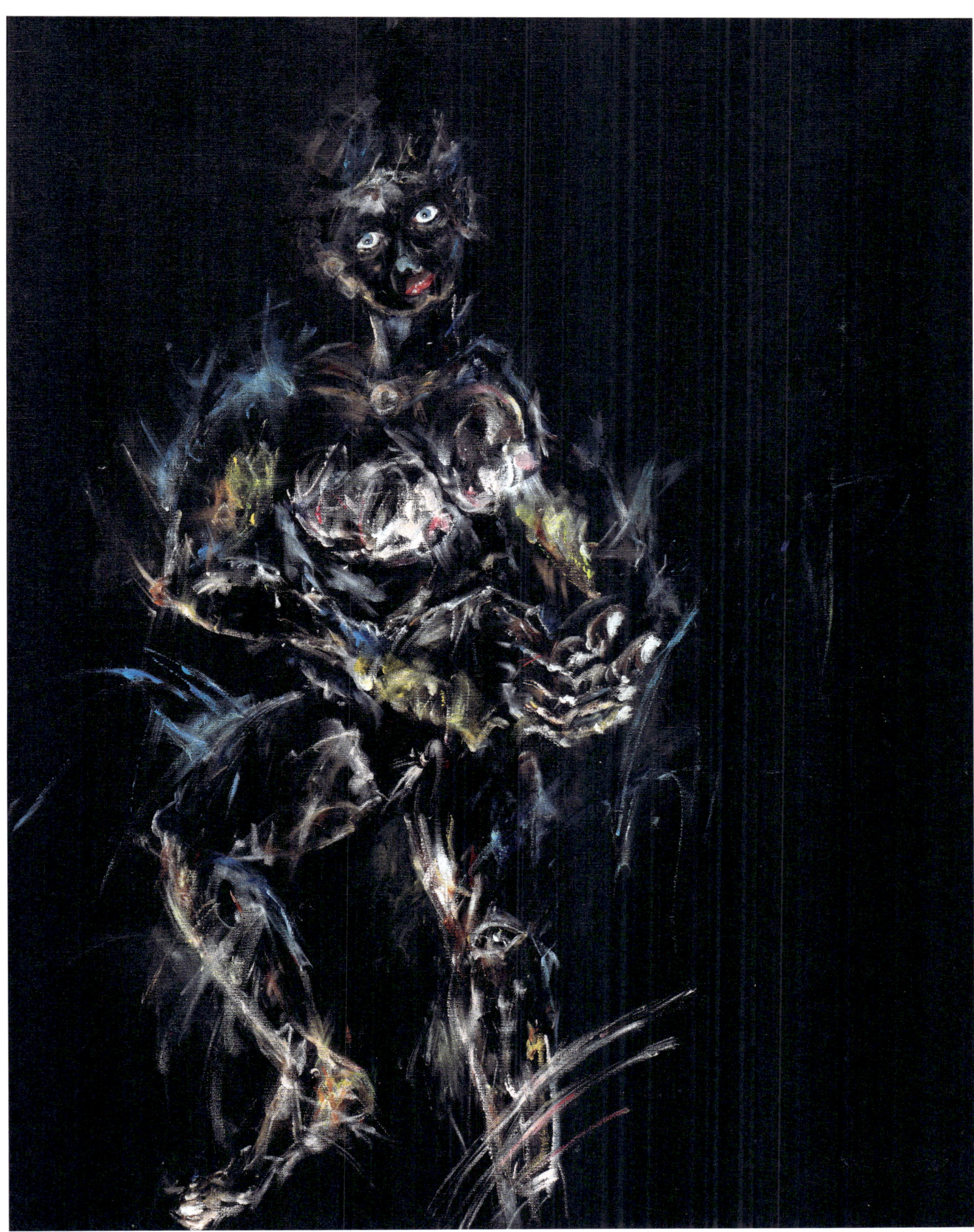

SOULEIMANE BARRY

Souleimane Barry (b. 1980 in Burkina Faso) considers his work experimental, as the fruit of his imagination influenced by his daily life. Avoiding all conformism, he "installs his elements without too much thought." In that regard, he particularly admires two of the greatest twentieth-century artists, Jean-Michel Basquiat and Francis Bacon, for their need to externalize tumultuous emotions. Using watercolor technique with acrylic paint as well as natural pigments, and even collage, Souleimane Barry lets the material guide him, creating forms and vague representations that are reworked according to what he seeks to explore. His source of inspiration remains the painted human figure in its plurality. He is particularly fond of portraits given their suitability for expressing emotions. His portrait series "Visage Anonyme" attests to the sensitivity with which Souleimane Barry represents the intensity of a feeling. As reflections of the soul, emotions transcribe our humanity as much as our own identity.

Essentially the artist wants to depict the human condition in a certain universalist manner but equally in its singularity, with each individual growing and evolving within a distinct cultural and social environment. An example is his work *Traditions*, which features a man surrounded by a chicken and a number of animist references such as a sacrificial altar or a studded totem. These cultural and religious codes have a strong symbolism that resonates differently depending on the people perceiving them. Having lived in France for a number of years, the artist contrasts his native culture of Burkina Faso with another reality, that of his daily life, which is rich with encounters. Travelling, moving around, but also being an expatriate broadens his universe. Consequently, the artist tends towards an intercultural dialogue that easily appeals to a wide audience. A practice that Souleimane Barry particularly enjoys is that of being able to exchange ideas with this audience in the presence of his works. The intriguing difference in perception between a European audience and his own raises questions for him, but also allows him to reflect on the subject that matters to him: the diversity of mankind.

ARMELLE DAKOUO

Souleimane Barry (geb. 1980 in Burkina Faso) versteht seine Arbeit als experimentell, als Frucht seiner Fantasie, die von seinem täglichen Leben beeinflusst wird. Er vermeidet jeglichen Konformismus, „setzt seine Elemente, ohne Fragen zu stellen". In diesem Sinne bewundert er vor allem zwei der größten Künstler des 20. Jahrhunderts, Jean-Michel Basquiat und Francis Bacon, für ihren Drang, ihre turbulente Gefühlswelt nach außen zu tragen. Durch die Verwendung der Aquarelltechnik, von Acrylfarbe und auch von natürlichen Pigmenten sowie sogar der Collage lässt sich Barry vom Material tragen und vage Formen und Darstellungen entstehen, die je nachdem, was er erforschen will, überarbeitet werden. Seine Inspirationsquelle bleibt der gemalte Mensch in seiner Vielfältigkeit. Das Porträt schätzt er besonders, da sich damit Gefühle gut ausdrücken lassen. Seine Porträtserie „Visage Anonyme" zeugt von der Sensibilität, mit der Barry die Tiefe eines Gefühls wiedergibt. Als Spiegelbild der Seele vermitteln Gefühle unser Menschsein ebenso wie unsere eigene Identität.

Im Wesentlichen will der Künstler unser Menschsein in seinen universalen, aber auch individuellen Dimensionen darstellen, da sich jeder Mensch in einem anderen kulturellen und sozialen Umfeld entwickelt. Ein Beispiel hierfür ist sein Werk *Traditions*, das einen Mann umgeben von einem Huhn und einer Reihe animistischer Referenzen zeigt, wie einem Opferaltar oder einem mit Nieten besetzten Totem. Diese kulturellen und religiösen Codes haben eine starke Symbolik, die auf jeden Menschen unterschiedlich wirkt. Der seit einigen Jahren in Frankreich lebende Künstler stellt die Kultur, in der er in Burkina Faso aufgewachsen ist, einer anderen Realität gegenüber, jener seines Alltags, die reich an Begegnungen ist. Das Reisen, das Sichfortbewegen, aber auch die Tatsache, dass er ein Auswanderer ist, erweitern sein Universum. So tendiert der Künstler zu einem interkulturellen Dialog, der ein breites Publikum anspricht. Barry schätzt es besonders, sich mit diesem vor seinen Werken auszutauschen. Der faszinierende Unterschied zwischen der Wahrnehmung eines europäischen Publikums und seiner eigenen stimmt ihn nachdenklich, erlaubt ihm aber auch, über das Thema, das ihm besonders wichtig ist, nachzudenken: der Mensch in seiner Vielfalt.

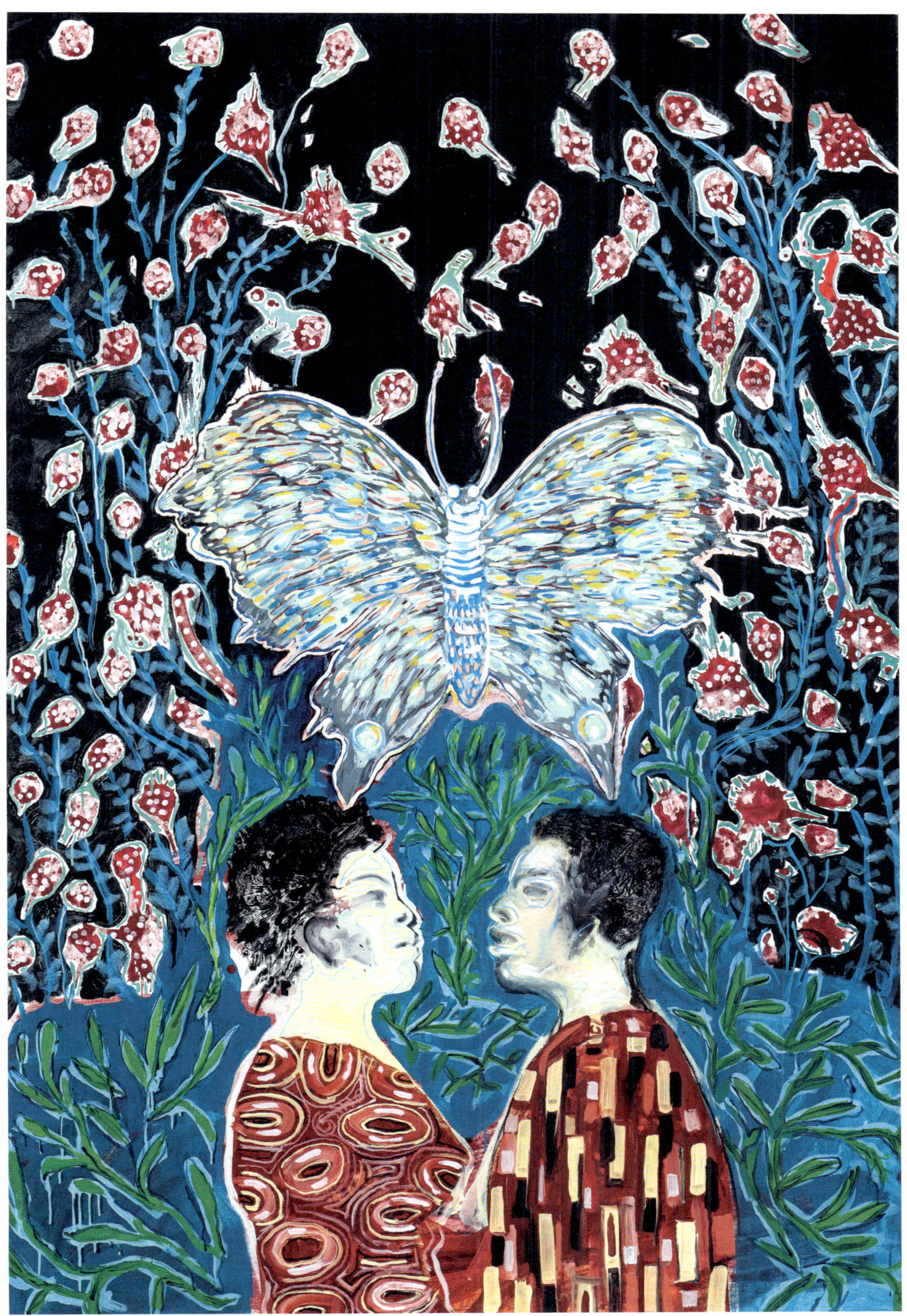

SOULEIMANE BARRY
Better Fly, 2020
Acrylic on canvas / Acryl auf Leinwand, 206 × 137 cm

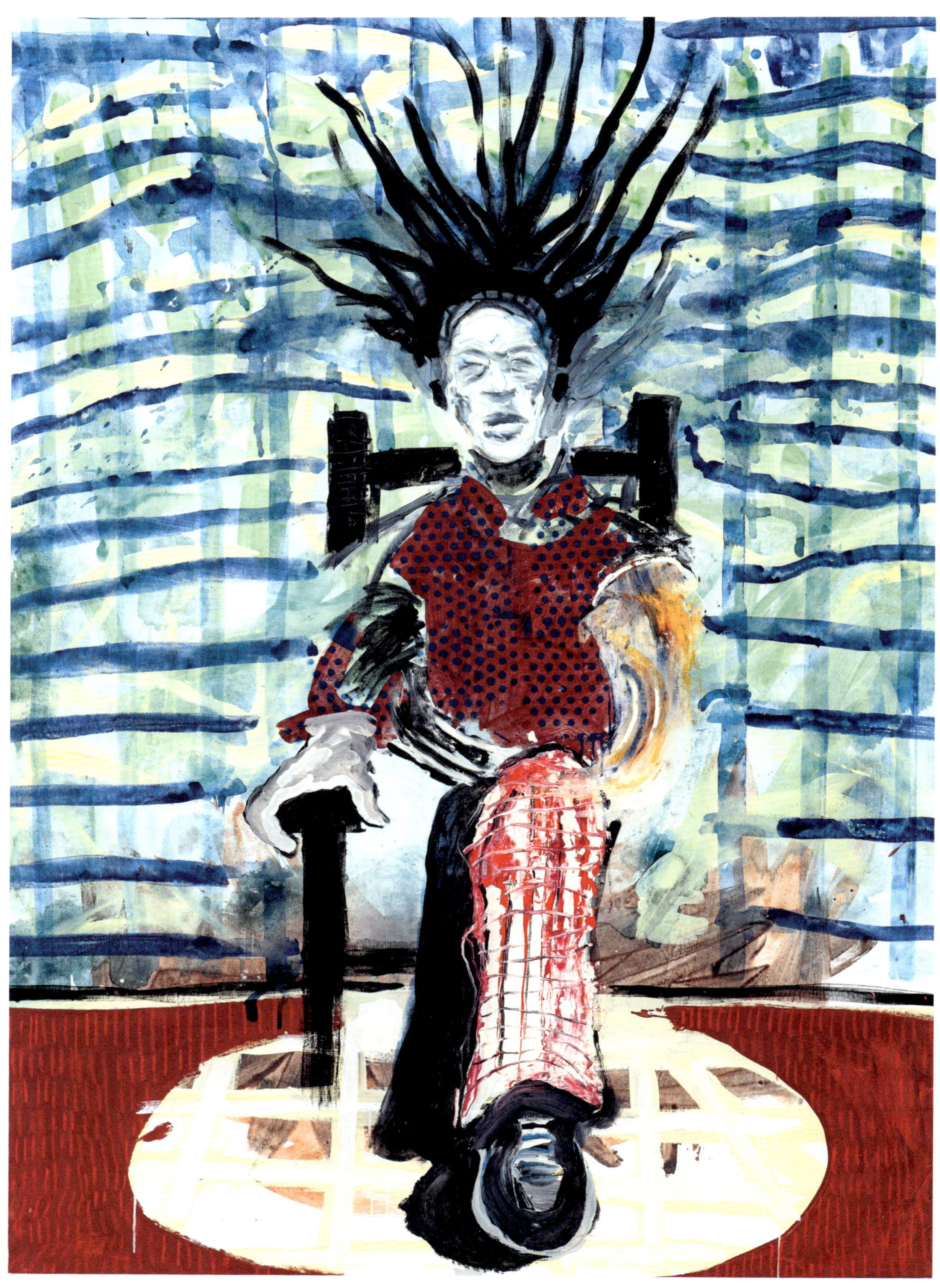

SOULEIMANE BARRY
Inspiration, 2020
Acrylic on canvas / Acryl auf Leinwand, 200 × 140 cm

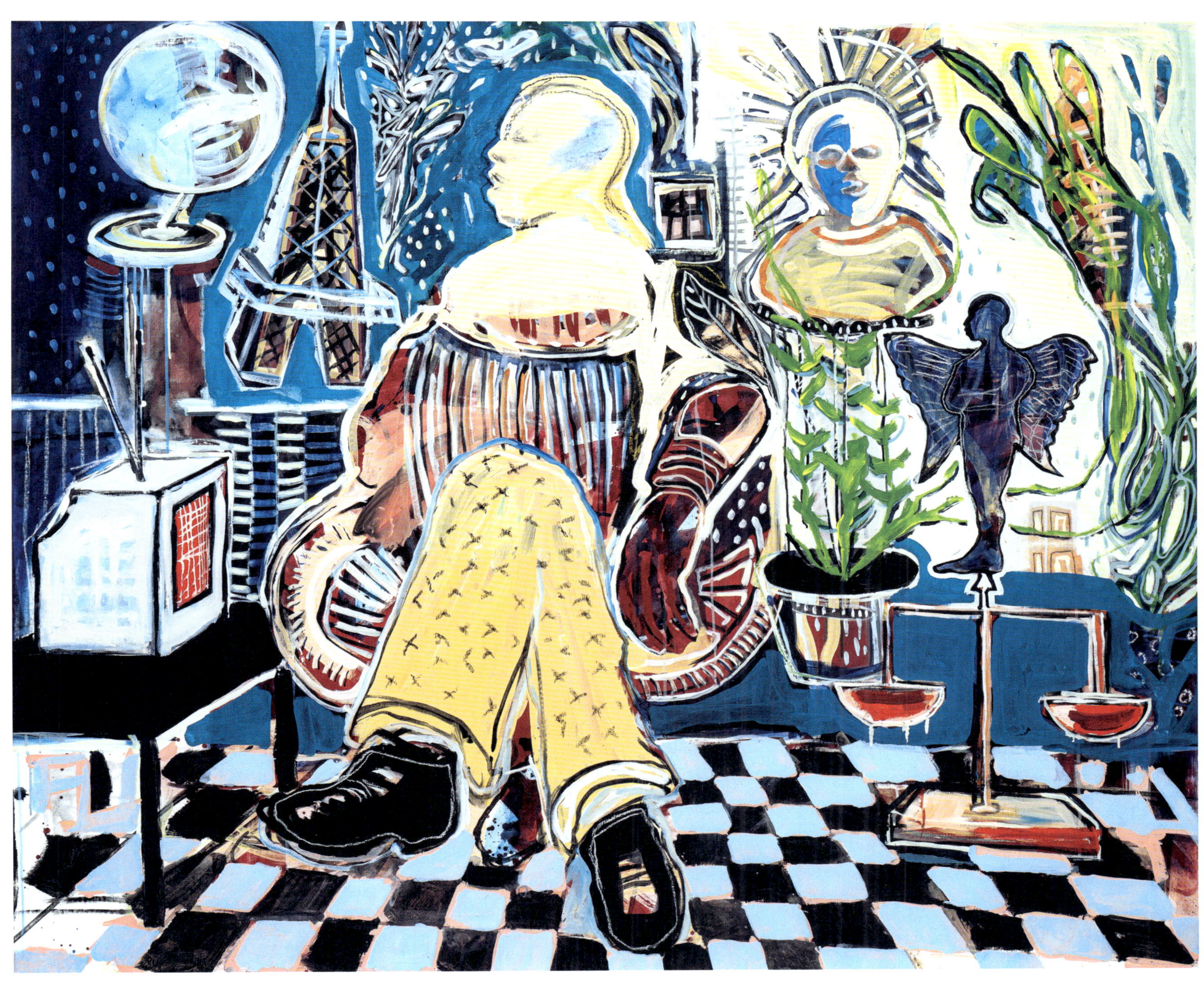

SOULEIMANE BARRY
Rêve d'ailleurs, 2020
Acrylic on canvas / Acryl auf Leinwand, 142 × 172 cm

EVERLYN NICODEMUS

Everlyn Nicodemus (b. 1954 in Marangu, Tanzania) has led a life marked by movement and trauma. Part of the African diaspora, she has lived in Sweden, France, Germany, Belgium, and Scotland (where she has lived and worked since 2008). Moving to Sweden with her first husband in 1973, she experienced racism for the first time: "When I came to Sweden, it was the first time I looked at my skin and said, 'Ah, I'm Black!'" Motivated by her experiences, she studied social anthropology at the University of Stockholm, wanting to understand why people treat each other differently. However, on a return trip to Tanzania in 1979, Nicodemus joined a group of aid workers who had come together to draw and paint, a pivotal event that instigated her artistic practice. Within six months she had a solo exhibition at the National Museum of Dar es Salaam.

Returning to Sweden, she began a prolific career that would be marked by her focus on the female and human experience, using the human form as the basis of her exploration of relationships, Black trauma, racism, and sexism. "When I started to paint, I first applied a form of direct and narrative representation which corresponded to my ideas as a student of social anthropology." Using her daughter, friends, and her second husband, the Swedish art historian, critic, and television producer Kristian Romare, as the subjects of her work, she created painted snapshots of her life, as with *Mother and Child* (1985). In 1987, Nicodemus suffered a major mental breakdown in France, where she had recently moved, and it was through her artistic practice that she recovered. Two key series emerged from this traumatic event; the "Silent Strength" series, which embodies her struggle to return to life and sanity, and the "Wedding" series, eighty-four paintings made over three years in Belgium: "A pictorial ballade about my meeting with Death, my being in his realm, my wrestling with him, and my way back to life and to a restored self." Simple brushstrokes delineate the forms, each series is marked by a limited palette, and a particular iconography: crosses, human skulls, windows, handprints, and flowers.

The tragedy of Nicodemus's forty-year career is that her ground-breaking artistic practice has been overshadowed by her academic and critical career. As a co-editor of *Modern Art in Africa, Asia and Latin America* and key contributor to *Third Text*, she has reshaped the way modern art from Africa is viewed, criticized, and understood.

NIAMH COGHLAN

Everlyn Nicodemus (geb. 1954 in Marangu, Tansania) blickt auf ein von Bewegung und Trauma geprägtes Leben zurück. Als Teil der afrikanischen Diaspora lebte sie in Schweden, Frankreich, Deutschland und Belgien, seit 2008 lebt und arbeitet sie in Schottland. Als sie 1973 mit ihrem ersten Ehmann nach Schweden zog, erlebte sie zum ersten Mal Rassismus: „Als ich nach Schweden kam, war das das erste Mal, dass ich mir meine Haut ansah und dachte: ‚Ah, ich bin Schwarz.'" Angetrieben von diesen Erfahrungen studierte sie an der Universität Stockholm Sozialanthropologie, um zu verstehen, weshalb Menschen einander ungleich behandeln. Bei einem Besuch in Tansania schloss Nicodemus sich einer Gruppe von Entwicklungshelfer:innen an, die zum Zeichnen und Malen zusammengefunden hatte – ein Schlüsselerlebnis, das den Anstoß für ihr künstlerisches Schaffen gab. Binnen sechs Monaten hatte sie eine Einzelausstellung im Nationalmuseum in Daressalam.

Wieder in Schweden, begann sie eine erfolgreiche Karriere, geprägt vom Fokus auf die menschliche, insbesondere weibliche Erfahrung, wobei die menschliche Gestalt zur Grundlage ihrer Erkundung von Beziehungen, Schwarzem Trauma, Rassismus und Sexismus wurde. „Als ich mit dem Malen anfing, nützte ich zunächst eine direkte und narrative Darstellungsform, wie sie meinen Vorstellungen als Studentin der Sozialanthropologie entsprach." Indem sie ihre Tochter, Freunde und ihren zweiten Ehemann, den schwedischen Kunsthistoriker, Kritiker und Fernsehproduzenten Kristian Romara, zu Motiven ihrer Arbeit machte, schuf sie gemalte Momentaufnahmen ihres Lebens, etwa in *Mother and Child* (1985). 1987 erlitt Nicodemus einen schweren Nervenzusammenbruch in Frankreich, wohin sie kurz zuvor gezogen war, von dem sie allein durch ihre Kunst genesen konnte. Aus diesem traumatischen Ereignis gingen zwei zentrale Serien hervor, „Silent Strength", die ihren Kampf um die Rückkehr ins Leben und zu geistiger Gesundheit verkörpert, und „Wedding", 84 Gemälde, die über drei Jahre in Belgien entstanden: „Eine Bildballade über meine Begegnung mit dem Tod, mein Verweilen in seinem Reich, mein Ringen mit ihm und meinen Weg zurück ins Leben und zu einem wiederhergestellten Selbst." Einfache Pinselstriche umreißen die Formen, jede Serie prägt eine reduzierte Farbpalette und eine spezielle Ikonografie: Kreuze, menschliche Schädel, Fenster, Handabdrücke und Blumen.

Das Tragische an Nicodemus' 40-jähriger Karriere ist, dass ihre bahnbrechende künstlerische Praxis im Schatten ihrer Laufbahn als Universitätslehrerin und Kritikerin stand. Als Mitherausgeberin von *Modern Art in Africa, Asia and Latin America* und wichtige Beitragende für *Third Text* hat sie die Art und Weise, wie moderne Kunst aus Afrika betrachtet und beurteilt wird, von Grund auf verändert.

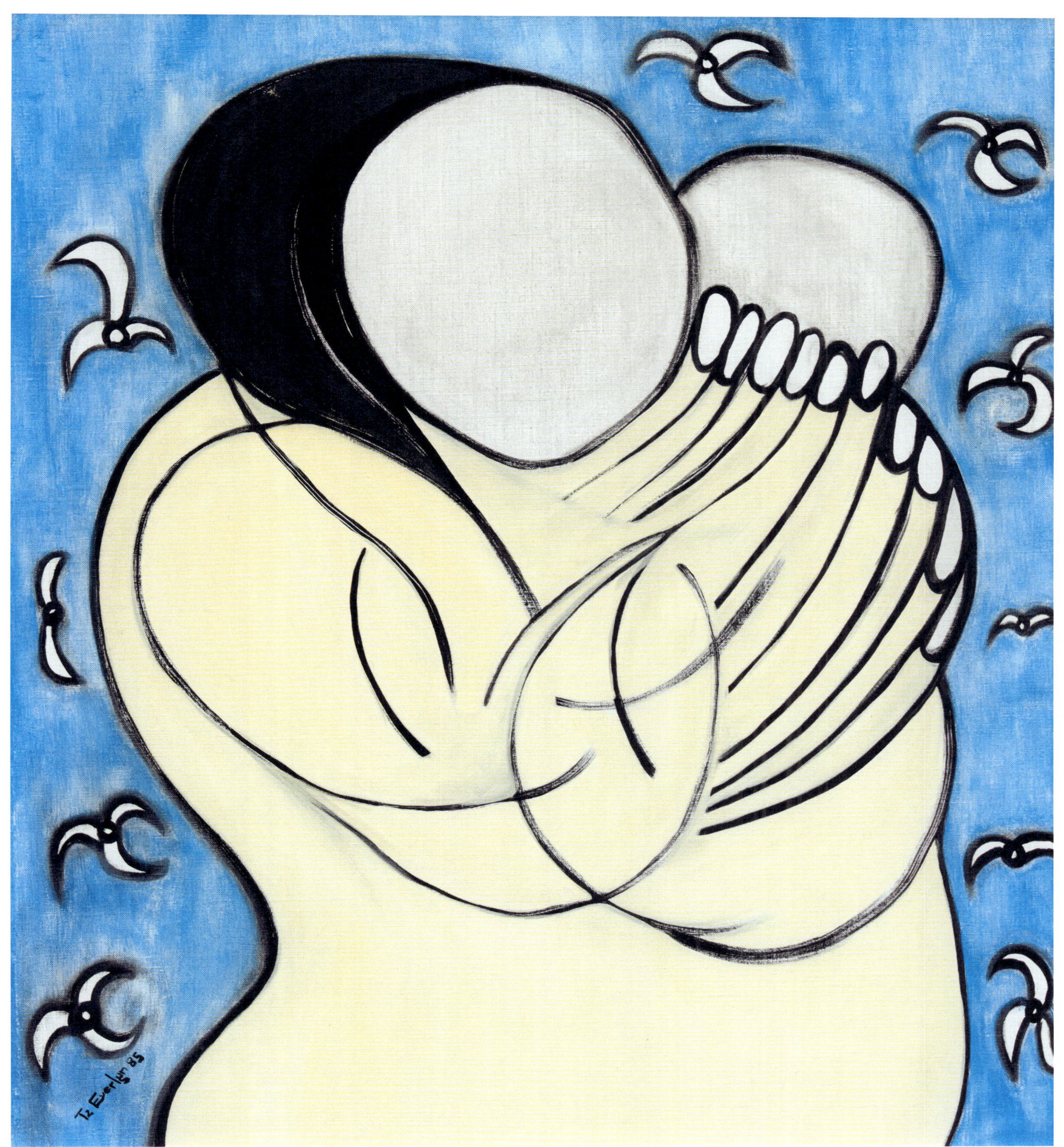

EVERLYN NICODEMUS
Mother and Child, 1985
Oil on canvas / Öl auf Le nwand, 77 × 69 cm

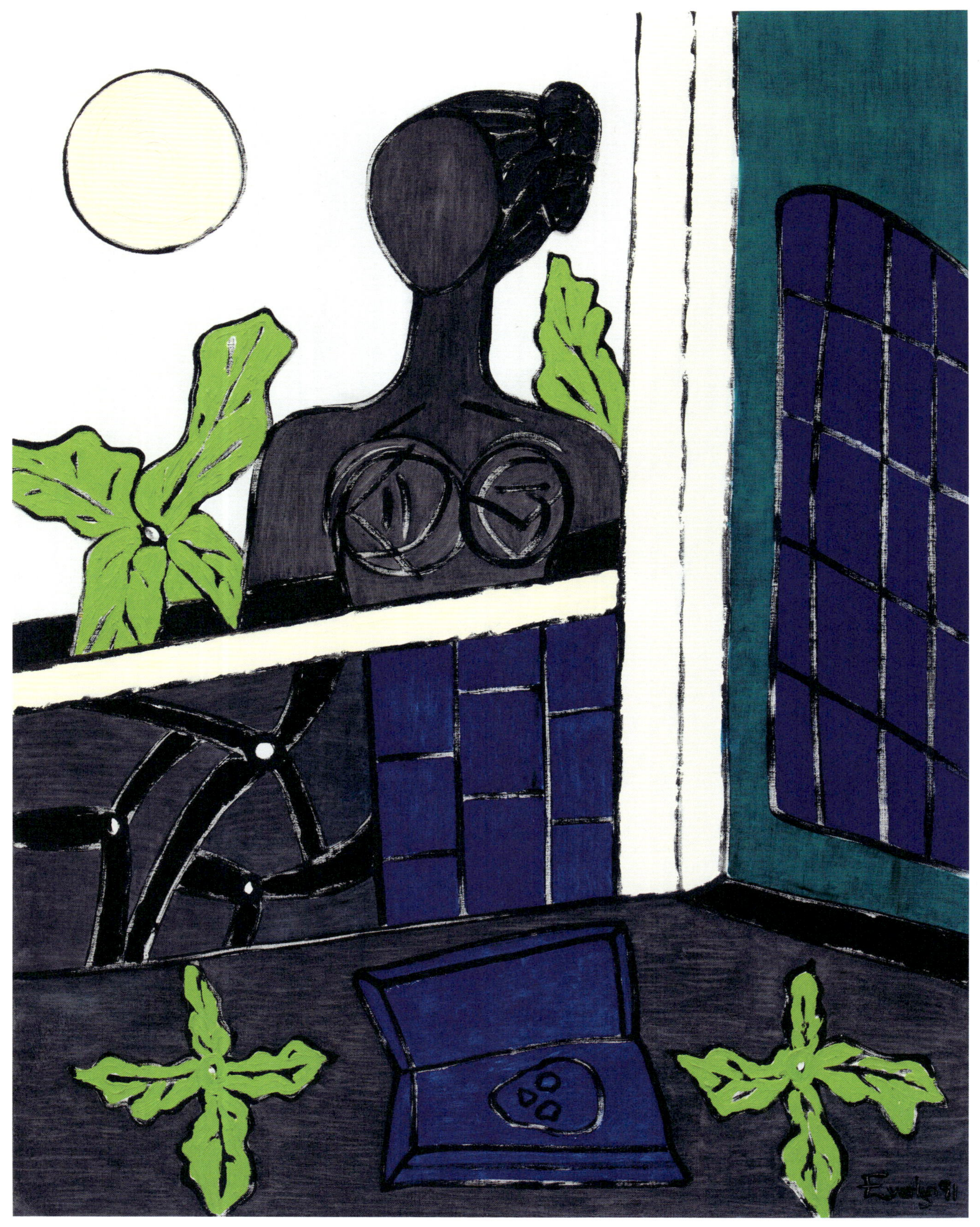

EVERLYN NICODEMUS
The Wedding No. 50, 1991
Oil on canvas / Öl auf Leinwand, 130 × 100 cm

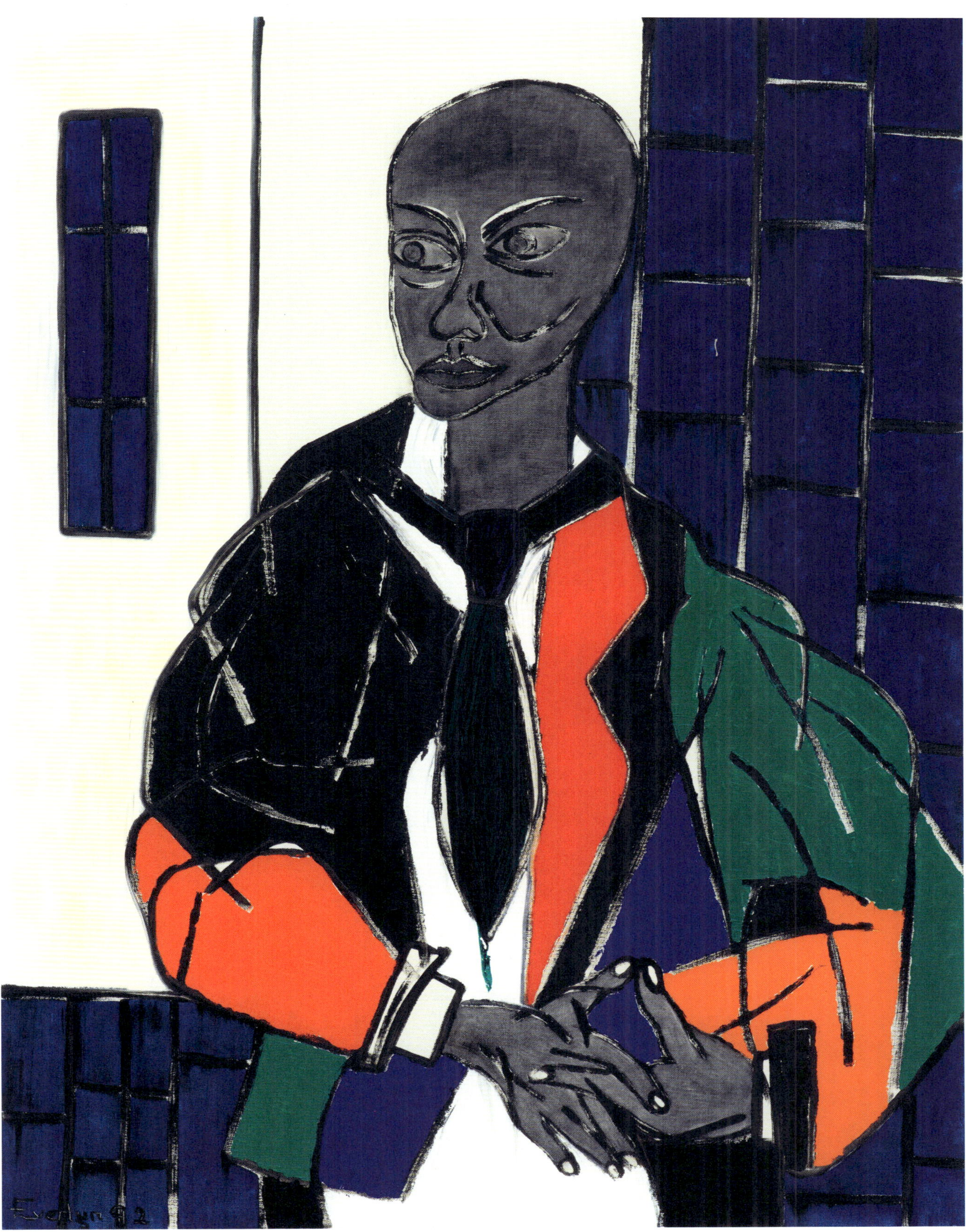

EVERLYN NICODEMUS
The Wedding No. 58, 1992
Oil on canvas / Öl auf Leinwand, 130 × 100 cm

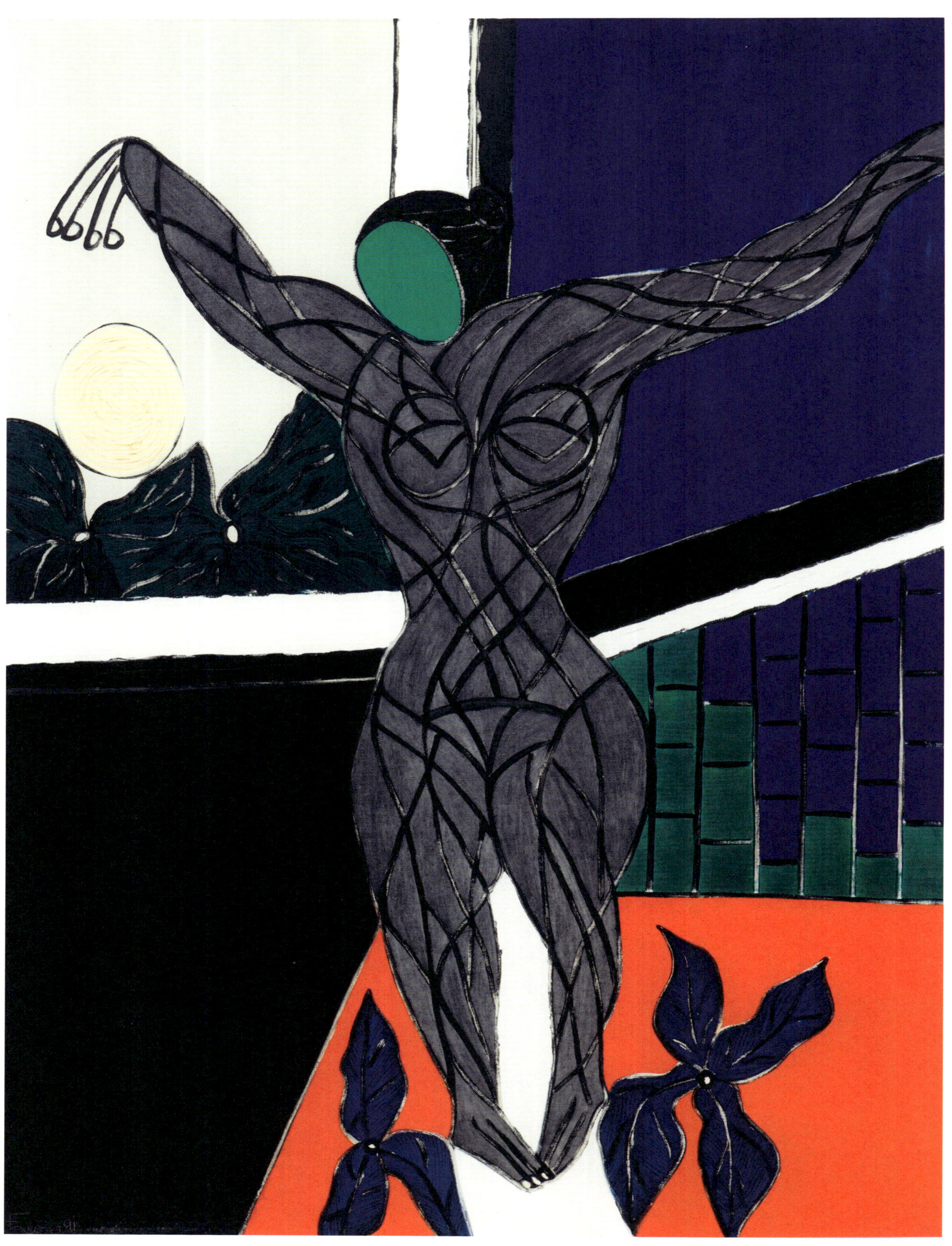

EVERLYN NICODEMUS
The Wedding No. 53, 1991
Oil on canvas / Öl auf Leinwand, 200 × 150 cm

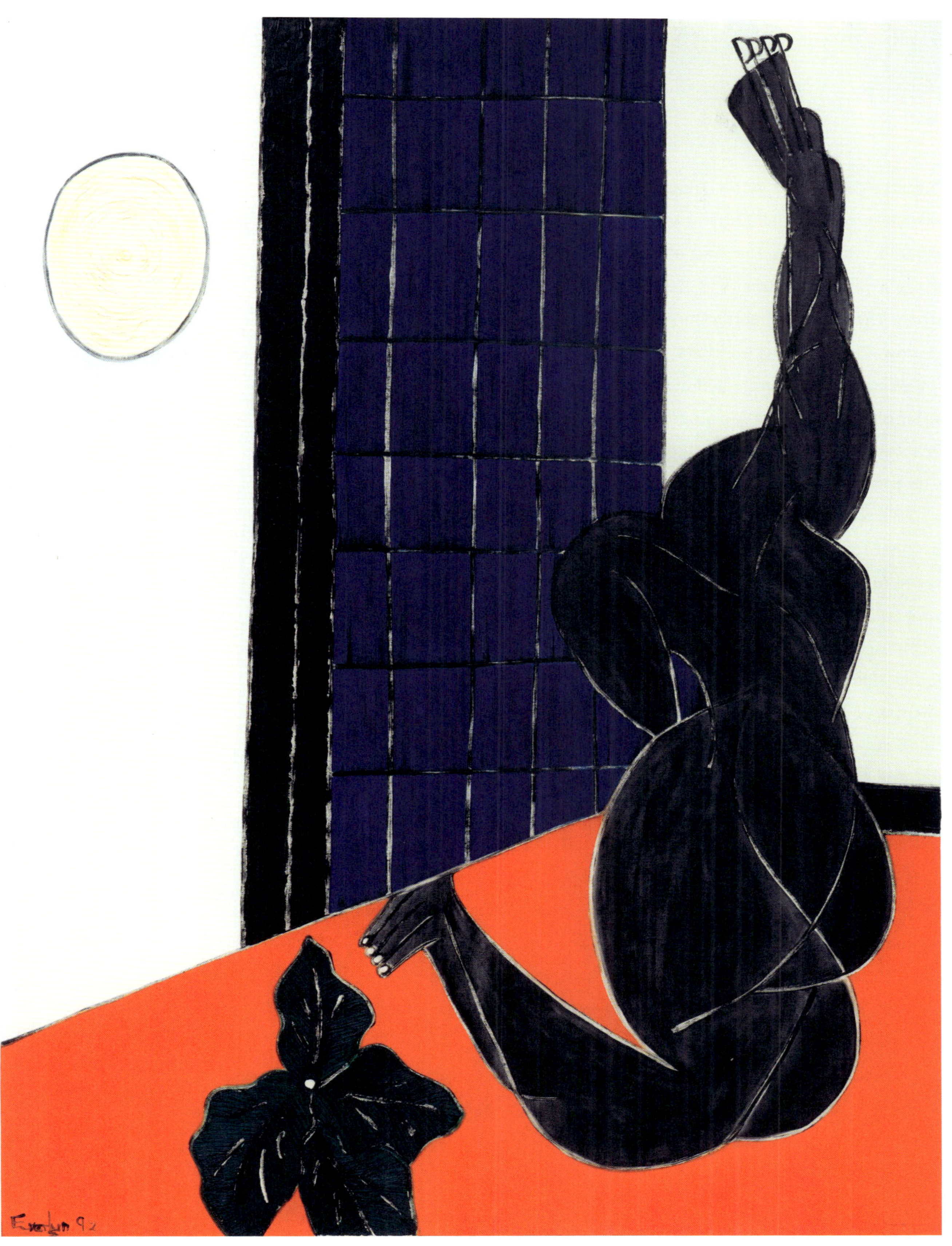

EVERLYN NICODEMUS
The Wedding No. 56, 1992
Oil on canvas / Öl auf Leinwand, 200 × 150 cm

TESFAYE URGESSA

In Tesfaye Urgessa's (b. 1983 in Addis Ababa, Ethiopia, lives and works in Nürtingen, Germany), current paintings—such as the series "No Country for Young Men"—frame and canvas form an entity overflowing with painting. Urgessa practices a physical, carnal-like style of painting in which color is intuitively applied. The artist fragments the pictorial space, deconstructs the illusionistic window. Figure and ground are interwoven, forming a complex, hybrid system that is part sculptural relief, part painterly surface, in which sequentially overlapping figures convey a certain dramaturgy and dynamism. Urgessa constructs psychological pictorial spaces where human vulnerability is the focus. The painted figures are anonymous, serial in their outward appearance, like soldiers marching in rank and file. The intertwined bodies symbolize interpersonal relationships and settings. Urgessa alludes to current migration movements—people struggling to survive, with an uncertain future in a foreign homeland. Yet the characters appear strong and self-determined, recalling boxers in a wrestling match, equipped with helmets, such as in *No Country for Young Men 15* from 2021.

Urgessa left his native Ethiopia in 2009 and studied painting at the State Academy of Fine Arts Stuttgart. "Foreignness" was something he experienced firsthand, the feeling of being constantly seen as "different." In 2011, the artist created his iconic body of work "Holy Criminals," portraits addressing how supposedly criminal "foreigners" are viewed.

Hiatus I (2017) is representative of Urgessa's post-Cubist pictorial compositions, with specific references to Picasso and primitivism in the form of the bull's head as a readymade montage of saddle with handlebars and African wooden masks. The painterly dismantled and deconstructed bodies and objects form a collaged-spatial pictorial structure, reminiscent of an existentialist stage. In addition to Expressionist-Cubist elements, Christian-Ethiopian icon and mural painting serve as sources of inspiration for Urgessa's painterly cosmos. Prominent examples are murals from around 1700 at the Debre Berhan Selassie monastery near the city of Gondar, now a UNESCO World Heritage Site.

In den aktuellen Gemälden von Tesfaye Urgessa (geb. 1983 in Addis Abeba, Äthiopien, lebt und arbeitet in Nürtingen, Deutschland), etwa dem Zyklus „No Country for Young Men", bilden Rahmen und Leinwand eine Einheit, auf der sich die Malerei ergießt. Urgessa praktiziert eine körperlich-fleischliche Malerei, in der die Farbe mit Sensibilität aufgetragen wird. Der Künstler zersplittert den Bildraum, dekonstruiert das illusionistische Fenster. Figur und Grund verweben sich zu einem komplexen, hybriden System zwischen skulpturalem Relief und malerischer Fläche, in dem sich die Figuren sequenziell überlagern und eine gewisse Dramaturgie und Dynamik vermitteln. Urgessa konstruiert psychologische Bildräume, die die Verletzbarkeit des Menschen in den Fokus setzen. Die gemalten Figuren sind anonym, seriell in ihrem äußeren Erscheinungsbild, wie in Reih und Glied marschierende Soldaten. Die ineinander verfangenen Körper symbolisieren zwischenmenschliche Relationen und Situationen. Urgessa spielt hierbei auf aktuelle Migrationsbewegungen an – Menschen, die um das nackte Überleben kämpfen, mit ungewisser Zukunft in einer fremden Heimat. Die Figuren wirken dennoch stark und selbstbestimmt, sind wie Boxer im Ringkampf, ausgestattet mit Helmen, wie etwa in *No Country for Young Men 15* von 2021.

Urgessa verließ 2009 sein Heimatland Äthiopien und studierte an der Staatlichen Akademie der Bildenden Künste Stuttgart Malerei. Er konnte am eigenen Leib das „Fremdsein" erfahren, das Gefühl, permanent als „anders" gelesen zu werden. 2011 entstand der ikonische Werkblock der „Holy Criminals", Porträts, in denen der Künstler den Blick auf die vermeintlich kriminellen „Fremden" thematisiert.

Hiatus I (2017) ist ein repräsentatives Beispiel für Urgessas postkubistisch-malerische Bildkomposition, mit dezidierten Bezügen auf Picasso und den Primitivismus in Gestalt des Stierkopfs als Readymade-Montage eines Sattels mit Lenkstange sowie afrikanischer Holzmasken. Die malerisch zerlegten und dekonstruierten Körper und Objekte bilden ein collagiert-räumliches Bildgefüge, einer existenzialistischen Bühne gleich. Neben expressionistisch-kubistischen Elementen ist die christlich-äthiopische Ikonen- und Wandmalerei Inspirationsquelle für Urgessas malerischen Kosmos. Ein prominentes Beispiel sind die um 1700 entstandenen Wandgemälde im Kloster Debre Berhan Selassie nahe der Stadt Gondar, das heute zum UNESCO-Weltkulturerbe zählt.

FLORIAN STEININGER

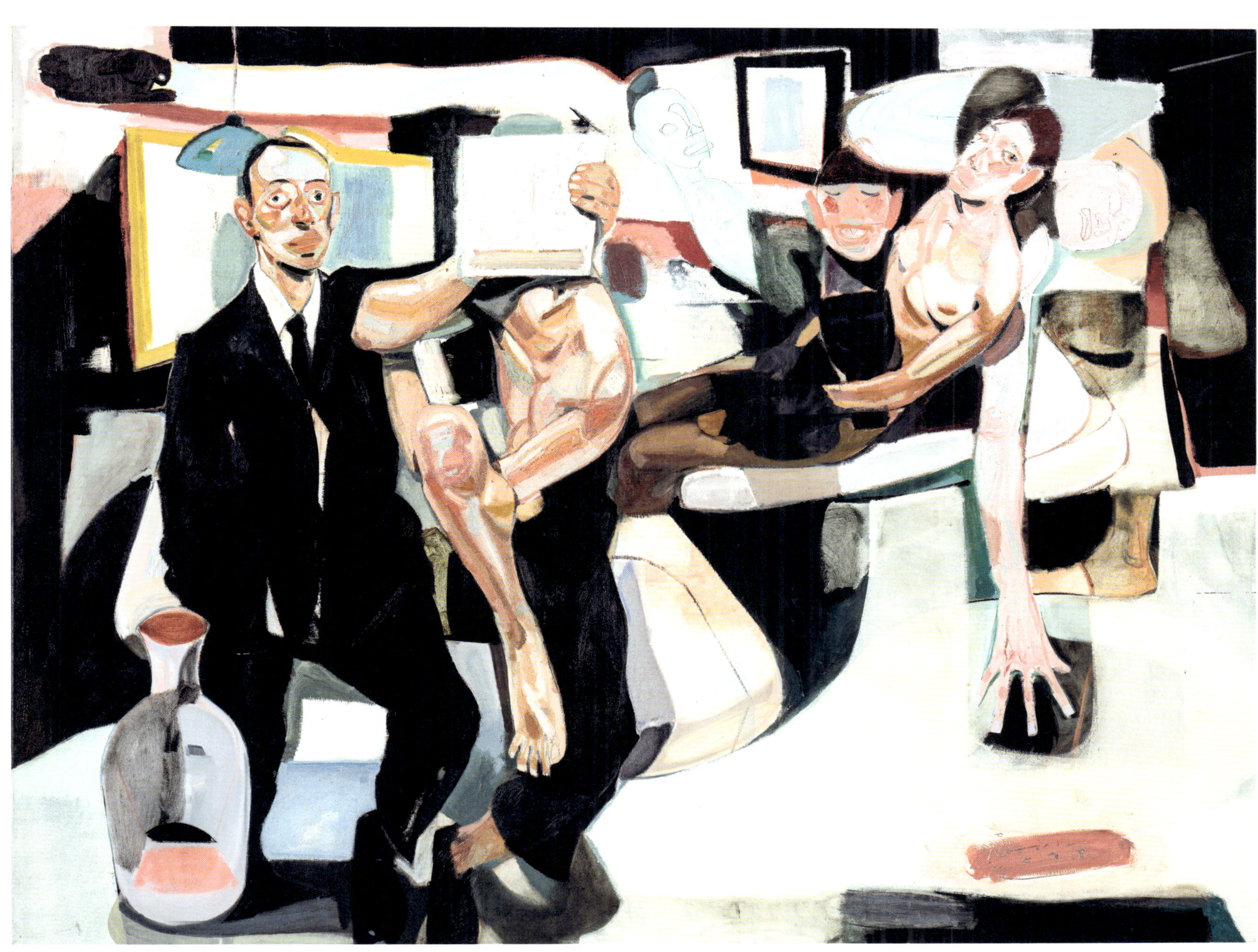

TESFAYE URGESSA
Trapped in Flesh, 2018
Oil on canvas / Öl auf Leinwand, 190 × 250 cm

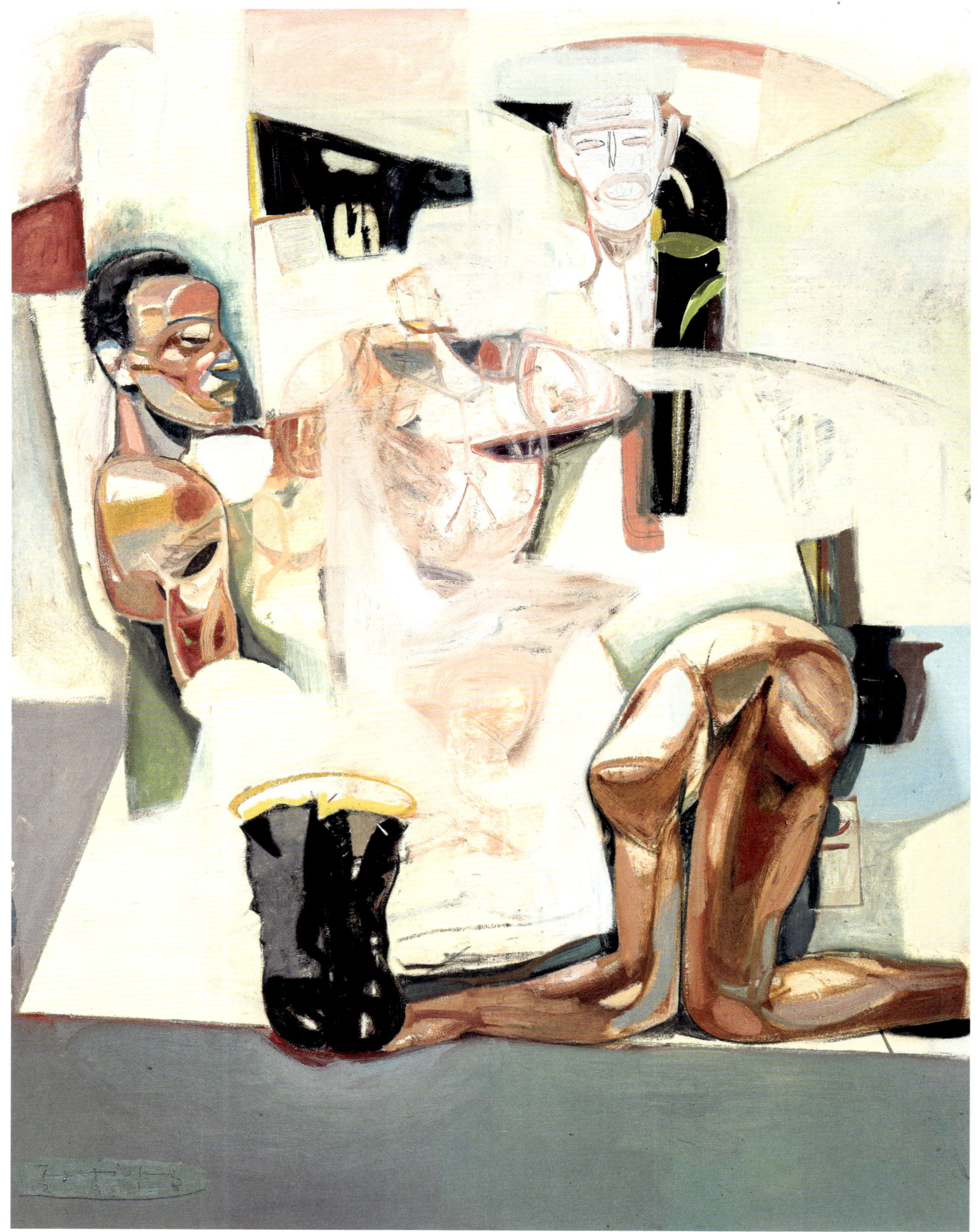

TESFAYE URGESSA
Devotion, 2018
Oil on canvas / Öl auf Leinwand, 170 × 130 cm

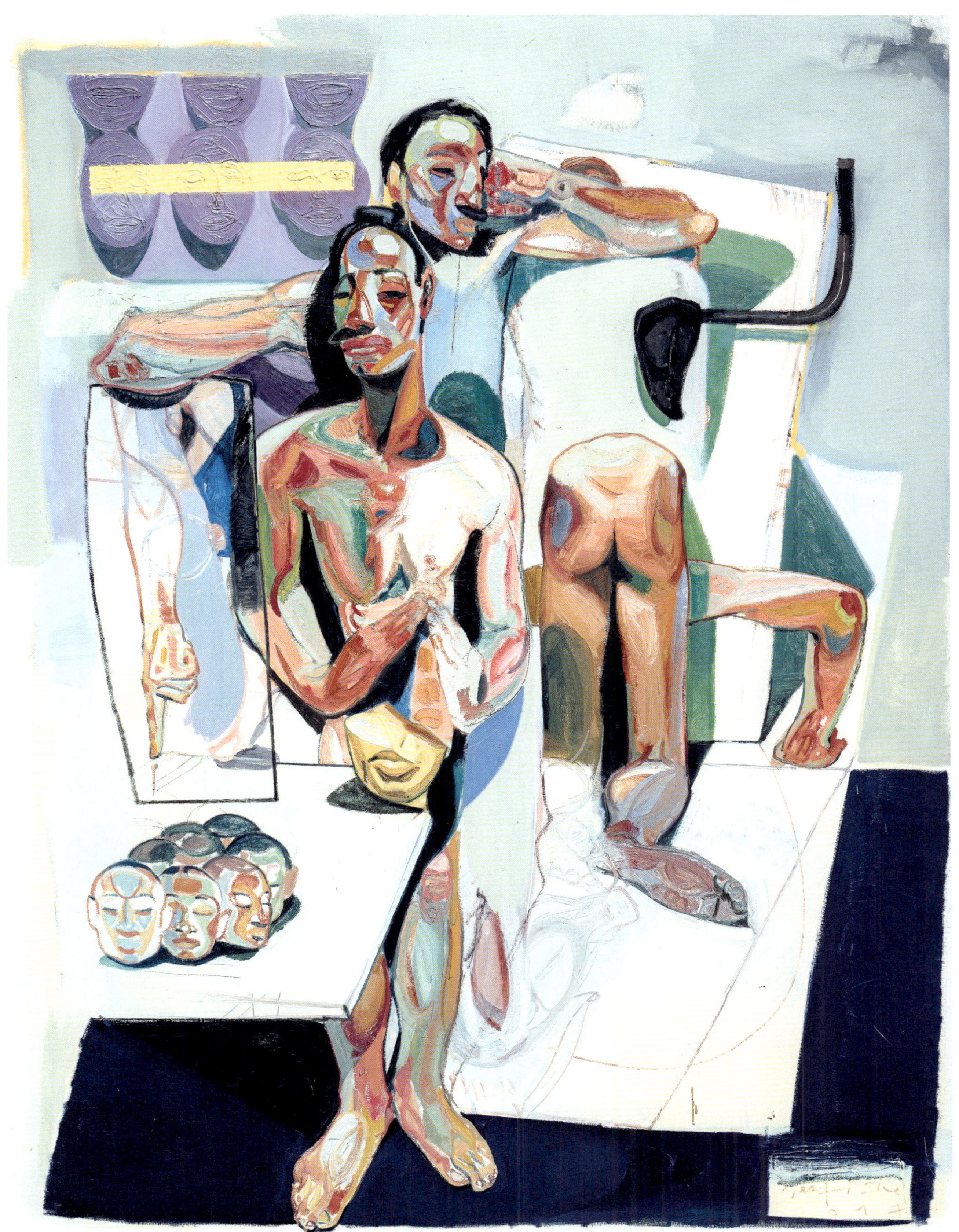

TESFAYE URGESSA
Hiatus I, 2017
Oil on canvas / Öl auf Leinwand, 200 × 150 cm

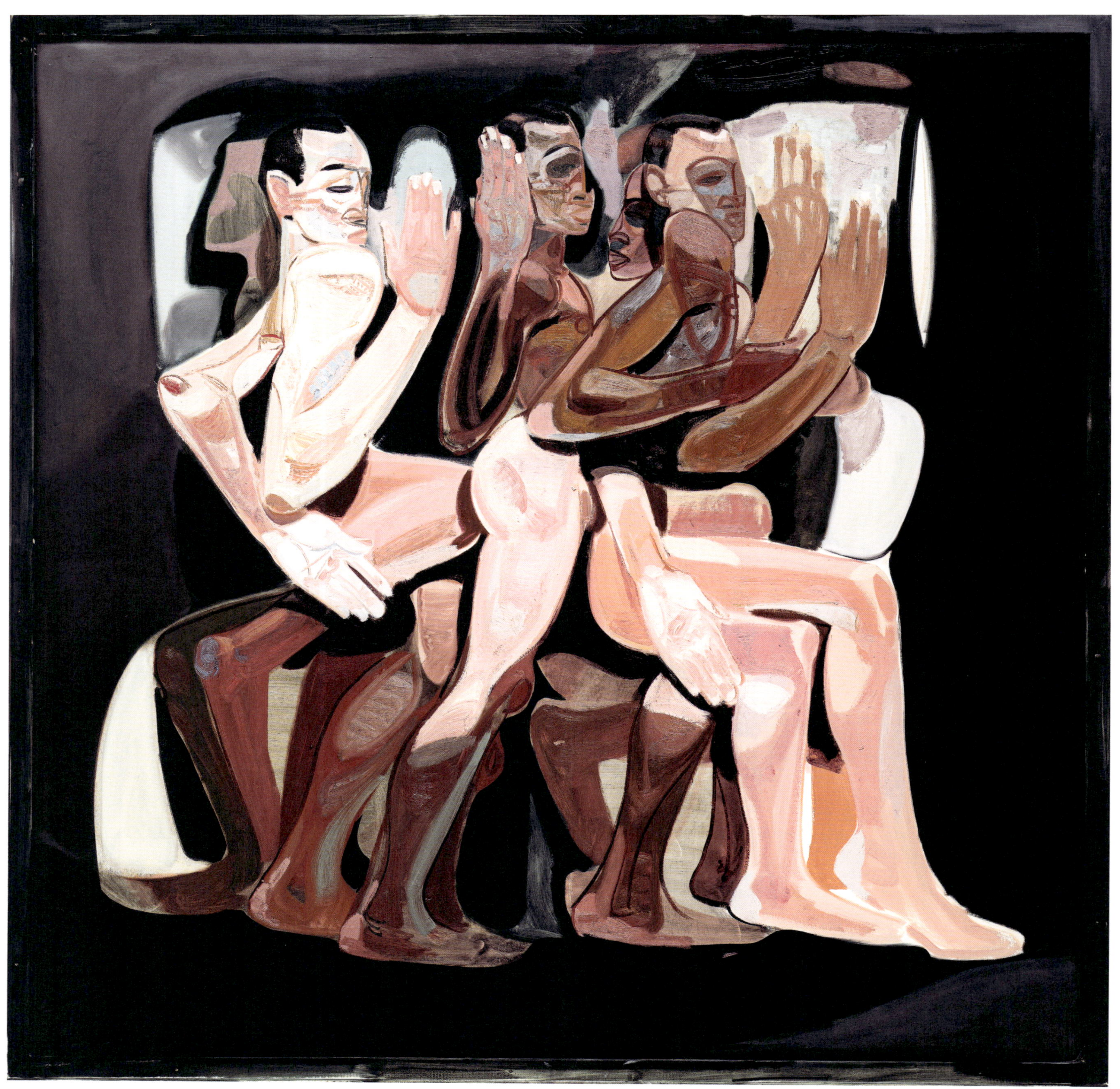

TESFAYE URGESSA
No Country for Young Men 19, 2021
Oil on canvas / Öl auf Leinwand, 180 × 180 cm

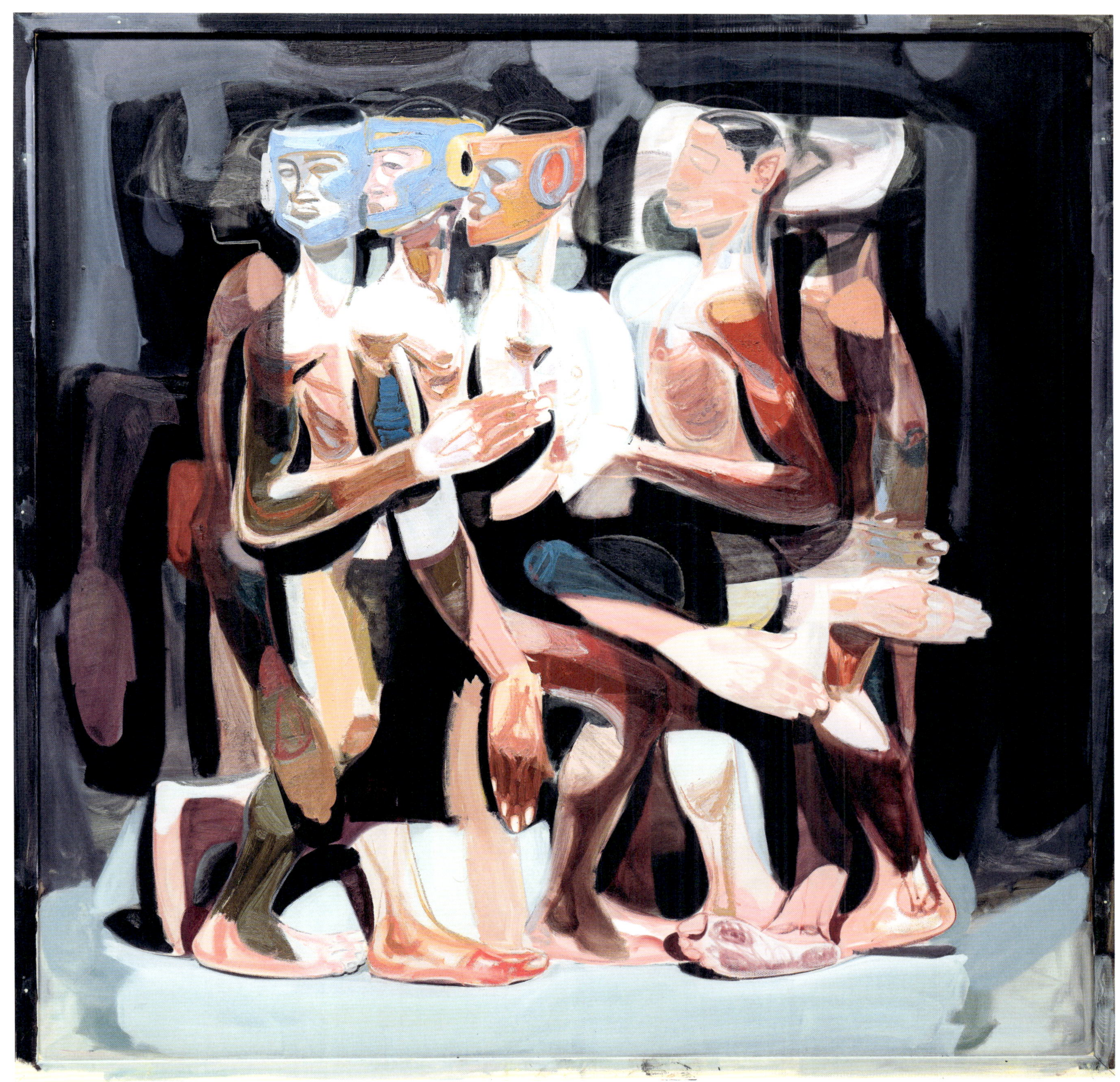

TESFAYE URGESSA
No Country for Young Men 15, 2021
Oil on canvas / Öl auf Leinwand, 180 × 180 cm

KIMATHI DONKOR

Kimathi Donkor (b. 1965 in Bournemouth, UK) creates works that re-imagine mythic, legendary, and domestic encounters across Africa and its global diasporas. He primarily works in paint, addressing both the way Western canonical art has erased Black subjectivity as well as how Western history has written out or diminished the role of Black historical figures such as Toussaint L'Ouverture and Harriet Tubman.

Donkor became aware of these figures while studying at Goldsmiths' College, University of London in the 1980s in part because of his own family connections to Jamaica, Nigeria, and Ghana. He became particularly interested in the way that the British education system at the time refused (and despite some progress, still refuses) to give these figures their historical due, or talk about the roles of colonialism, slavery, oppression, and empire that are central to British history.

Donkor subsequently became involved in a number of community initiatives in Brixton, the main site of the uprisings by the Black British community against state and police injustice in the 1980s. This experience fed into a number of later works that focused on police brutality against members of the Black British community such as Cynthia Jarrett and Cherry Groce. Donkor also developed a number of paintings reviving Black historical figures. In all these works Donkor references and plays with the style of Western canonical history paintings, in order to re-insert the erased Black figure back into one of the most recognizable visual idioms. His work can be seen as not simply reviving Black historical figures or remembering Black victims of police and societal brutality but also as an act of actively diversifying the canon.

St. Iphigenia LMN (2011) is a key painting in Kimathi Donkor's revival of female Black historical figures. Iphigenia, an Ethiopian princess, was converted to Christianity by Matthew the Apostle. She refused to marry King Hirtacus whose subsequent attempt to destroy her house with fire was thwarted by the spirit of the previously martyred Matthew. Iphigenia was later celebrated especially in Brazil, Cuba, and Peru as a Black Madonna, and it is thought that Black slaves started her cult there. This painting, like others by Donkor, re-imagines this Black female historical figure as a contemporary subject in a setting that draws on Western canonical art, subtly highlighting the erasure of figures such as St. Iphigenia from that narrative.

NIRU RATNAM

Kimathi Donkor (geb. 1965 in Bornemouth, England) reimaginiert in seinen Arbeiten mythische, legendäre und alltägliche Begebenheiten in Afrika und Afrikas Diaspora. Er arbeitet überwiegend malerisch und thematisiert sowohl die Ausblendung Schwarzer Subjektivität in der kanonischen westlichen Kunst als auch die Art und Weise, wie Schwarze historische Persönlichkeiten wie Toussaint L'Ouverture oder Harriet Tubman aus der westlichen Geschichtsschreibung getilgt oder in ihrer Bedeutung geschmälert wurden.

Donkor wurde im Laufe seines Studiums am Goldsmiths' College der University of London auf diese historischen Figuren aufmerksam, unter anderem aufgrund seiner eigenen familiären Verbindungen nach Jamaika, Nigeria und Ghana. Sein Interesse galt insbesondere dem Umstand, dass das britische Bildungssystem sich damals weigerte (und ungeachtet einiger Fortschritte bis heute weigert), diesen die ihnen gebührende historische Bedeutung einzuräumen oder die Rolle von Kolonialismus, Sklaverei, Unterdrückung und Imperialismus zu thematisieren.

In der Folge beteiligte Donkor sich an einer Reihe von Gemeinschaftsaktionen im Londoner Stadtteil Brixton, Hauptschauplatz des Aufstandes der britischen Schwarzen Community gegen Unrecht vonseiten des Staates und der Polizei in den 1980er-Jahren. Diese Erfahrung schlug sich in einer Anzahl späterer Arbeiten nieder, die sich mit der Polizeigewalt gegen Mitglieder der britischen Schwarzen Community wie Cynthia Jarrett oder Cherry Groce befassten. Donkor entwickelte auch eine Serie von Gemälden, in denen er Schwarze historische Persönlichkeiten wieder aufleben lässt. In all diesen Werken nimmt er spielerisch Bezug auf den Stil kanonischer westlicher Historienmalerei, um die ausgelöschten Schwarzen Figuren wieder in eines der vertrautesten visuellen Idiome einzufügen. Sein Werk ist somit nicht einfach als Vergegenwärtigung Schwarzer historischer Persönlichkeiten oder als Erinnerung an Schwarze Opfer polizeilicher und gesellschaftlicher Gewalt zu sehen, sondern auch als ein Akt der bewussten Diversifizierung des Kanons.

St. Iphigenia LMN (2011) ist ein Schlüsselwerk in Kimathi Donkors Vergegenwärtigung Schwarzer historischer Frauengestalten. Die äthiopische Prinzessin Iphigenia wurde vom Apostel Matthäus zum Christentum bekehrt. Sie weigerte sich, König Hirtacus zu heiraten, woraufhin dieser versuchte, ihr Haus niederzubrennen, was durch den Geist des inzwischen zum Märtyrer gewordenen Matthäus vereitelt wurde. Iphigenia wurde später insbesondere in Brasilien, Kuba und Peru als Schwarze Madonna verehrt, und man nimmt an, dass dieser Kult von Schwarzen Sklaven eingeführt wurde. Wie andere Bilder Donkors reimaginiert auch dieses die historische Schwarze Frauengestalt als zeitgenössisches Sujet in einem Setting, das auf die kanonische westliche Kunst anspielt und damit auf subtile Weise die Ausradierung von Figuren wie der Heiligen Iphigenia aus diesem Narrativ hervorhebt.

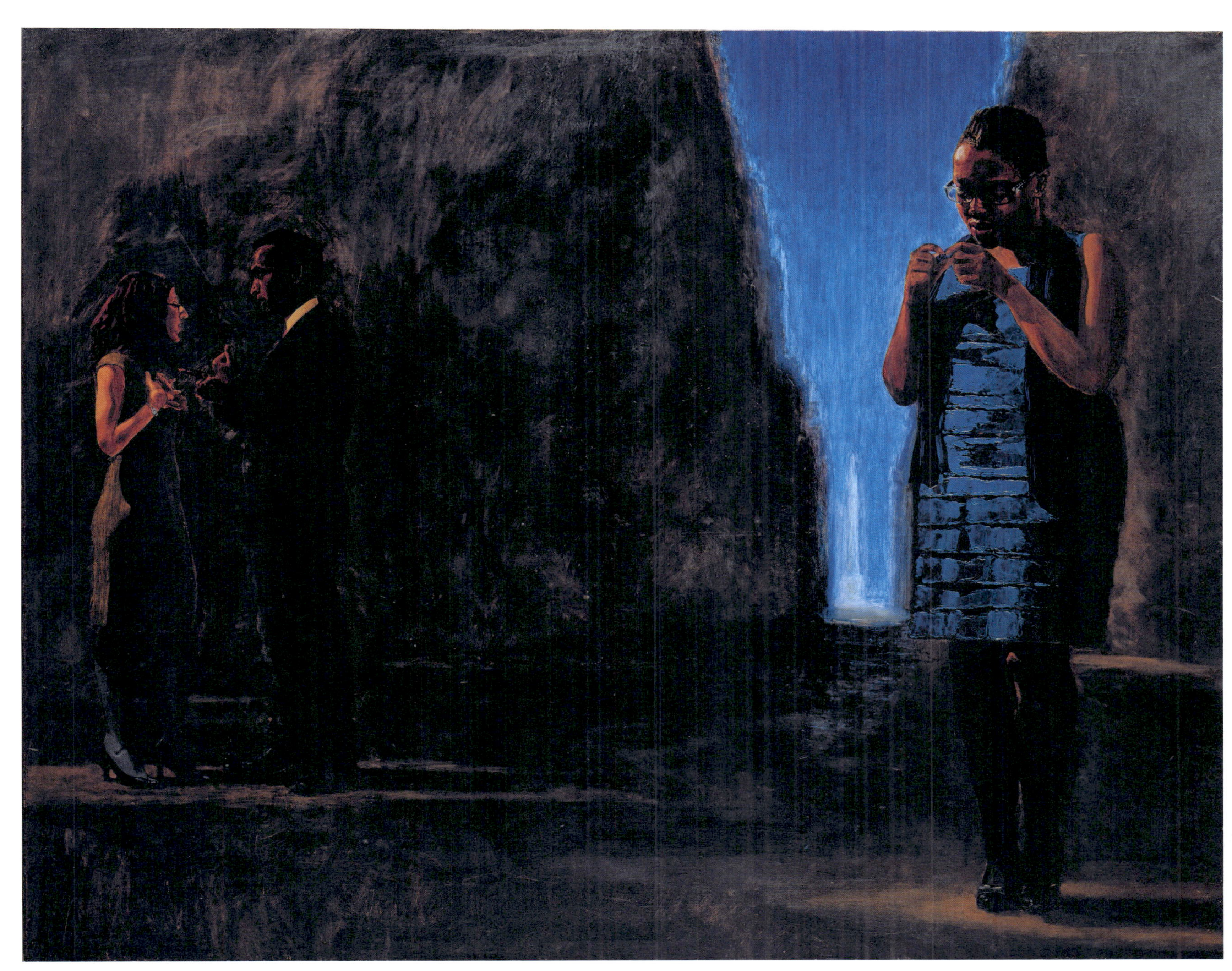

KIMATHI DONKOR
St. Iphigenia LMN, 2011
Oil on canvas / Öl auf Leinwand, 120 × 150 cm

MATTHEW EGUAVOEN

In his work, Matthew Eguavoen (b. 1988 in Nigeria) addresses the societal, economic, and political aspects of the complex intersectionality facing Nigerians across various facets of life. Drawing from classic painting and representing current trends, Eguavoen's portraits mirror his own fears and questions about life.

His portraits reflect his thoughts regarding the society in which he lives and continues to evolve, including matters of family and immigration, as well as the consequences of post-colonialism. He offers a glimpse into the human side of social and political issues. His subjects grow and adapt within familiar environments, representing a personal experience of contemporary life.

Matthew Eguavoen's series on family alludes to the challenges and impacts of parenthood. To be a parent is to become decentered, to put your child before yourself. Depicted and highlighted are the various relationship pairings that emerge within the family setting, the complicities created, as well as the ties that bind them.

Eguavoen's collection of self portraits, sometimes referred to as "crypto portraits" given their hidden, enigmatic nature, revolves around the arrival of his first child. In a frank and personal way, they convey his feelings about his new fatherhood and how it has changed his conception of the world and his relationship with his partner. The neutral expressions and piercing gazes of his portraits leave room for interpretation. Although tenderness is evident, the portraits at times also bear witness to the baby blues, where parenthood is accompanied by its share of questioning and doubts. The series follows the stages that Matthew Eguavoen himself experienced on his journey to becoming a parent: from the difficulties he finally overcame, to his pride of being a father. The titles of his works such as *Iyaniwura (Mother is as precious as gold)* express the importance of the female figure: companion and mother—as precious as gold.

Matthew Eguavoen's art, while rooted in a classical-portrait tradition, is part of the Black Vanguard, a form of figuration that strongly champions its origins and culture, influenced by the world of fashion. Under his brushstrokes, art, fashion, and social issues merge, reflecting his generation.

MICHAËLA HADJI-MINAGLOU

In seinem Werk thematisiert Matthew Eguavoen (geb. 1988, Nigeria) gesellschaftliche, wirtschaftliche und politische Aspekte der komplexen intersektionalen Machtverhältnisse, mit der Nigerianer:innen sich in unterschiedlichen Lebensbereichen konfrontiert sehen. Eguavoens Porträts, die von der klassischen Malerei ausgehen, aber heutige Trends repräsentieren, spiegeln seine eigenen Ängste und Fragen an das Leben wider.

Seine Porträts reflektieren sein Denken über die Gesellschaft, in der er lebt und sich fortwährend weiterentwickelt; das schließt Fragen von Familie und Einwanderung genauso ein wie die Folgen des Postkolonialismus. Er gewährt einen Einblick in die menschliche Seite sozialer und politischer Themen. Seine Figuren wachsen in vertraute Umgebungen hinein; sie stehen für eine persönliche Erfahrung des zeitgenössischen Lebens.

Matthew Eguavoens Serie über die Familie befasst sich mit den Anforderungen und Auswirkungen des Elternseins. Elternschaft heißt, sich selbst nicht mehr in den Mittelpunkt und das eigene Kind über sich zu stellen. Dargestellt und beleuchtet werden die verschiedenen Beziehungspaare, die sich innerhalb der Familie herausbilden, die Komplizenschaften, die dabei entstehen, sowie auch die Bande, die sie zusammenhalten.

Eguavoens Kollektion von Selbstporträts, manchmal in Anbetracht ihres geheimen und rätselvollen Wesens auch als „Kryptoporträts" bezeichnet, kreisen um die Ankunft seines ersten Kindes. Auf offene und persönliche Weise vermitteln sie seine Gefühle über die neue Vaterschaft und wie sie sein Weltbild und seine Beziehung zu seiner Partnerin verändert hat. Der neutrale Gesichtsausdruck und die durchdringenden Blicke der Porträtierten lassen Raum für Interpretation. Obwohl die Zärtlichkeit offensichtlich ist, zeugen die Porträts gelegentlich auch vom Babyblues, wenn das Elternsein von vielen Fragen und Zweifeln begleitet wird. Die Serie folgt den Stadien, die Eguavoen selbst auf seinem Weg zur Elternschaft durchlebte: von den Schwierigkeiten, die er letztendlich überwand, bis zum Stolz, Vater zu sein. Die Titel seiner Arbeiten wie *Iyaniwura (Mother is as precious as gold)* geben der Bedeutung der Frauenfigur Ausdruck: Gefährtin und Mutter – kostbar wie Gold.

Matthew Eguavoens Kunst ist zwar in der klassischen Porträttradition verwurzelt, aber auch Teil der Schwarzen Avantgarde, einer Form von Figuration, die sich für ihre Ursprünge und Kultur starkmacht und von der Welt der Mode beeinflusst ist. Unter seinen Pinselstrichen verschmelzen Kunst, Mode und soziale Fragen zu einem Spiegelbild seiner Generation.

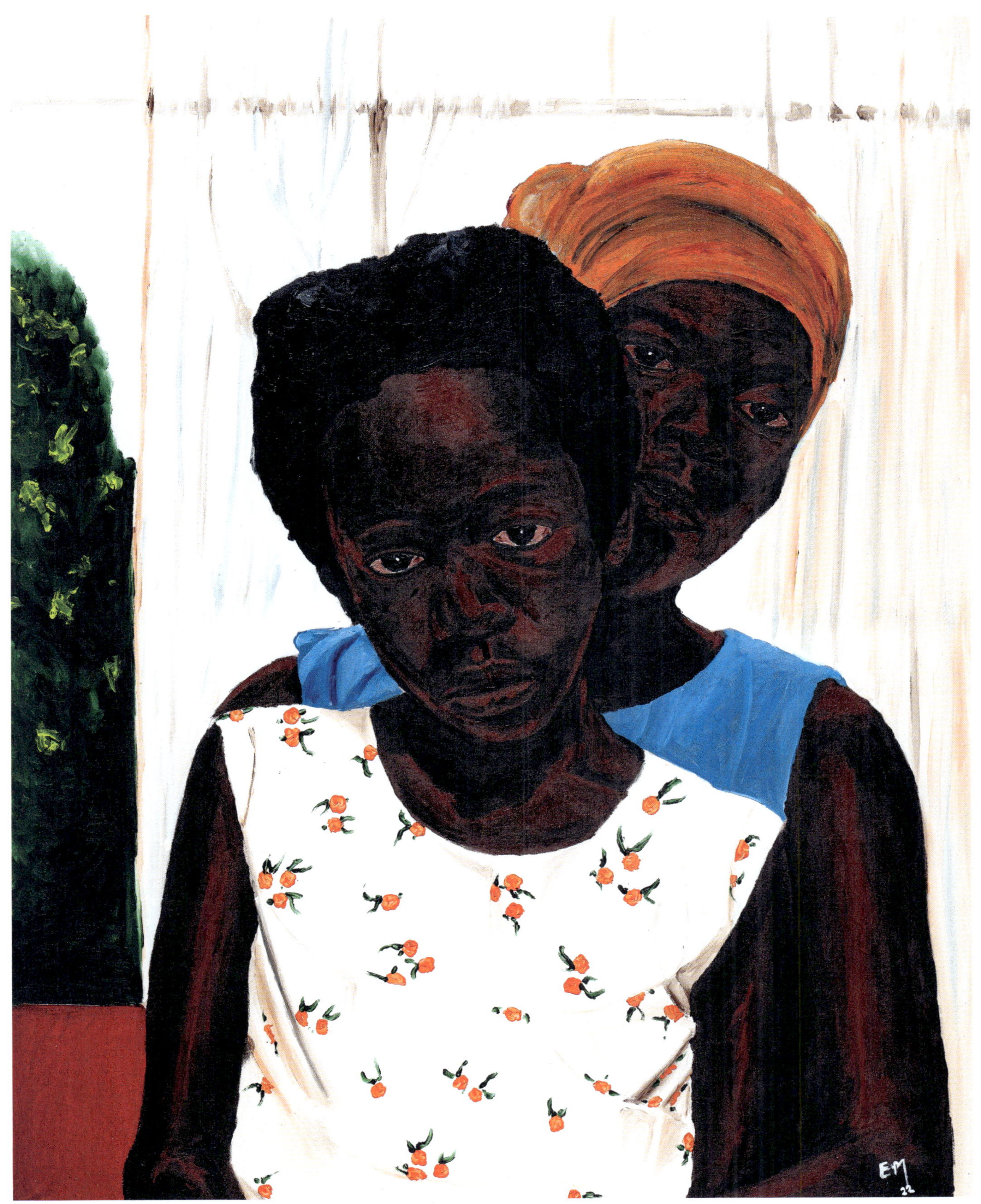

MATTHEW EGUAVOEN
Iyaniwura (Mother is as precious as gold), 2022, Acrylic and oil on canvas / Acryl und Öl auf Leinwand, 130 × 100 cm

BOLUWATIFE OYEDIRAN

Historical personalities and emblematic scenes from religious paintings make up the pictorial vocabulary of Boluwatife Oyediran (b. 1997 in Ogbomosho, Nigeria). The Nigerian painter creates alternate histories by changing the skin complexion of widely known historical figures. Centering on the history of cotton growing, his compositions seek to correct long-held notions of Black identity, power, fashion, and monarchy. In so doing, he demonstrates that established representations of power are not immutable. By challenging how traditional icons are portrayed, his powerful images put forth new icons and convey hope. Far from being fatalistic, the works suggest potential new paths forward and assert that every voice counts. Boluwatife Oyediran borrows from the codes of ethnocentric occidental art to cast people of color in a favorable light and to question conceptions of power and norms. He substitutes the usual heroes of religious and political imagery with those who have been historically cast aside or erased by the spheres of power. Boluwatife Oyediran changes the skin color of major figures in European history. From Queen Elizabeth II to Pope John Paul II and Napoleon, who he embodies in a self-portrait, he shakes up historical representations of power and racist hierarchies. He calls for the inclusion of people of color who have been historically marginalized, exploited, excluded, and underrepresented by reversing this inadequate representation and giving them back their share of power. He upends stereotypes and instills new values; even if subversive, his work is above all optimistic. Oyediran does not take an accusatory stance. On the contrary, he advocates for a better future without reproducing past mistakes. He proposes to rethink pre-existing hierarchies and representations of power through a new reading of history. The artist explains "I met someone who once told me that my figures appear to be phoenixes rising out of their own ashes (the cotton fields), in glory and splendor. I quite agree with that."

Historische Persönlichkeiten und emblematische Szenen aus religiösen Gemälden bilden das Bildvokabular von Boluwatife Oyediran (geb. 1997 in Ogbomosho, Nigeria). Der nigerianische Maler schafft alternative Versionen der Geschichte, indem er die Hautfarbe bekannter historischer Figuren ändert. Seine Kompositionen, die sich auf die Geschichte des Baumwollanbaus konzentrieren, suchen lang bestehende Auffassungen von Schwarzer Identität, Macht, Mode und Monarchie zu korrigieren. Dabei führt er vor Augen, dass etablierte Darstellungen von Macht nicht unveränderlich sind. Indem er hinterfragt, wie traditionelle ikonische Figuren porträtiert werden, stellen seine machtvollen Bilder neue Ikonen vor und vermitteln Hoffnung. Weit davon entfernt, fatalistisch zu sein, weisen die Arbeiten neue Wege und beharren darauf, dass jede Stimme zählt. Oyediran entlehnt die Codes der ethnozentrischen westlichen Kunst, um People of Color in ein positives Licht zu setzen und Auffassungen von Macht und Normen zu hinterfragen. Er ersetzt die üblichen Held:innen religiöser und politischer Bilder durch jene, die historisch gesehen beiseitegeschoben oder aus den Sphären der Macht entfernt wurden. Indem Oyediran bedeutenden Gestalten der europäischen Geschichte – von Königin Elisabeth II. über Papst Johannes Paul II. bis zu Napoleon, den er in einem Selbstporträt verkörpert – eine andere Hautfarbe verleiht, bringt er historische Darstellungen von Macht und rassistische Hierarchien ins Wanken. Er fordert die Einbeziehung von People of Color, die historisch marginalisiert, ausgebeutet, ausgeschlossen und unterrepräsentiert waren, indem er die unzulängliche Repräsentation revidiert und ihnen ihren Anteil an der Macht zurückgibt. Er stellt Stereotype auf den Kopf und vermittelt neue Werte; auch wenn es subversiv ist, ist sein Werk vor allem optimistisch. Oyediran nimmt keine anklagende Haltung ein. Er tritt im Gegenteil für eine bessere Zukunft ein, ohne die Fehler der Vergangenheit zu wiederholen. Er schlägt vor, bestehende Hierarchien und Machtrepräsentationen durch eine neue Lesart der Geschichte zu überdenken. Der Künstler erklärt: „Ich bin einmal jemandem begegnet, der mir gesagt hat, dass meine Figuren wie Phönixe aus ihrer eigenen Asche (den Baumwollfeldern) in Herrlichkeit und Pracht aufzusteigen scheinen. Dem stimme ich durchaus zu."

MICHAËLA HADJI-MINAGLOU

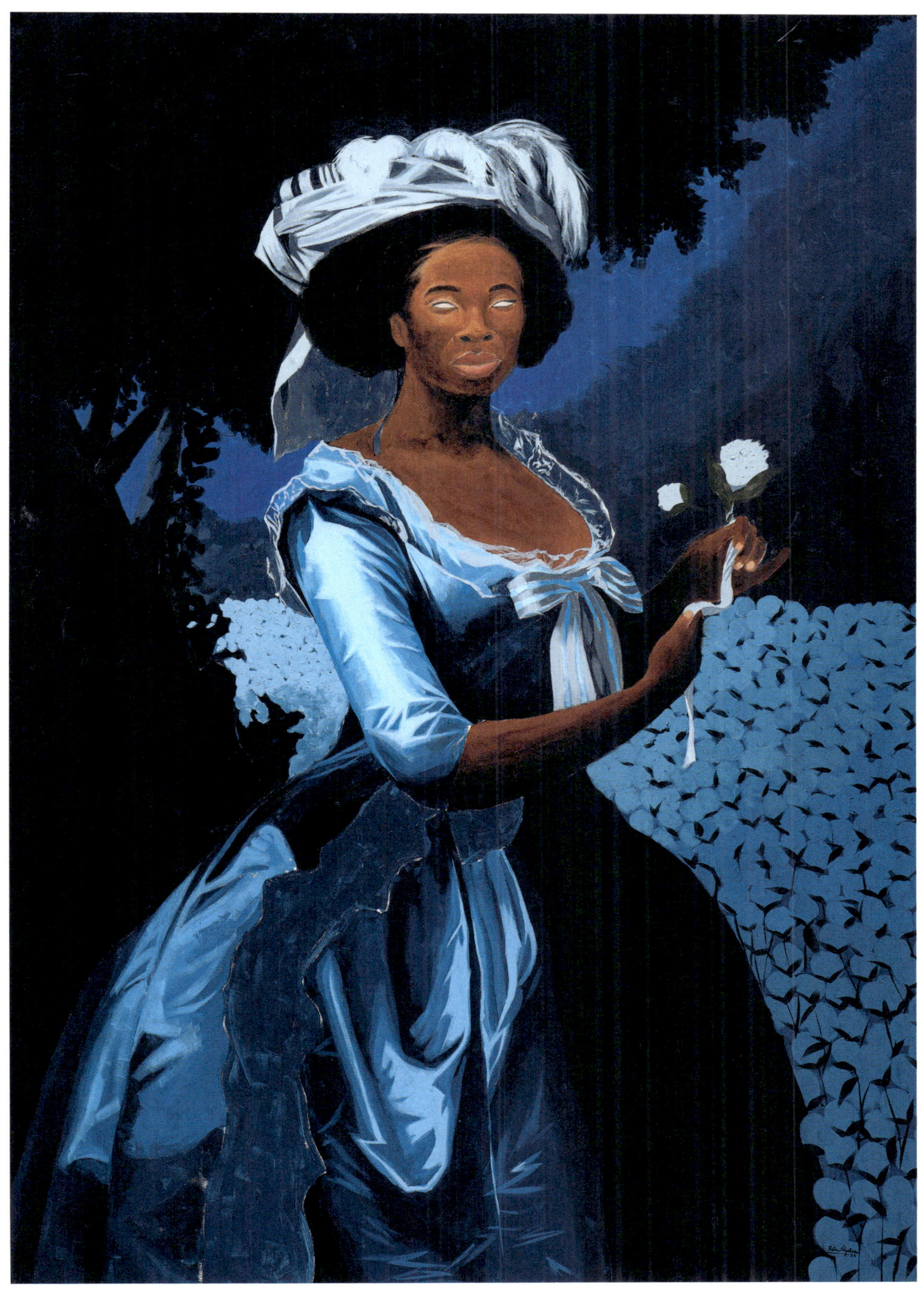

BOLUWATIFE OYEDIRAN
Lady with a Boll, 2021
Acrylic on canvas / Acryl auf Leinwand, 170 × 118 cm

BOUVY ENKOBO

Seeking inspiration for his painting in scenes of everyday life, Bouvy Enkobo is careful never to let his art succumb to the flat realism of ordinary reportage. In his strolls around urban Kinshasa and elsewhere, the artist always manages to capture moments suspended in time, when images touch the mind and reality gives rise to dreams. Each painting seems to capture the deep and poetic character of human situations we can no longer see: a man putting down his travel bag, his gaze lost in the distance; a vagrant lying on the ground with his dog, companions suffering in misery. Like scenes from cinematic Neorealism, reality conquers the poetry of images in which the street, the city, and current events become the stage for an aesthetic that engages equally with the humanist photography of Brassaï, the meanderings of Aragon's urban prose, and the elation of New Realists receptive to the untamed beauty of our city walls. To poeticize this urban expressionism, Bouvy Enkobo plays with the disparity between explicit figurative painting and sculptural, deconstructed backgrounds, giving his paintings the appearance of the torn posters of Villeglé or Hains. This technique of mixing collage and acrylic allows the artist to intensify his characters' presence. They seem to float, strangely detached from their brightly colored, unsettled backgrounds. To this end, the artist has become a collector of posters, gathering them exclusively in Kinshasa to introduce a visual reference to the streets of his capital into his paintings. But unlike the poster artists, Bouvy Enkobo is not content by simply displaying the shreds. Employing subtle elements of collage and décollage, the artist uses the shreds like visual catalysts contributing to the color dynamic and duality of his painting.

Playing with this tension between the abstract and the figurative makes it easier for Bouvy Enkobo to express the precious alliance of dream and reality that brings each scene we encounter to life.

The Congolese artist (b. 1981 in Kinshasa) deterritorializes his painting by appropriating the codes of an art that is traditionally almost exclusively focused on the representation of men of European decent to highlight the condition of people of color.

Following in the footsteps of artists like Kerry James Marshall, he implicitly reflects the general lack of representation of people of color in the canon of images that form the basis of art history. This explains the unusual effect of some paintings whose subjects seem to be directly inspired by an iconic representation of Western painting.

PHILIPPE GODIN

Bouvy Enkobo sucht in Szenen des täglichen Lebens nach Inspiration für seine Malerei, wobei er darauf achtet, seine Kunst nie dem platten Realismus einer gewöhnlichen Reportage zu opfern. Dem Künstler gelingt es, bei seinen Streifzügen durch Kinshasa und anderorts diese Augenblicke einzufangen, in denen das Bild die Gedanken streift und die Realität Träume hervorbringt. Jedes Gemälde scheint die Tiefe und Poesie menschlicher Situationen festzuhalten, die wir nicht mehr zu sehen vermögen: Ein Mann, der seine Reisetasche abstellt, sein Blick schweift in die Ferne; ein Landstreicher, der mit seinem Hund am Boden liegt, Gefährten im Elend. Wie in Szenen des filmischen Neorealismus erobert die Realität eine Bildpoetik, in der Straße, Stadt und Ereignisse zum Schauplatz einer Ästhetik werden, die an die humanistische Fotografie von Brassaï, das Umherschweifen der Stadtprosa von Aragon und die Begeisterung der Nouveaux Réalistes, die für die raue Schönheit der Mauern unserer Städte empfänglich sind, anknüpft.

Um diesen urbanen Expressionismus zu poetisieren, spielt Enkobo mit der Diskrepanz zwischen der expliziten figurativen Malerei und den plastischen, dekonstruierten Hintergründen, die seinen Leinwänden die Anmutung von Plakatabrissen von Villeglé oder Hains verleihen. Diese Technik, die Collage und Acryl kombiniert, ermöglicht es dem Künstler, die Präsenz seiner Figuren zu verstärken. Sie scheinen zu schweben und heben sich auffällig von den unruhigen, bunten Hintergründen ab. Der Maler ist zum Sammler von Plakaten geworden, die er ausschließlich in Kinshasa zusammenträgt, um etwas vom visuellen Rauschen der Straßen der Metropole in seine Bilder einzubringen. Doch im Gegensatz zu den Plakatkünstlern begnügt sich Enkobo nicht damit, die Papierschnipsel auszustellen. Vielmehr nutzt er diese durch den subtilen Einsatz von Collage und Décollage als plastische Elemente, die zur Dynamik des Kolorits und Dualität seiner Malerei beitragen.

Das Spiel mit der Spannung zwischen Abstraktion und Figuration erleichtert es Enkobo, die Verbindung von Traum und Wirklichkeit zum Ausdruck zu bringen, die jede Szene, die sich unserem Blick offenbart, belebt.

Der kongolesische Künstler (geb. 1981, Kinshasa) deterritorialisiert die Malerei, indem er sich die Codes dieser Kunst, die sich traditionell fast ausschließliche auf die Darstellung von Männern europäischer Herkunft konzentriert, aneignet, um die Situation von People of Color zu verdeutlichen.

In der Nachfolge von Künstler:innen wie Kerry James Marshall verweist er implizit auf den Mangel an Darstellungen von People of Color in dem Bildkanon, der das Fundament der Kunstgeschichte bildet. Daher rührt die ungewöhnliche Wirkung einiger Gemälde, deren Sujets von ikonischen Darstellungen der westlichen Malerei inspiriert zu sein scheinen.

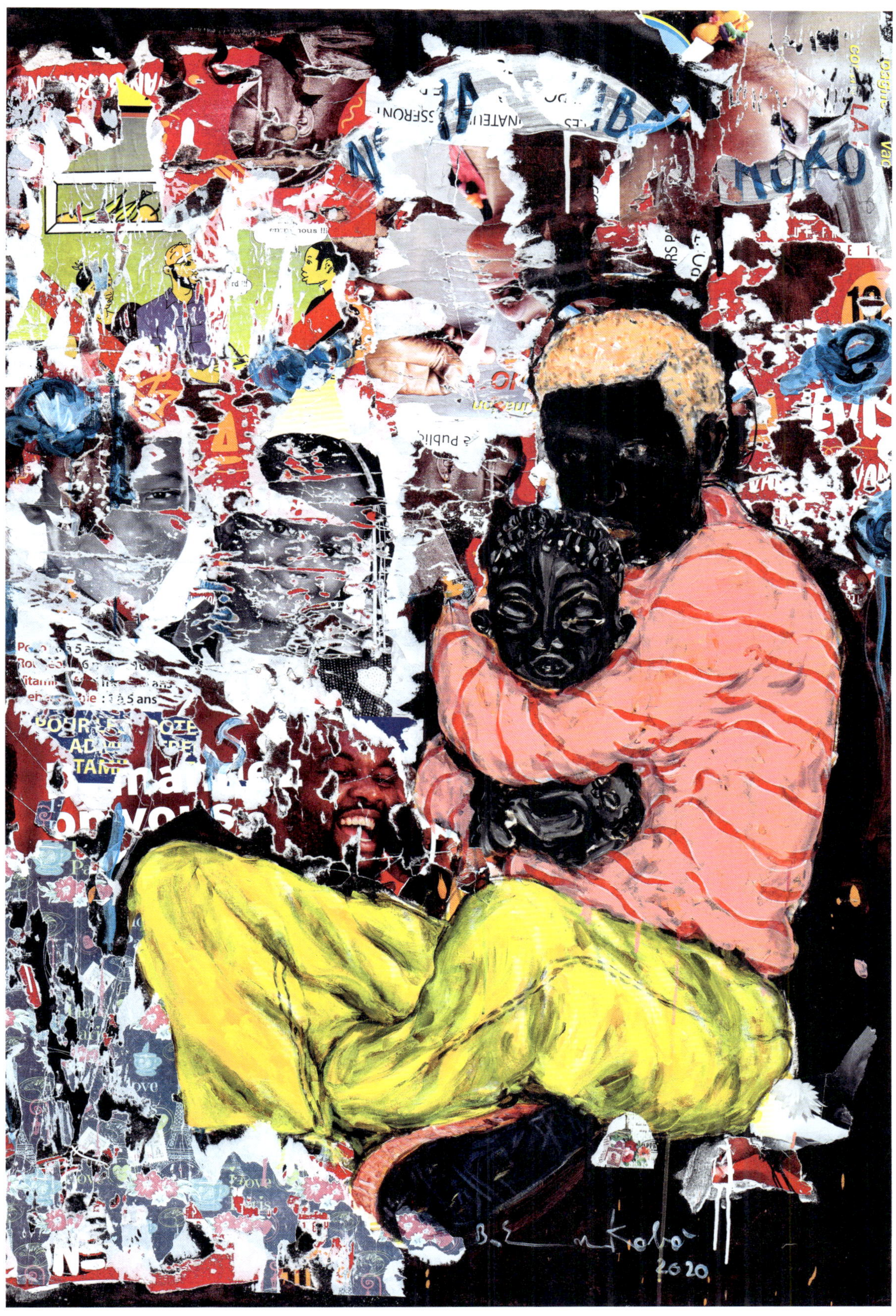

BOUVY ENKOBO

MANSEBA (Oncle), 2022, Acrylic, collage and charcoal on canvas /
Acryl, Collage und Kohle auf Leinwand, 150 × 100 cm

BOUVY ENKOBO
L'Évolué, 2022, Acrylic, collage and charcoal on canvas /
Acryl, Collage und Kohle auf Leinwand, 180 × 140 cm

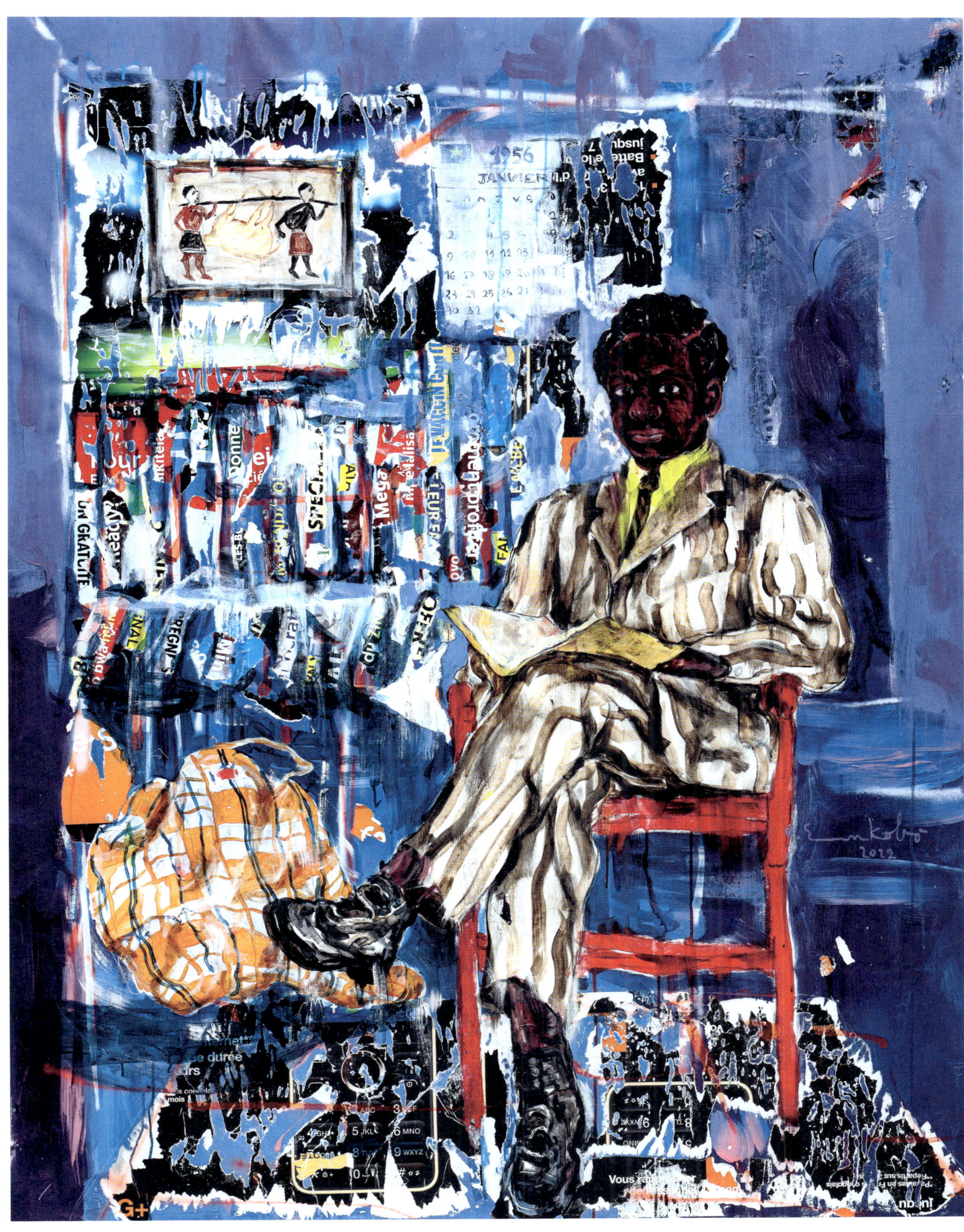
1956
JANVIER

JEAN DAVID NKOT

In his most recent works, Jean David Nkot (b. 1989 in Douala, Cameroon) investigates the exploitation of raw materials in Africa: the underlying conditions, the economic and political framework, and the implications for humanity and the environment. The work included in the exhibition situates three female miners in the center of the image as if seated atop a throne, holding their tools, and owning the space. They appear strong, resilient, dignified.
Portraiture traditions in the Western arts canon have historically been the prerogative of royalty and the upper class, mostly excluding people of color unless depicted through a colonial/postcolonial lens. With his portraits of mine workers, Nkot reclaims agency on their behalf, as the viewer must gaze up and pay attention. His subjects are not waiting on the audience to bestow them with worth; Nkot's placement already provides this added layer of power.
Nkot constructs his artistic narrative from three layers. The base or "molecule map," inspired by Swiss artist Thomas Hirschhorn, is intended to visually represent the subjects' connection to their environment. This is of considerable relevance when exploring mining's impact on humans and land since they are intrinsically linked.
The details of waterways and roads cover the painting like veins, becoming part of human bodies, and continuously circulating life, heritage, history, and identity. Landscape and identity cannot be separated as landscape holds many cultural and ontological markers, yet the exact location remains abstract and does not need to be defined in detail.
As raw materials are extracted from scarred land, the veins of roads and rivers also become scars as they appear across the canvas, across bodies. They offer a narrative of healing and future. Wisdom and generational knowledge are passed on. Like Nkot paying heed to painters who preceded him, this goes beyond artistic gesture or abstract nods to art history. Like the tales of a griot, history is alive in the people.
The second and third layers—applied with acrylic and India ink—create portraits of defiance and hope, claiming visibility and refusing to be objectified. Not in life, not in art. As Nkot guides us through his painting, his aesthetic choices key us in to the essential meaning of the work, where he leaves us to continue the effort.

In seinen jüngsten Werken thematisiert Jean David Nkot (geb. 1989 in Douala, Kamerun) die Ausbeutung von Rohstoffen in Afrika: die zugrundeliegenden Gegebenheiten, die ökonomischen und politischen Rahmenbedingungen sowie die Auswirkungen auf Mensch und Umwelt. Die in der Ausstellung gezeigte Arbeit rückt drei Minenarbeiterinnen ins Zentrum des Bildes. Wie auf einem Thron sitzend, ihre Werkzeuge in den Händen, beherrschen sie den Bildraum. Sie erscheinen stark, unverwüstlich, würdevoll.
Porträts waren in der westlichen Kunsttradition historisch dem Adel und der Oberschicht vorbehalten; People of Color waren weitgehend ausgeschlossen, außer sie wurden aus einem kolonialen oder postkolonialen Blickwinkel wiedergegeben. Mit seinen Porträts von Minenarbeiter:innen fordert Nkot in deren Namen Selbstbestimmung ein, denn die Betrachtenden müssen hochblicken und ihnen Aufmerksamkeit zollen. Die Porträtierten warten nicht darauf, dass das Publikum ihnen Wertschätzung entgegenbringt; Nkots Platzierung verleiht ihnen bereits jene zusätzliche Ebene der Macht.
Nkot konstruiert sein Narrativ anhand dreier Schichten. Die Basis oder „Molekül-Landkarte", inspiriert von dem Schweizer Künstler Thomas Hirschhorn, soll die Verbindung der Porträtierten mit ihrer Umwelt visuell darstellen. Dies ist vor allem für die Untersuchung der Auswirkungen des Bergbaus auf Mensch und Natur von großer Bedeutung, die untrennbar miteinander verbunden sind. Darstellungen von Flüssen und Straßen durchziehen das Gemälde wie Adern, verschmelzen mit den Körpern, lassen Leben, Kultur, Geschichte und Identitäten zirkulieren. Landschaft und Identität lassen sich nicht voneinander trennen, da Landschaften kulturelle und auch ontologische Kennzeichen aufweisen; der genaue Ort bleibt aber abstrahiert, muss nicht im Detail definiert werden. So wie dem vernarbten Land Rohstoffe extrahiert werden, verwandeln sich auch die Adern aus Straßen und Flüssen zu Narben, die sich über die Leinwand, über die Körper ziehen. Sie bieten eine Erzählung von Heilung und Zukunft. Weisheit und das Wissen von Generationen werden weitergegeben. Wie Nkot, der früheren Künstlergenerationen Respekt zollt, ist dies mehr als eine künstlerische Geste oder eine abstrakte kunsthistorische Referenz. Wie die Erzählungen eines Griot, ist die Geschichte in den Menschen lebendig.
Die zweite und dritte Schicht, die er mit Acryl und Tusche kreiert, schaffen Porträts voller Widerstandskraft und Hoffnung; sie erheben Anspruch auf ihre Sichtbarkeit und lassen sich nicht objektifizieren – weder im Leben noch in der Kunst. Nkot führt uns durch seine Malerei. Seine ästhetischen Entscheidungen weisen uns auf die zentrale Bedeutung seiner Arbeit hin, und er überlässt es uns, die Bemühungen fortzuführen.

HEIKE DEMPSTER

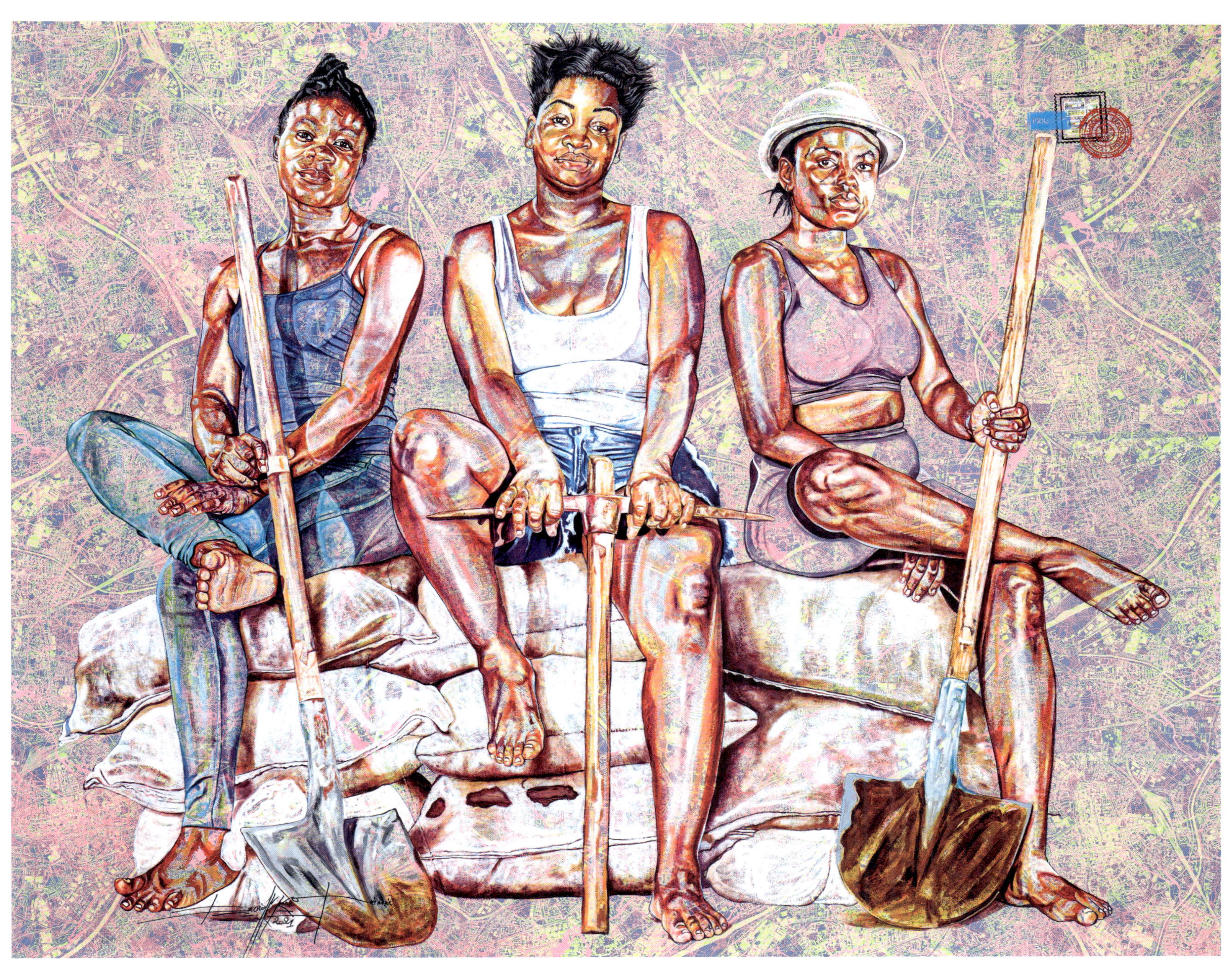

JEAN DAVID NKOT
www.Les reines@des mines.org, 2021
Acrylic on canvas / Acryl auf Leinwand, 236 × 294,6 cm

TURIYA MAGADLELA

South African artist Turiya Magadlela (b. 1978) studied at the National School of Arts, the University of Johannesburg, and the Rijksakademie van beeldende kunsten in Amsterdam, where she began experimenting with materials and craft in her practice. The artist employs a multidisciplinary approach in her figurative work, crafting portraits that blend oil paint and sewing or embroidery, making use of nylon pantyhose, Apartheid prison sheets, and uniforms to bring each work to life. Patches of variously colored tights add a filmy, ethereal element to the artist's historically relevant themes.

In her art-making, Magadlela carefully selects textiles that give voice to a society she considers not only gendered, but radicalized, while drawing from her experiences as a Black woman, South African, and mother. The multimedia artist cuts, stitches, and folds her textiles across wooden frames, creating captivating scenes that invite the public to join the metaphor: celebrating womanhood while criticizing the eroticization and violence committed against Black bodies in South Africa and around the world. Each work is multilayered and nuanced, showcasing the subject in an almost erotic, voyeuristic fashion, creating scenes that make it seem as though the viewer is peering through a film to access the subject underneath.

Magadlela's series "Untitled" (2020) depicts oil-painted subjects covered in semi-transparent layers of nylon and cotton tights and thread. Magadlela applies the fabric to her works in methodical, rectangular shapes, with small holes and variations in color creating a filter, if you will, through which to view the painting. In some works, the viewer makes eye contact with the subject, taking in the features and intricacies of the person's face through individual pieces of fabric. In others, a single eye might be hidden from view as a result of a darker textile, the fabric creating a palpable distance. In another work from the series, a group of nude women are seated together, lounging in an interior setting, unaware of the viewer's gaze from the other side of the fabric. The separation is insurmountable; to gaze at Magadlela's paintings is to feel overwhelmed with curiosity, desperate to access the other side of the fabric. In every work, the artist takes politically charged materials, softens them, and makes them entirely her own. This is the power, and the beauty, of the feminine experience through her lens.

Magadlela won the FNB Art Prize in 2015 and was shortlisted for the Jean-François Prat Prize in 2017. Her work has been exhibited extensively across the globe.

CHARLES MOORE

Die südafrikanische Künstlerin Turiya Magadlela (geb. 1978) studierte an der National School of the Arts, der Universität Johannesburg und der Rijksakademie van beeldende kunsten in Amsterdam, wo sie begann, mit Materialien und Handarbeit zu experimentieren. Die Künstlerin verfolgt in ihrem figurativen Werk einen multidisziplinären Ansatz und gestaltet Porträts, die Ölmalerei mit Näh- oder Stickarbeit verbinden; sie verwendet Nylonstrumpfhosen, Gefängnisbettlaken aus der Zeit der Apartheid und Uniformen, um jedes Werk zum Leben zu erwecken. Flecken verschiedenfarbiger Strumpfhosen fügen den historisch relevanten Sujets der Künstlerin ein hauchfeines, ätherisches Element hinzu.

In ihrem Schaffen wählt Magadlela mit Sorgfalt Textilien aus, die einer Gesellschaft, die sie nicht nur als vergeschlechtlicht, sondern auch als radikalisiert erachtet, eine Stimme verleihen, wobei sie aus ihrer Erfahrung als Schwarze Frau, Südafrikanerin und Mutter schöpft. Die Multimediakünstlerin schneidet, näht und faltet Textilien auf Holzrahmen und schafft so fesselnde Szenen, die das Publikum einladen, auf die Metapher einzugehen: Weiblichkeit zu feiern und zugleich die Erotisierung von und die in Südafrika und auf der ganzen Welt verübte Gewalt an People of Color zu kritisieren. Jede Arbeit ist vielschichtig und nuanciert und zeigt das Motiv auf beinahe erotische, voyeuristische Weise; dabei entstehen Szenen, die den Anschein erwecken, als erspähten die Betrachtenden durch einen dünnen Film hindurch das Sujet dahinter.

Magadlelas Serie „Untitled" (2020) zeigt in Öl gemalte Menschen, bedeckt von halbtransparenten Schichten aus Nylon- und Baumwollstrumpfhosen und Fäden. Sie bringt den Stoff systematisch in rechteckigen Formen auf ihre Werke auf, wobei kleine Löcher und Farbvariationen einen Filter bilden, durch den man das Gemälde betrachtet. Bei einigen Werken sieht man der abgebildeten Person in die Augen und nimmt durch einzelne Stoffstücke Gesichtszüge und Details wahr. Bei anderen wird ein einzelnes Auge durch einen dunkleren Stoff verdeckt, wodurch eine spürbare Distanz entsteht. In einer weiteren Arbeit aus der Serie sitzt eine Gruppe nackter Frauen entspannt in einem Innenraum, ohne der Blicke der Betrachtenden von der anderen Seite des Stoffes gewahr zu sein. Die Trennung ist unüberwindlich; wer Magadlelas Bilder betrachtet, wird von Neugier überwältigt, will auf die andere Seite des Stoffes gelangen. Für jede Arbeit verwendet die Künstlerin politisch aufgeladene Materialien, nimmt ihnen die Schärfe und macht sie sich zu eigen. Das ist die Kraft und die Schönheit der weiblichen Erfahrung aus ihrer Sicht.

2015 gewann Magadlela den FNB-Kunstpreis, 2017 stand sie auf die Shortlist für den Jean-François Prat Prize. Ihre Arbeiten wurden vielfach international ausgestellt.

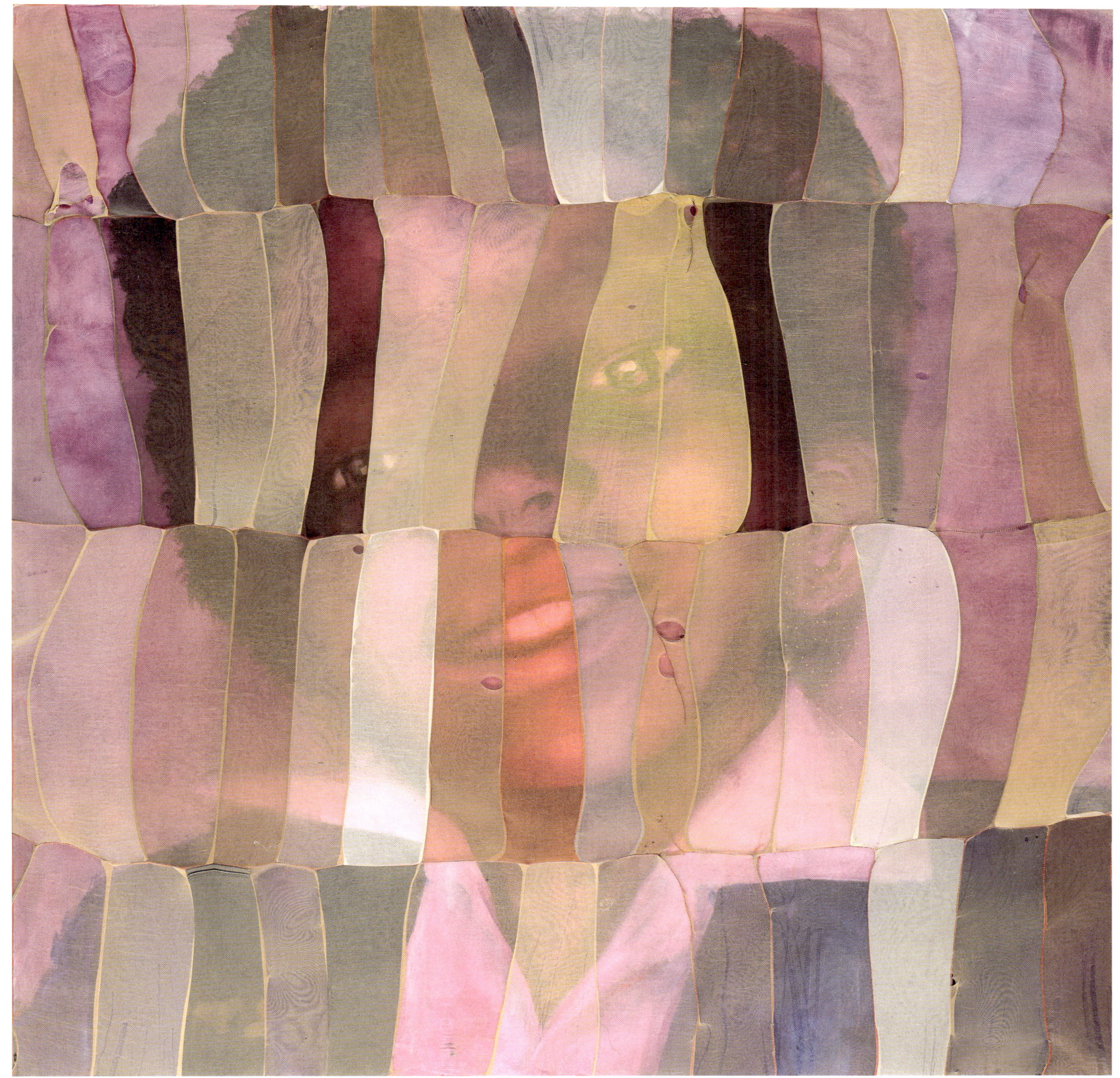

TURIYA MAGADLELA

Untitled, 2020, Oil, nylon and cotton pantyhose, thread and sealant on canvas / Öl, Nylon- und Baumwollstrumpfhosen, Fäden und Versiegelungsmittel auf Leinwand, 200 × 199 cm

BASIL KINCAID

Basil Kincaid (b. 1986 in St. Louis, US) works from mind, body, and spirit, acting in the role of a griot, summoning enhanced insight, visions, truths, and dreams that tell not only his personal story but the history of his people. Stitching quilts gives Basil a sense of belonging to his ancestral homeland. His family has been involved in quilt making for over one-hundred years and he feels compelled to carry on this family tradition. Basil continues this artistic tradition in order to uplift and honor the women in his family whose quilts were underappreciated and never received recognition. He feels guided by the spirit of his paternal grandmother Eugenia Kincaid, his greatest influence, with the creation of each quilt.

Working within the tradition of improvisational assemblage, Kincaid uses quilting to illustrate his personal and cultural identity. Employing an intuitive collage technique, involving piecing together a variety of textiles, woven, and hand-embroidered work, he produces large compositions in a laborious and time-consuming process. The impact of Kincaid's work lies not only in the sheer splendor of visual impact, but also in the exuberance of color and collective message. Kincaid draws on the geometric patterns of West African textiles and embroidery to explore the link between the US and his adopted country of Ghana, and highlight his family, historical markers, and personal stories. Kincaid creates work that challenges us in intellectually and aesthetically compelling ways. His pieces are both incredibly powerful and poetic, uniting seductive elements and socially germane messages. Exploring the intimate interconnections between body and mind, as well as ethnicity, gender, and sexuality, he pushes his visual language to the brink, causing the viewer to pause and contemplate. Fascinating, ambiguous, and provocative, Basil Kincaid's unassailably remarkable figurative compositions are absolute genius, with the best yet to come.

Basil Kincaid (geb. 1986, St. Louis, USA) arbeitet mit Geist, Körper und Seele und übernimmt die Rolle eines Griots, der tiefere Einsichten, Visionen, Wahrheiten und Träume heraufbeschwört, die nicht nur seine persönliche Geschichte erzählen, sondern auch die seines kulturellen Hintergrundes. Quilts zu nähen, gibt Basil ein Gefühl der Zugehörigkeit zur Heimat seiner Vorfahren. Seine Familie widmet sich seit über hundert Jahren der Herstellung von Quilts, und er fühlt sich dieser Familientradition verpflichtet. Basil führt die künstlerische Tradition fort, um die Frauen in seiner Familie hervorzuheben und zu ehren, deren Quilts zu wenig gewürdigt wurden und nie Anerkennung fanden. Bei der Gestaltung jedes Quilts fühlt er sich vom Geist seiner Großmutter väterlicherseits, Eugenia Kincaid, die ihn am meisten beeinflusst hat, geleitet.

In der Tradition der improvisierten Assemblage nutzt Kincaid das Quilten, um seine persönliche und kulturelle Identität zu vermitteln. Mit einer intuitiven Collagetechnik, bei der er eine Vielzahl von Textilien, darunter gewebte und handgestickte Erzeugnisse, zusammenfügt, erschafft er in einem arbeitsintensiven und zeitaufwendigen Prozess große Kompositionen. Die Wirkung von Kincaids Werken resultiert nicht nur aus der schieren Pracht der Gestaltung, sondern auch aus dem Reichtum an Farben und allgemeingültigen Botschaften. Kincaid greift auf die geometrischen Muster westafrikanischer Textilien und Stickereien zurück, um die Verbindung zwischen den USA und seiner Wahlheimat Ghana zu erkunden und um seine Familiengeschichte, historische Ereignisse und persönliche Geschichten hervorzuheben. Er schafft Werke, die uns intellektuell und auf ästhetisch überzeugende Weise herausfordern. Seine Arbeiten sind zugleich unglaublich kraftvoll und poetisch und vereinen verführerische Elemente und gesellschaftlich relevante Botschaften. Indem er die intimen Verbindungen zwischen Körper und Geist sowie zwischen Ethnie, Geschlecht und Sexualität erforscht, führt er seine Bildsprache an ihre Grenze, was die Betrachter:innen zum Innehalten und Nachdenken anregt. Faszinierend, mehrdeutig und provokativ – Basil Kincaids unbestreitbar bemerkenswerte figurative Kompositionen sind absolut genial – und das Beste kommt erst noch.

CAROLYN L. MAZLOOMI

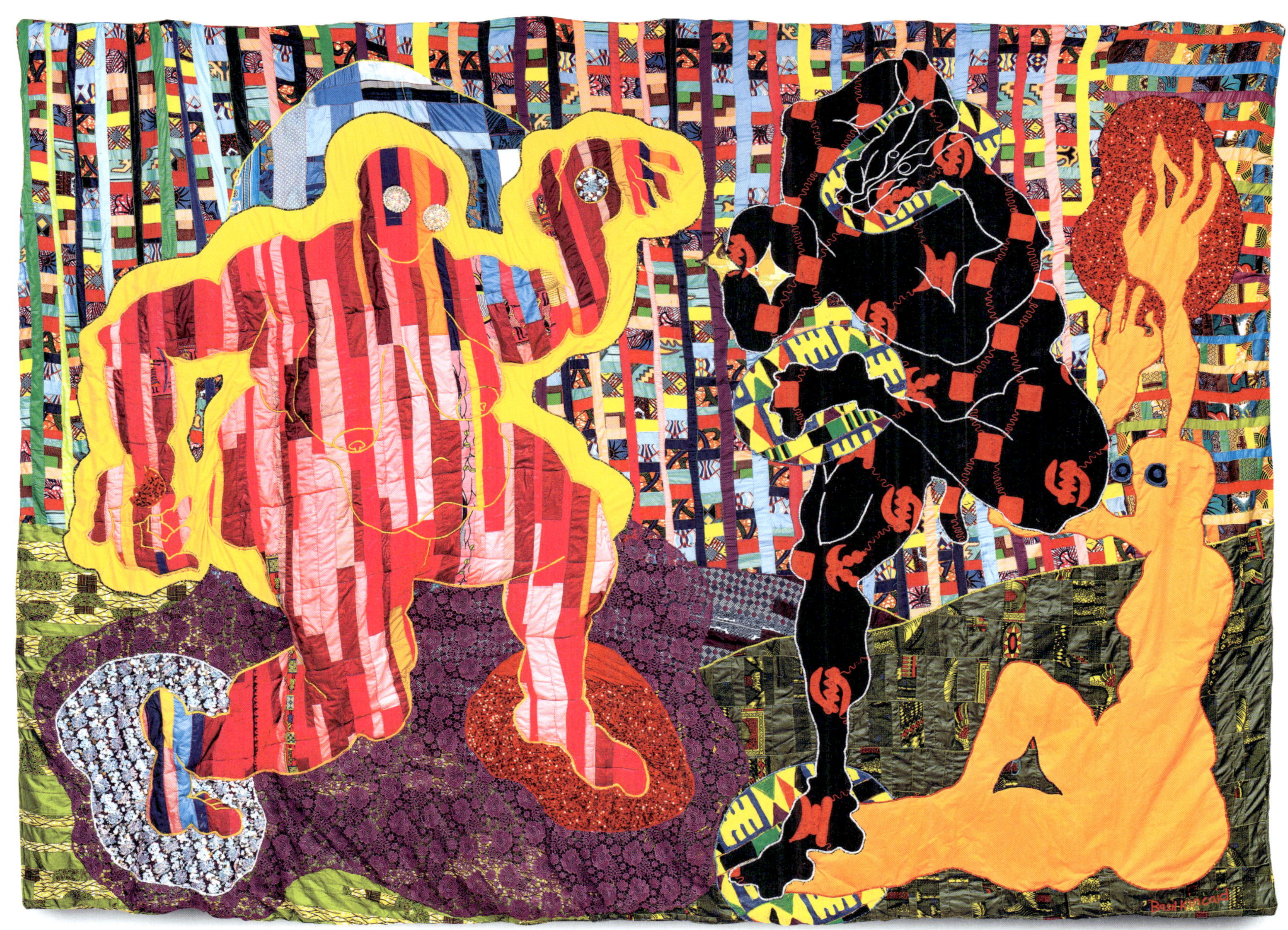

BASIL KINCAID
Origins of the Earth, 2020–2022
Quilt, 269,2 × 396,2 cm

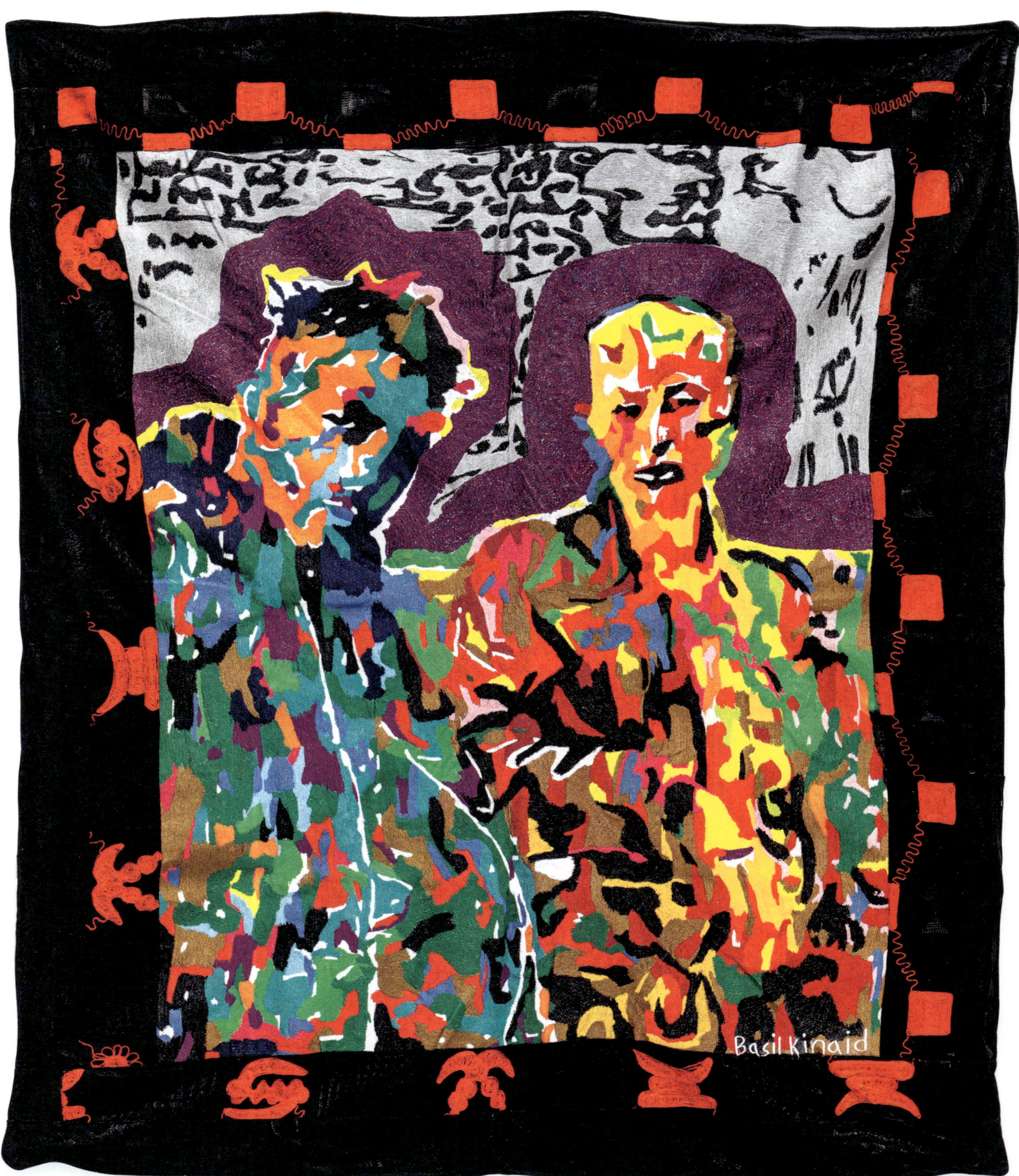

112

BASIL KINCAID
Kennedy and Nasir, 2021/22, Embroidery and handwoven cotton fiber on canvas /
Stickerei und handgefertigtes Baumwollgewebe auf Leinwand, 200,7 × 165,1 cm

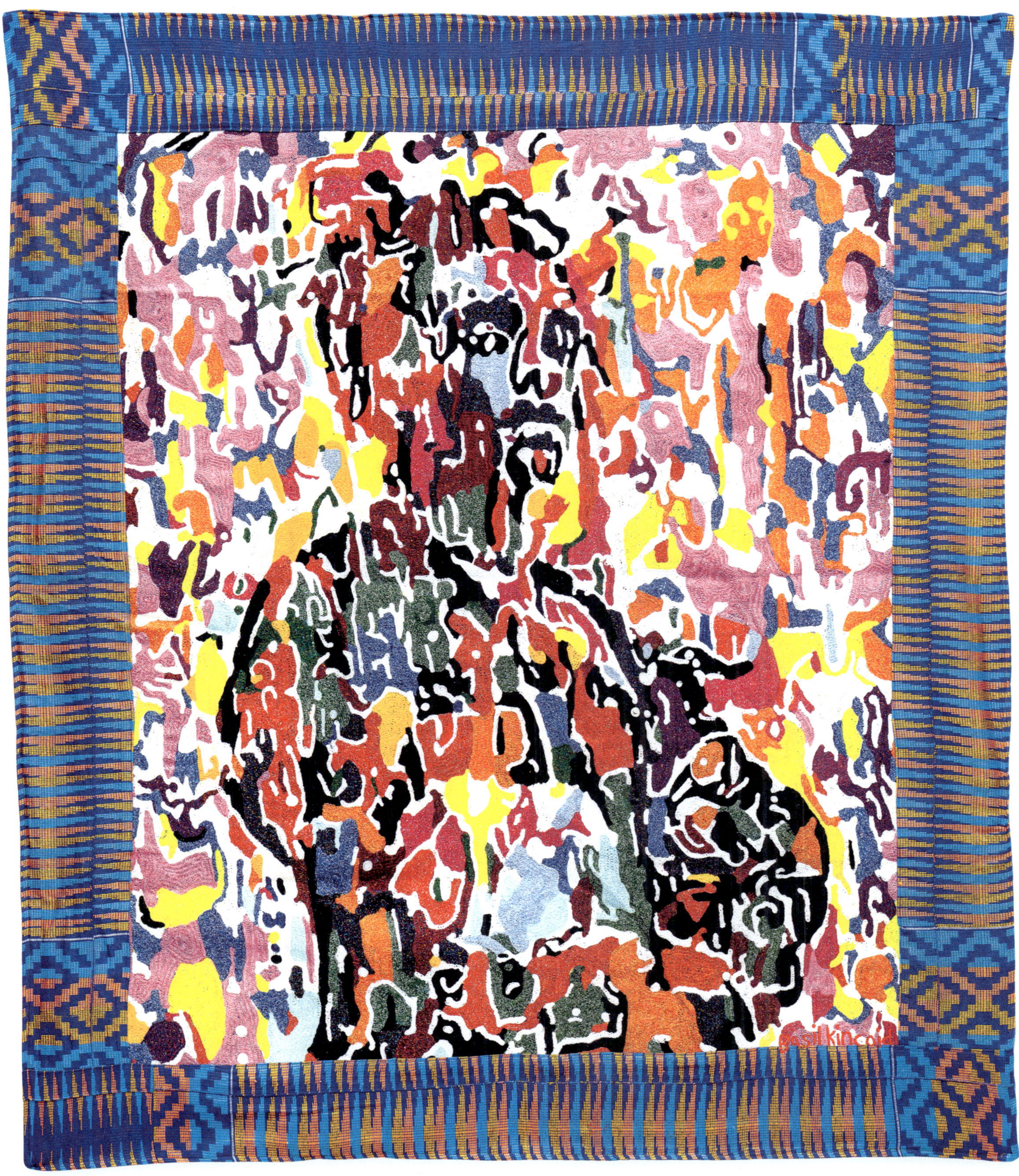

BASIL KINCAID
Kenturah Davis, 2021/22, Embroidery and handwoven fiber on canvas / Stickerei und handgefertigtes Gewebe auf Leinwand, 185,4 × 154,9 cm

CHRISTOPHER MYERS

Christopher Myers was born in New York in 1974. He is an artist and writer whose transdisciplinary work is rooted in storytelling. Myers delves into the margins of the historical archive to reconstruct narratives that parse the slippages between fact and fiction. His diverse practice spans textiles, performance, film, stained-glass, and sculptural objects often created in collaboration with artisans from around the globe. In his hand-stitched appliqué textile works, Myers explores transcultural hybridities and mythologies. His deeply researched projects filter collective and personal histories through the transformative materiality of narrative. Myers depicts individual figures as contemporary icons, condensing the signs and symbols of their spiritual and historic journeys into syncretic portraits that speak powerfully to the present. For Myers, there is a connection between the material form of the works and the histories they explore. He writes: "Just as quilts are made from scraps of fabric, the mythologies of global liberation movements are made from a mixture of religious stories from all around the world." To create his textile artworks, Myers uses appliqué, a technique that appears often in quilting and banner making, and has developed as a tangible union of diverse cultural and visual practices. Each tapestry creates an emblematic space for hybridized narratives to unfold.

Christopher Myers wurde 1974 in New York geboren. Er ist ein Künstler und Schriftsteller, dessen transdisziplinäre Arbeit im Geschichtenerzählen ihren Ursprung hat. Myers taucht in die Randbereiche des historischen Archivs ein, um Narrative zu rekonstruieren, die die Übergänge von Fakten und Fiktion ausloten. Seine vielgestaltige künstlerische Praxis umfasst Textilien, Performance, Film, Glasmalerei und skulpturale Objekte, die oft in Zusammenarbeit mit Kunsthandwerker:innen aus der ganzen Welt entstehen. In seinen textilen Arbeiten mit handgestickten Applikationen erkundet Myers transkulturelle Hybriditäten und Mythologien. Seine gründlich recherchierten Projekte filtern kollektive und persönliche Geschichten durch das transformative Wesen des Narrativs. Myers stellt individuelle Figuren als zeitgenössische Ikonen dar und verdichtet die Zeichen und Symbole ihres spirituellen und historischen Werdegangs zu synkretistischen Porträts, die eine starke Aussagekraft für die Gegenwart haben. Für Myers besteht eine Verbindung zwischen der materiellen Form der Werke und den Geschichten, die sie ergründen. Er schreibt: „So wie Quilts aus Stoffresten hergestellt werden, bestehen die Mythologien der globalen Befreiungsbewegungen aus einer Mischung von religiösen Geschichten aus der ganzen Welt." Für seine textilen Kunstwerke setzt Myers Applikationsstickerei ein, eine Technik, die häufig beim Quilten oder dem Nähen von Bannern angewendet wird und sich als eine greifbare Verbindung verschiedener kultureller und visueller Praktiken entwickelt hat. Jeder Bildteppich schafft einen symbolischen Raum, in dem sich hybridisierte Narrative entfalten können.

SARAH STENGEL

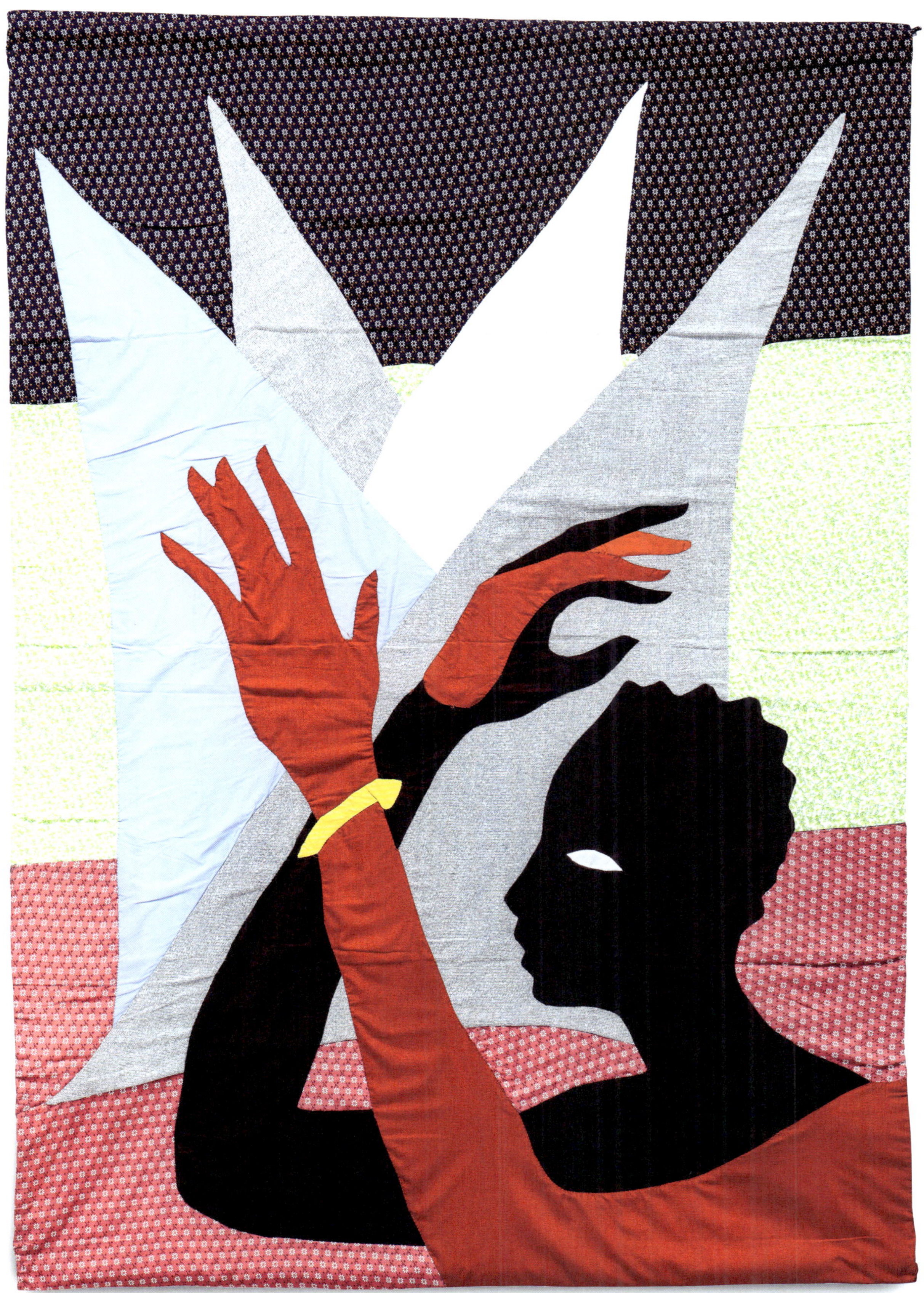

CHRISTOPHER MYERS
Orient Overseas (Sail), 2019
Applied fabric / Applizierter Stoff, 218,5 × 150 cm

CHRISTOPHER MYERS
Wovoka Speaks, 2020–2022
Applied fabric / Applizierter Stoff, 183 × 122 cm

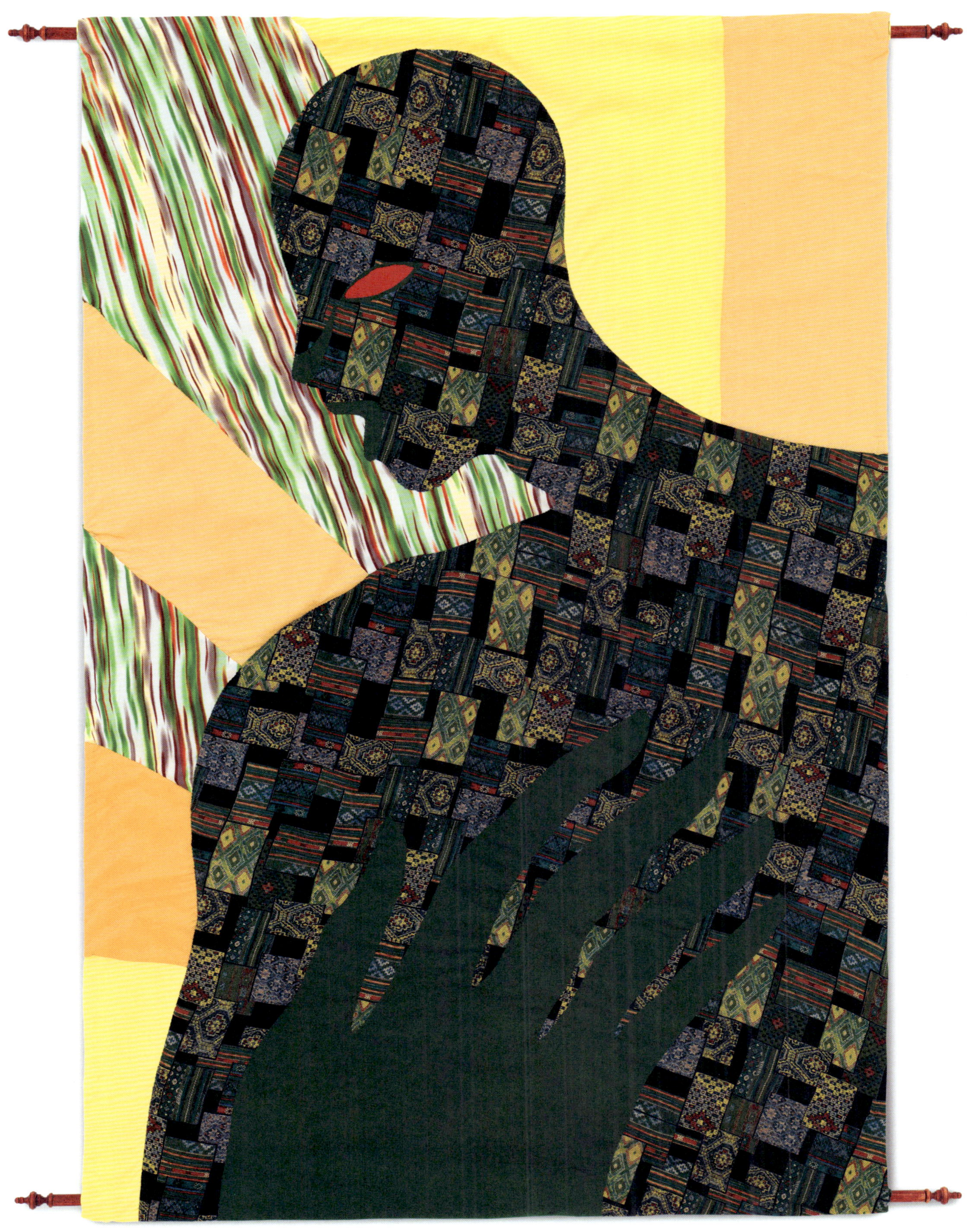

JOSIE LOVE ROEBUCK

"Who am I? Am I who they say I am?" are those centuries-old questions that many of us subliminally ask ourselves time and time again. And in the midst of a new dawn, artist Josie Love Roebuck (b. 1995) is no different as she allows me to journey with her while carefully speaking her truth in the moment: "I am a bi-racial woman, adopted by a white family," she asserts adamantly. She leans forward, listening clearly to every word I say. Her responses are direct; making it clear that who she is manifests in the visual poetry of her art. Through all of the pain that she has endured throughout the more than two decades of her life on earth, Roebuck's knowledge of family, perseverance, and triumphs are gifted to those who view her variety of images. I am reminded of the hidden treasures that peep through a great storyline waiting for a researcher to notice. That hidden jewel becomes the one that makes the story a bestseller. Roebuck has mastered this technique in her images using flowers and other forms of material culture.

In Roebuck's *Not Blood, But Blood*, she uses tulips to represent unconditional love when she speaks about her brother who was also adopted into the same family. Although both siblings were born to different birth parents, they have a sacred bond. Her use of screen printing on fabric embellished with oil pastel, ribbon, yarn, beads, embroidery floss, and buttons bring this two-dimensional fiber work to life. Roebuck makes sure that we all recognize that the brother she grew up with is not her twin; this is written multiple times on the tapestry between the two of them. This seemed to be an assumption made by onlookers because of their skin color due to the African ancestry they both possess.

A multi-faceted artist, Josie Love Roebuck continues to approach the making of her art as a journey to discover her "whole self." Like the piecing together of her patchworks, each creation brings her closer to "knowing," serving as an example for others who want the same thing.

„Wer bin ich? Bin ich die Person, für die ich gehalten werde?" – jahrhundertealte Fragen, die sich viele von uns unterschwellig immer wieder stellen. Und mitten in einem neuen Aufbruch tut dies auch die Künstlerin Josie Love Roebuck (geb. 1995), die mich mit auf die Reise nimmt, während sie bedachtsam ihre Wahrheit in diesem Augenblick ausspricht: „Ich bin eine Frau gemischter Ethnizität, die von einer weißen Familie adoptiert wurde", stellt sie entschieden fest.

Sie beugt sich vor und horcht aufmerksam auf jedes meiner Worte. Ihre Antworten sind direkt und machen deutlich, dass in der visuellen Poesie ihrer Kunst zutage tritt, wer sie ist. Durch allen Schmerz hindurch, den sie in den mehr als zwei Jahrzehnten ihres Erdenlebens ertragen hat, schenkt Roebuck denjenigen, die die Vielfalt ihrer Bilder betrachten, ihr Wissen über Familie, Beharrlichkeit und Triumphe. Ich fühle mich an die verborgenen Schätze erinnert, die in einer großen Geschichte schlummern und darauf warten, entdeckt zu werden. Das versteckte Juwel, das die Geschichte zum Bestseller machen wird. Roebuck perfektioniert diese Technik in ihren Bildern unter Einsatz von Blumen und anderen Formen der materiellen Kultur.

In *Not Blood, But Blood* verwendet sie Tulpen als Ausdruck ihrer bedingungslosen Liebe zu ihrem Bruder, der in dieselbe Familie adoptiert wurde. Wenngleich beide Geschwister unterschiedliche leibliche Eltern haben, besteht zwischen ihnen ein heiliges Band. Der Einsatz von Siebdruck, Ölkreide, Band, Garn, Perlen, Stickseide und Knöpfen erweckt diese zweidimensionale Textilarbeit zum Leben. Roebuck stellt sicher, dass wir alle erkennen, dass der Bruder, mit dem sie aufgewachsen ist, nicht ihr Zwilling ist – das steht mehrfach zwischen den beiden auf der Tapisserie geschrieben. Es scheint, als wäre das aufgrund ihrer beider Hautfarbe, die auf ihre gemeinsame afrikanische Herkunft zurückgeht, die Annahme vieler Betrachter:innen gewesen.

Als vielseitige Künstlerin betrachtet Josie Love Roebuck die Herstellung ihrer Kunst als eine Reise zur Entdeckung ihres „ganzen Ichs." Wie das Zusammensetzen ihrer Patchworks bringt jede Kreation sie dem „Wissen" näher und gibt ein Bespiel für andere, die dasselbe wollen.

MYRAH BROWN GREEN

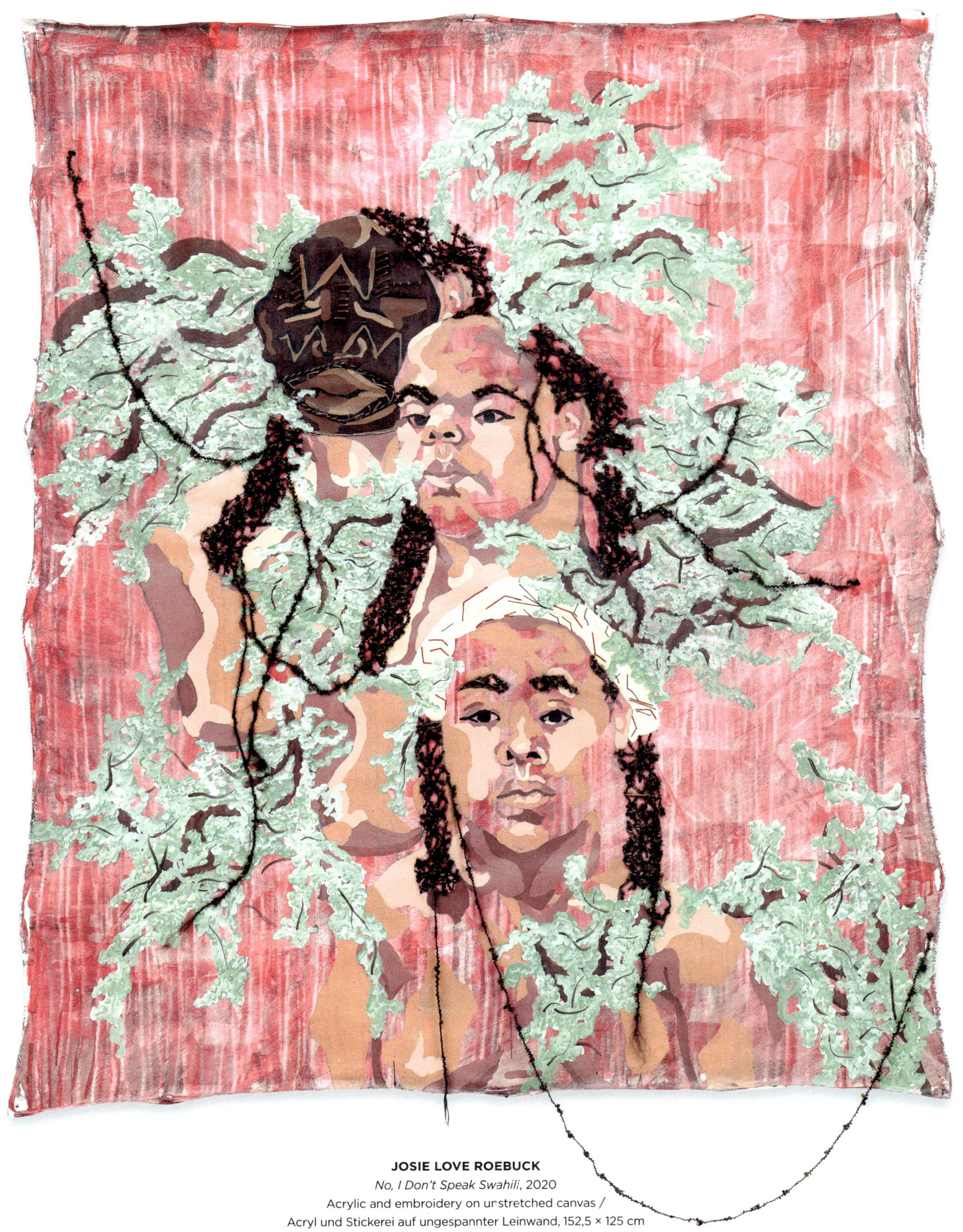

JOSIE LOVE ROEBUCK
No, I Don't Speak Swahili, 2020
Acrylic and embroidery on unstretched canvas /
Acryl und Stickerei auf ungespannter Leinwand, 152,5 × 125 cm

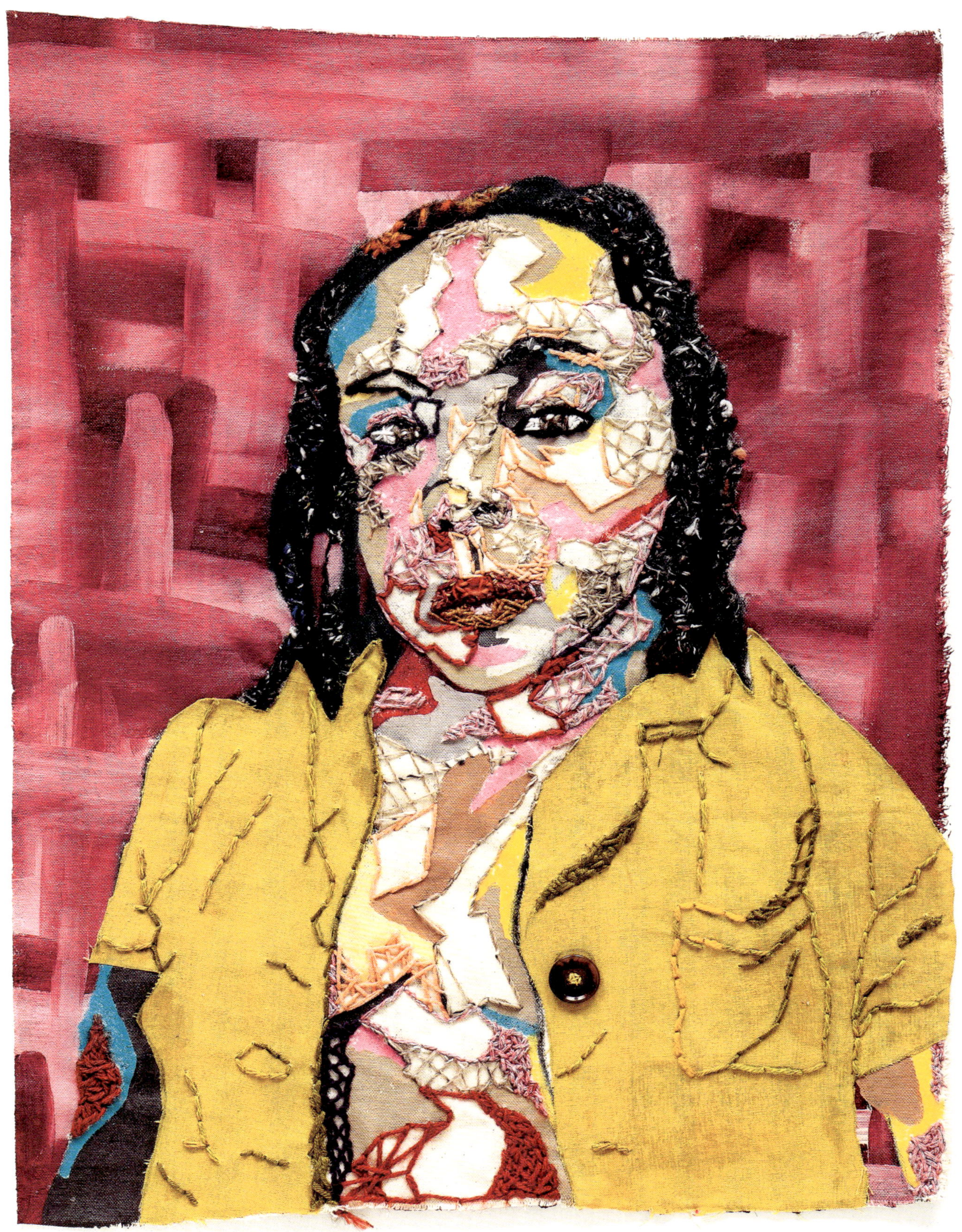

JOSIE LOVE ROEBUCK
I Am Biracial: 49% England, Wales, and Northwestern Europe, 2020, Acrylic, oil pastel, charcoal, fabric, and yarn on unstretched canvas / Acryl, Ölpastell, Kohle, Stoff und Garn auf ungespannter Leinwand, 61 × 45,7 cm

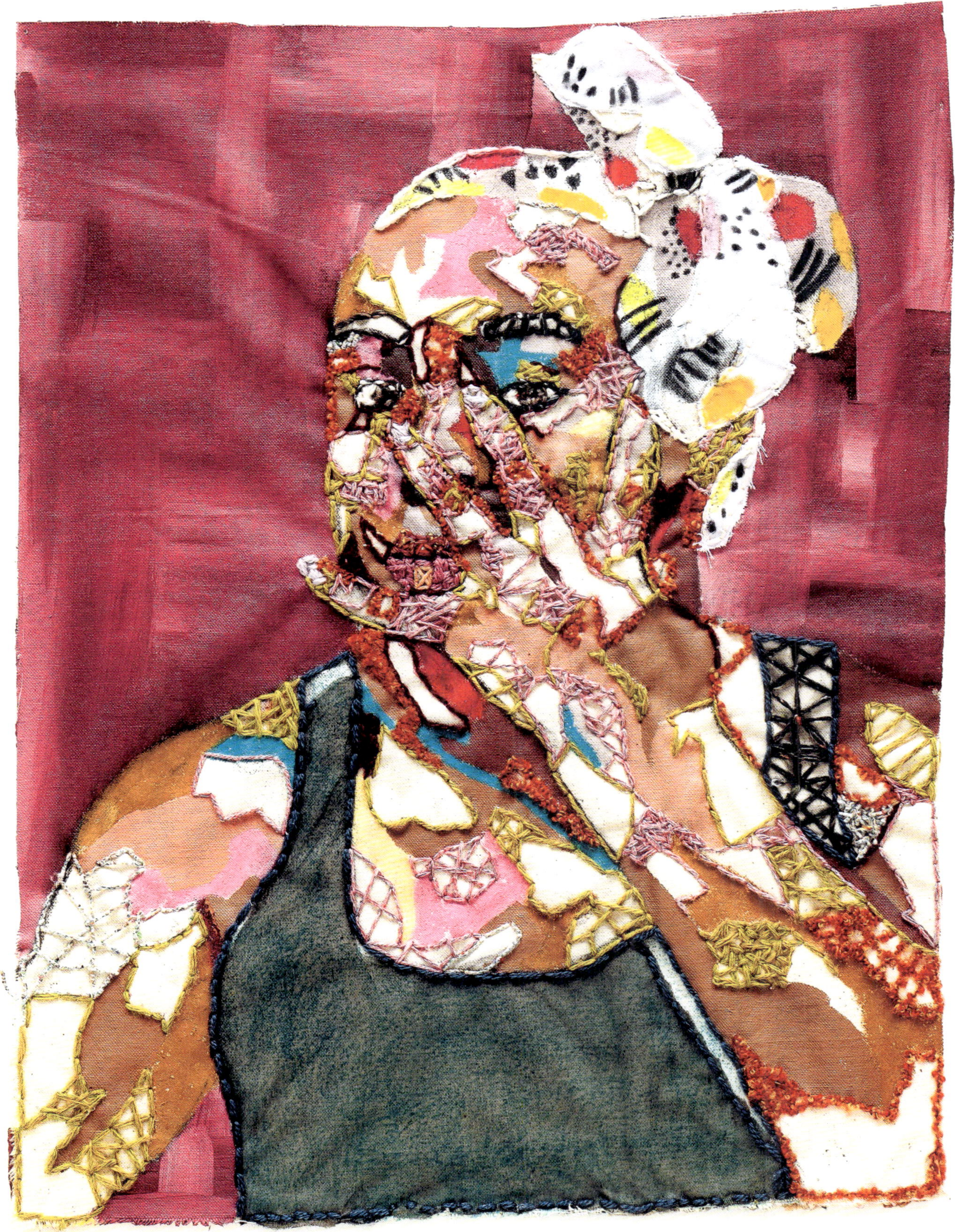

JOSIE LOVE ROEBUCK
I Am Biracial: 24% Nigeria, 10% Cameroon, Congo & Southern Bantu People, 6% Mali, and 3% Ghana, 2020, Acrylic, oil pastel, charcoal, fabric and yarn on unstretched canvas / Acryl, Ölpastell, Kohle, Stoff und Garn auf ungespannter Leinwand, 61 × 45,7 cm

JOSIE LOVE ROEBUCK
The Unseen, 2019, Acrylic, soft pastel, charcoal and yarn on unstretched canvas / Acryl, weiches Pastell, Kohle und Garn auf ungespannter Leinwand, 183 × 154 cm

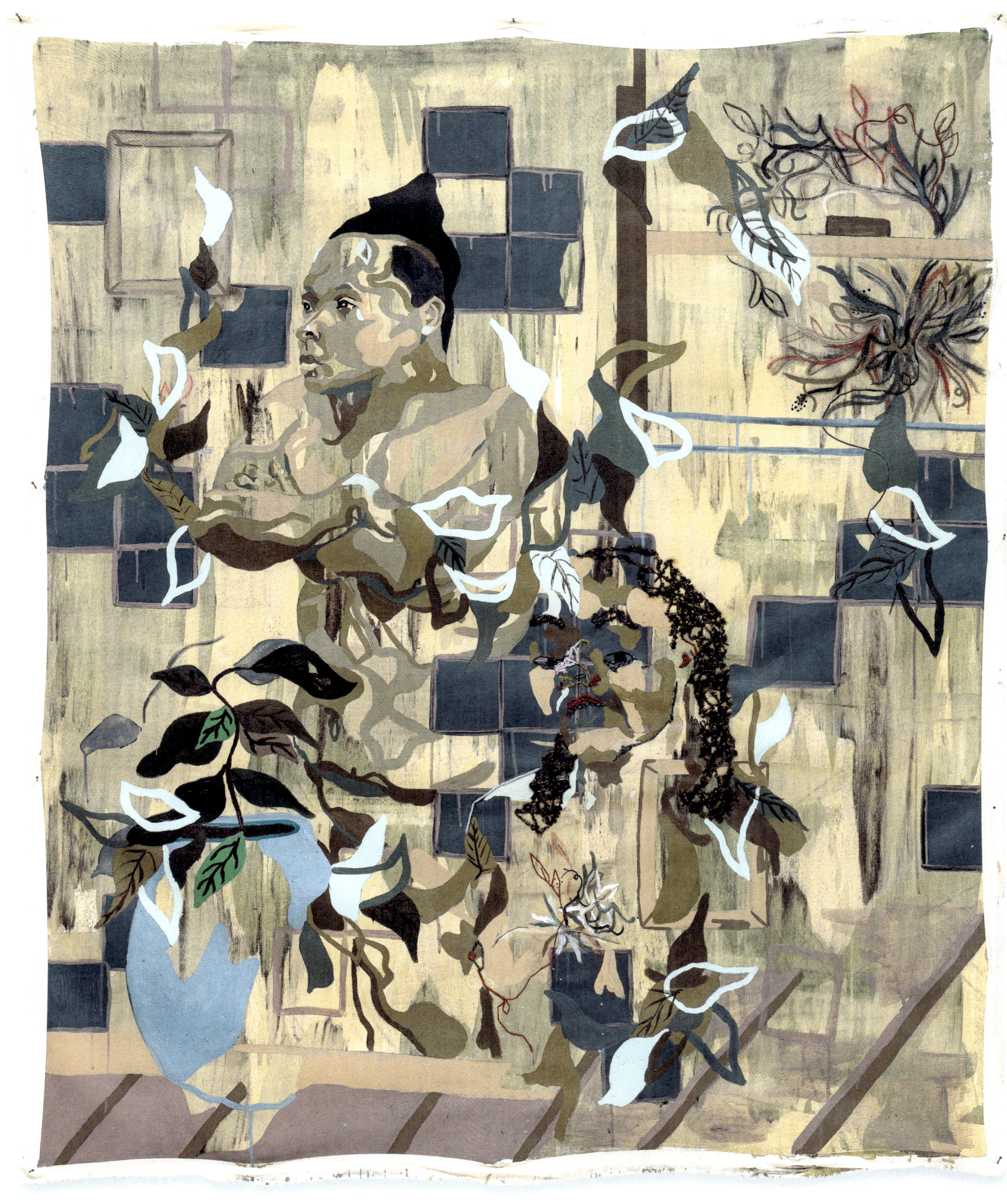

REPRESENTATION MATTERS

FLORIAN STEININGER

The focus of the Krems exhibition is on contemporary African portraiture and the question of how Black identity and individual representation are negotiated. Against the backdrop of the Black Lives Matter movement, the artists emphatically affirm the presence of the Black body, which has been marginalized or even ignored throughout the history of art.

MADELEINE

In the history of painting, where people of color appeared, they were noticeably relegated to the backgrounds, to the verge of disappearing. Often, they were depicted as clownish oddities, or as nameless slaves or servants—think of the maidservant with a bouquet in Manet's painting *Olympia* (1863).
A somewhat untypical painterly representation of a person of color is Marie-Guillemine Benoist's portrait of a maid from around 1800 in the Louvre, whose identity and individuality were restored as a consequence of the exhibition *Le Modèle noir de Gericault à Matisse* at the Musée d'Orsay in Paris in 2019 (fig. 1). The curators were able to identify the historical person behind the *Portrait d'un femme noire*: Madeleine, the housekeeper of Benoist's brother-in-law. The painting was created at a time when slavery had already been abolished in France's Caribbean colonies; it has since become an icon for human rights, freedom, and women's emancipation. The neoclassical-style portrait depicting Madeleine in three-quarter view seated on a feudal-era furniture piece is comparable to Jacques-Louis David's portrait of a woman, *Madame Récamier* (1800), also from the Louvre. Madeleine's nudity, however, constitutes an important difference; an unclothed portrayal of a respectable European woman would have been unthinkable at the time. The Parisian painter, however, also had to endure harsh criticism for her "exotic" portrait of a woman, attesting to racist attitudes. It was branded a "black spot" in the context of the Salon de Paris. The painting nevertheless found its way into the Louvre's collection in 1818 as a *Portrait d'une négresse*, and to this day it remains the only "Black portrait" in the collection.

Der Fokus der Kremser Ausstellung liegt auf der zeitgenössischen afrikanischen Porträtmalerei und der Frage, wie in dieser „Black Identity" und individuelle Repräsentation verhandelt werden. Vor dem Hintergrund der Black-Lives-Matter-Bewegung unterstreichen die Künstler:innen entschieden die Präsenz des Schwarzen Körpers, der in der Geschichte der Kunst bislang an den Rand gedrängt oder gar ausgeblendet wurde.

MADELEINE

Wo People of Color in der Geschichte der Malerei vorkamen, rückten sie merklich in den Hintergrund, an den Rand des Verschwindens. Oft wurden sie als clowneskes Kuriosum oder als namenlose Sklav:innen oder Dienstbot:innen dargestellt – man denke an die Dienerin mit Blumenstrauß in Manets Gemälde *Olympia* (1863).
Eine eher ungewöhnliche malerische Abbildung einer Person of Color ist das um 1800 von Marie-Guillemine Benoist geschaffene Porträt einer Magd aus dem Louvre, die im Zuge der Ausstellung *Le Modèle noir de Gericault à Matisse* im Pariser Musée d'Orsay 2019 ihre Identität und Individualität zurückerlangte (Abb. 1). Die Kurator:innen konnten die historische Person hinter dem *Portrait d'un femme noire* identifizieren: Madeleine, die Haushälterin von Benoists Schwager. Das Gemälde entstand in einer Zeit, als die Sklaverei in Frankreichs karibischen Kolonien bereits abgeschafft worden war; seither ist es eine Ikone für Menschenrechte, Freiheit und die weibliche Emanzipation geworden. Das Porträt ist im neoklassizistischen Stil gehalten und zeigt Madeleine in Dreiviertelansicht auf einem feudalen Möbel, vergleichbar mit Jacques-Louis Davids Frauenporträt der *Madame Récamier* (1800), ebenfalls aus dem Louvre. Ein gewichtiger Unterschied liegt jedoch in der Nacktheit der Madeleine; die entblößte Darstellung einer ehrbaren Europäerin wäre zu dieser Zeit undenkbar gewesen. Allerdings musste die Pariser Malerin für ihr „exotisches" Damenporträt auch harsche Kritik einstecken, die von rassistischem Denken zeugt. Im Rahmen des Salon de Paris wurde es als „schwarzer Fleck" gebrandmarkt. Als *Portrait d'une négresse* fand das Gemälde 1818 dennoch Einzug in die Bestände des Louvre, bis heute ist es das einzige „Black Portrait" der Sammlung.

1
Marie-Guillemine Benoist
Portrait d'une femme noire, 1800
Oil on canvas / Öl auf Leinwand, 81 × 65 cm
Musée du Louvre, Paris

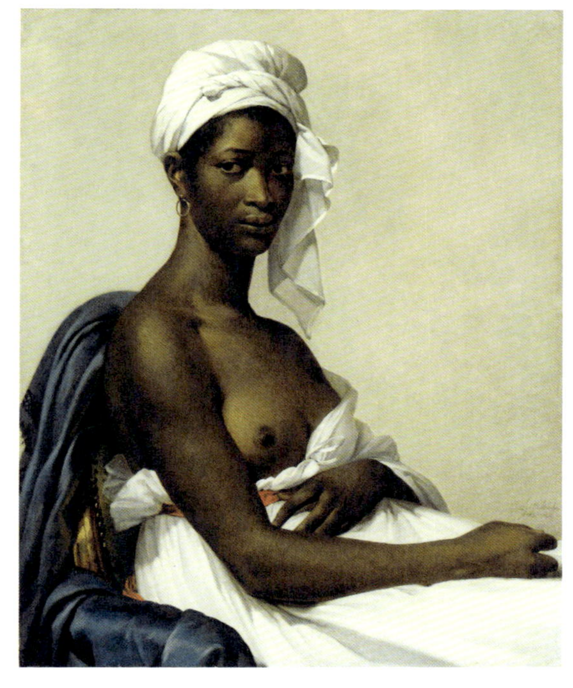

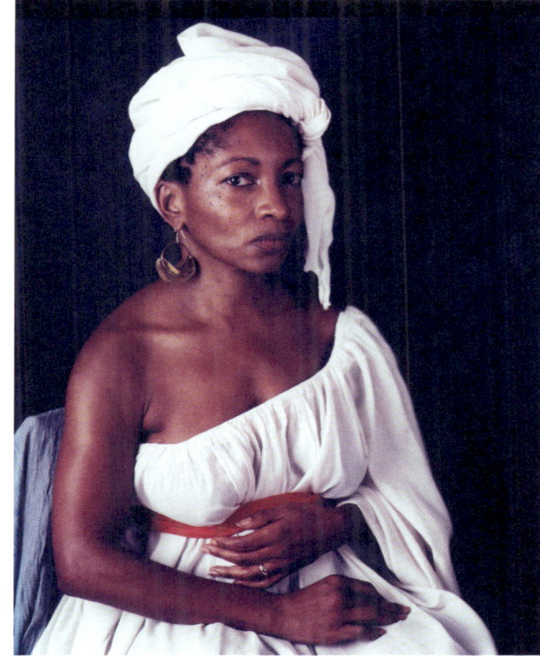

2
Maud Sulter
Bonnie Greer, 2002
Colour polaroid print / Farbpolaroid-Druck, 80,4 × 56 cm
National Portrait Gallery, London

The pop singer Beyoncé and her partner Jay-Z shot their video *Apeshit* inside the famous Parisian museum in 2018, in which they reference the Madelaine portrait, linking it directly to Leonardo's *Mona Lisa* (1503–19), the most famous artwork in the world. Here Madeleine is reinterpreted as the Black Mona Lisa, a symbol of Black empowerment and Black identity. In the music clip, dancers from communities of color also pose in front of Jacques-Louis David's 1807 historical painting of Napoleon's coronation, who reinstated slavery in 1802. In another scene, two dancers with white turbans recreate David's 1800 portrait of *Madame Récamier*. Maud Sulter, a Scottish photo artist, writer, and feminist with family roots in Ghana, also took up Benoist's portrait of Madeleine in one of her large-format Polaroids, creating a photographic homage to the Black icon in 2002. The work's title *Bonnie Greer* (fig. 2) corresponds to the name of the woman photographed wearing a white turban. Sulter reconstructs buried histories of Black women, making them the focus of her photographs.

Die Popsängerin Beyoncé und ihr Partner Jay-Z drehten 2018 in den Räumlichkeiten des berühmten Pariser Museums ihr Video *Apeshit*, in dem sie auf das Madelaine-Porträt referieren und es in unmittelbaren Konnex mit Leonardos *Mona Lisa* (1503–1519), dem bekanntesten Kunstwerk der Welt, bringen: Madeleine als die Schwarze Mona Lisa interpretierend, als Symbol für Black Empowerment und Black Identity. In dem Musikclip posieren Tänzerinnen aus Communities of Color auch vor Jacques-Louis Davids Historiengemälde von 1807 von der Krönung Napoleons, der 1802 die Sklaverei wieder eingeführt hatte. In einer weiteren Szene stellen zwei Tänzerinnen mit weißem Turban Davids Porträt der *Madame Récamier* von 1800 nach. Auch Maud Sulter, schottische Fotokünstlerin, Literatin und Feministin mit familiären Wurzeln in Ghana, greift in einem ihrer großformatigen Polaroids Benoists Madeleine-Porträt auf und schuf so 2002 eine fotografische Hommage an die Schwarze Ikone. Der Werktitel *Bonnie Greer* (Abb. 2) entspricht dem Namen der mit weißem Turban fotografierten Frau. Sulter rekonstruiert verschüttete Geschichten Schwarzer Frauen und stellt sie ins Zentrum ihrer Fotografien.

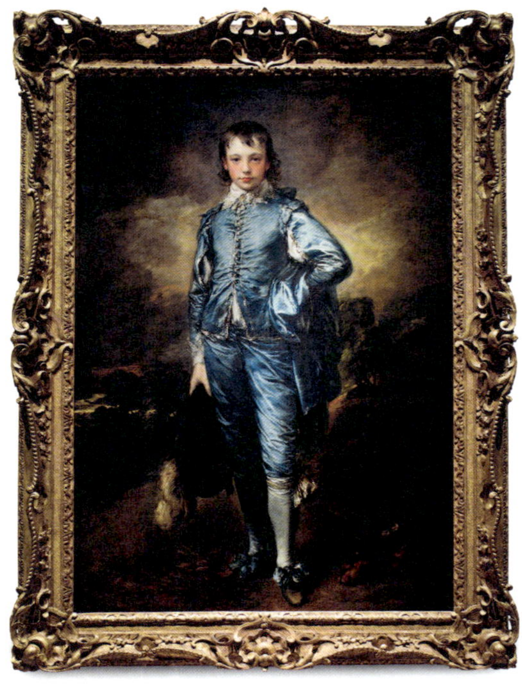

3
Thomas Gainsborough
The Blue Boy, 1770
Oil on canvas / Öl auf Leinwand, 179,4 × 123,8 cm
The Huntington Library, Art Museum, and Botanical Gardens

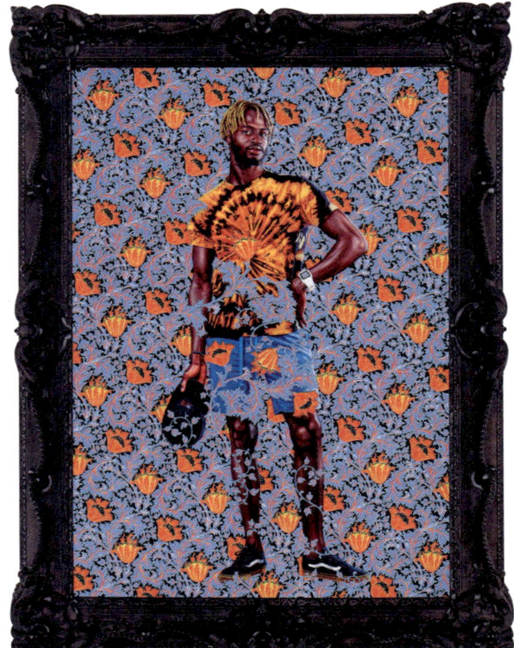

4
Kehinde Wiley
A Portrait of a Young Gentleman, 2021
Oil on linen / Öl auf Leinen, 179,1 × 124,8 cm
Collection of The Huntington Library, Art Museum, and Botanical Gardens; Commissioned through Roberts Projects, Los Angeles; Gift of Anonymous Foundation, Anne F. Rothenberg, Terry Perucca and Annette Serrurier, the Philip and Muriel Berman Foundation, and the WHH Foundation. Additional support is provided by Laura and Carlton Seaver, Kent Beiden and Dr. Louis Re, and Faye and Robert Davidson.

BLACK COWBOYS AND ICONIC WOMEN OF COLOR

The artists presented in Krems are also involved in the reorientation of the representation of people of color. Otis Kwame Kye Quaicoe's portraits are painterly manifestations of Black identities. Quaicoe's impasto application of paint and the chromatic intensity and power of the garments and surroundings are striking. Faces and skin, on the other hand, are rendered in gray, like in a black-and-white photograph. "We should be in front, because we've been at the back door for so long. It is up to us to change that."[1] Among his most popular series of works are the "Black Cowboys," heroic Black icons that seek to rectify the image of the white cowboy modeled after Clint Eastwood (cat. p. 49). In actuality, the first cowboys also came from communities of color. Today the Compton Cowboys live this rectified myth of the mounted hero. In the Los Angeles suburb of Compton, they confront racist stereotypes against African American people. Quentin Tarantino, in turn, casts in the heroic role of a cowboy in *Django Unchained* (2012) a slave who frees his beloved Brunhilde from the plantation owner's clutches and rides off with her into the night in the film's finale. In one scene at the plantation, Django dons a garish costume. Here the director cites Thomas Gainsborough's monumental portrait of a regal boy, *The Blue Boy* (1770), in the Thornton Portrait Gallery

BLACK COWBOYS UND ICONIC WOMEN OF COLOR

An dieser Neuorientierung in der Darstellung von People of Color haben auch die in Krems gezeigten Künstler:innen teil. Otis Kwame Kye Quaicoes Porträts sind malerische Manifestationen Schwarzer Identitäten. Markant ist Quaicoes pastoser Farbauftrag sowie die intensive koloristische Kraft der Gewänder und der Umgebung. Gesichter und Haut sind hingegen in Grau gehalten, wie auf einer Schwarz-Weiß-Fotografie. „Wir sollten vorn dabei sein, nachdem wir so lang an der Hintertür gestanden sind. Es liegt an uns, das zu ändern."[1] Zu seinen populärsten Werkgruppen zählen die „Black Cowboys", heroische Schwarze Ikonen, die das weiße Cowboy-Image à la Clint-Eastwood korrigieren (Kat. S. 49). Tatsächlich kamen die ersten Cowboys auch aus Communities of Color. Heute leben die Compton Cowboys diesen korrigierten Mythos des berittenen Helden. In Compton, einem Vorort von Los Angeles, bekämpfen sie rassistische Stereotype gegenüber afroamerikanischen Menschen. Quentin Tarantino wiederum lässt in *Django Unchained* (2012) einen Sklaven in die heroische Rolle des Cowboys schlüpfen; dieser befreit seine Geliebte Brunhilde aus den Fängen des Plantagenbesitzers und reitet mit ihr im Finale des Films in die Nacht davon. In einer Szene auf der Plantage ist Django grotesk kostümiert. Hier zitiert der Regisseur Thomas Gainsboroughs monumental-royales Bubenporträt *The Blue Boy* (1770), das sich in der Thornton Portrait Gallery

at the Huntington Museum of Art in San Marino, California (fig. 3). Kehinde Wiley, Barack Obama's portraitist, a leading artist of new African American figurative painting, and creator of dazzling pop works, was also inspired by Gainsborough's *The Blue Boy*. He painted a teenager in skater pants in a contrapposto pose and exhibited the opulently framed work opposite the old master painting as an emblematic, representative portrait (fig. 4).

"The main idea of my work is representation, documentation as well as celebrating and showing new ways of approaching Blackness,"[2] states Amoako Boafo regarding his iconic-expressionist portrait paintings. The artist, who also hails from Ghana, creates heads and hands with finger painting; their lively structure is reminiscent of Egon Schiele's expressive figurations of Viennese Modernism. Clothing and background are mostly monochrome or ornamental and reference elements of Viennese Art Nouveau. Boafo studied at the Academy of Fine Arts Vienna and was inspired by Schiele and Klimt. His most recent work includes the 2021 portrait painting *Kennedy* (cat. p. 25), whose subject is Kennedy Yanko, a US artist known for her painterly sculptures created from scrap metal. The finger-painting depicts the artist in the form of a portrait bust before a monochrome, white background. Human beings as individuals are the unwavering focus of Boafo's portraits.

1 Amah-Rose Abrams, "Kwesi Botchway and Otis Kwame Kye Quaicoe. Encounters," in *Elephant*, no. 45 (2021): 72.

2 Amoako Boafo in Johannes Luxner, "Wiener Moderne Revisited," in *Vienna, Intl.*, no. 2 (2022): 15.

im Huntington Museum of Art in San Marino, Kalifornien, befindet (Abb. 3). Auch Kehinde Wiley, Barack Obamas Porträtist und ein führender Künstler der neuen afroamerikanischen figurativen Malerei mit schillernd-poppigen Werken, ließ sich von Gainsboroughs *Blauem Knaben* inspirieren. Er malte einen Jugendlichen mit Skaterhose in Kontrapoststellung und stellte das Gemälde, gleichfalls in opulenter Rahmung gefasst, gegenüber dem Altmeistergemälde als repräsentatives Porträt aus (Abb. 4).

„Die Hauptidee meines Schaffens ist die Repräsentation, das Dokumentieren sowie das Feiern und Aufzeigen neuer Wege, sich dem Schwarzsein zu nähern",[2] so Amoako Boafo zu seinen ikonisch-expressionistischen Porträtgemälden. Kopf und Hände formt der ebenfalls aus Ghana stammende Künstler mittels Fingermalerei, ihre belebte Struktur erinnert an Egon Schieles ausdrucksstarke Figurationen der Wiener Moderne. Kleidung und Hintergrund sind zumeist monochrom oder ornamental gestaltet und referieren auf Elemente des Wiener Jugendstils. Boafo studierte an der Akademie der bildenden Künste Wien und ließ sich von Schiele und Klimt inspirieren. Zu seinen neuesten Arbeiten zählt das Porträtgemälde *Kennedy* von 2021 (Kat. S. 25). Die Bildprotagonistin ist Kennedy Yanko, eine US-amerikanische Künstlerin, die malerische Skulpturen aus Metallschrott erschafft. Das Gemälde zeigt die Künstlerin büstenhaft in reiner Fingermalerei auf monochrom weißem Grund. Der Mensch als Individuum steht in Boafos Porträts stets im Mittelpunkt.

1 Amah-Rose Abrams, „Kwesi Botchway and Otis Kwame Kye Quaicoe. Encounters", in: *Elephant*, Nr. 45, 2021, S. 72 (Übers. v. Michael Strand).

2 Amoako Boafo in Johannes Luxner, „Wiener Moderne Revisited", in: *Vienna, Intl.*, Nr. 2 (2022), S. 15.

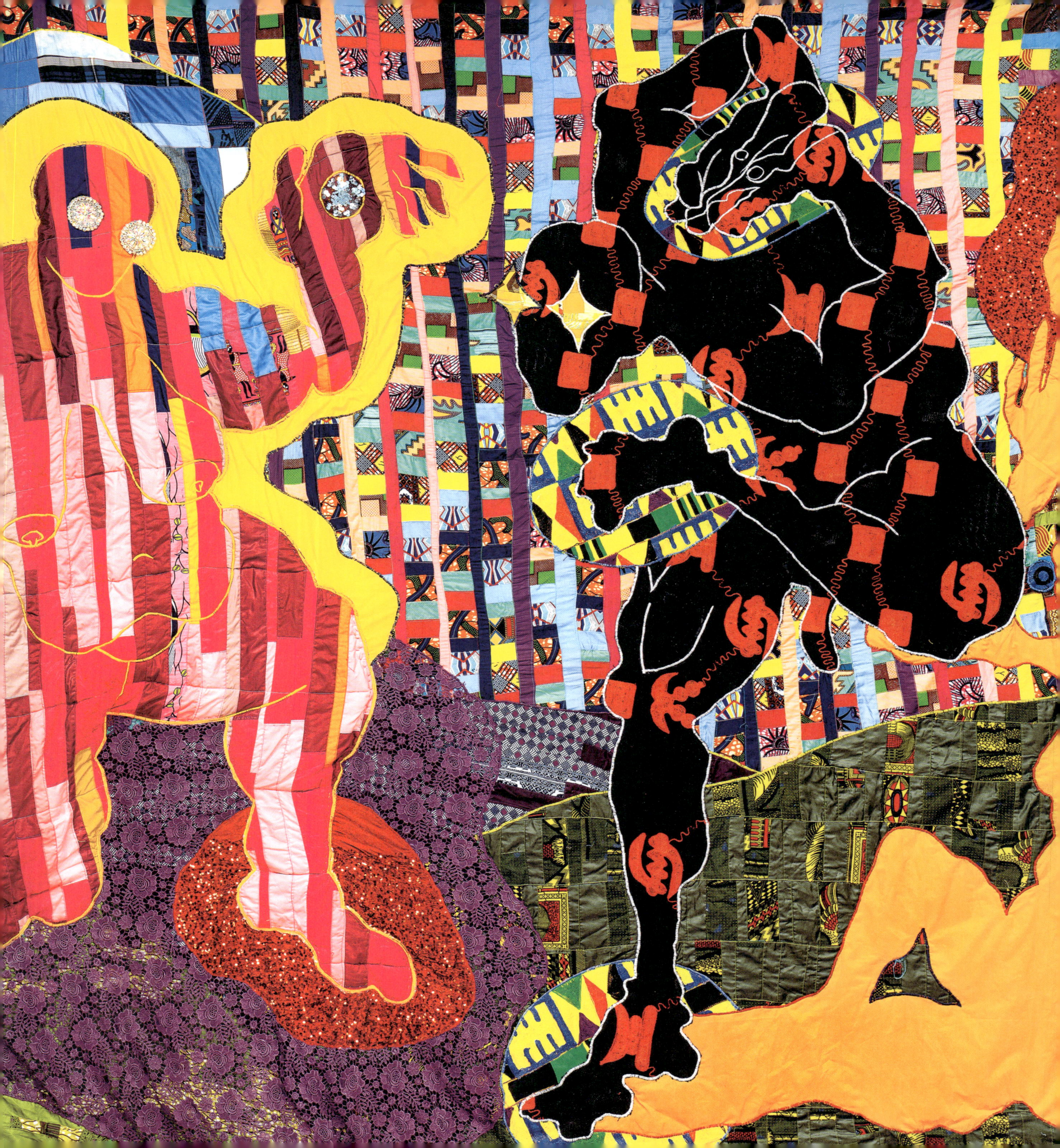

SHARIAT COLLECTIONS

AMIR SHARIAT IN CONVERSATION WITH / IM GESPRÄCH MIT FLORIAN STEININGER

FLORIAN STEININGER: Amir, how did you get into art? Was there a seminal moment?
AMIR SHARIAT: When we arrived in Vienna from Iran more than forty years ago, my father was already over sixty and was forced to rethink his life to keep the family afloat. We had lost everything, both my father's printing company—he had been the owner and publisher of the leading business magazine—as well as my mother's medical practice. So instead, he devoted himself to his passion—art—and became an art dealer. My brother and I often tagged along with him to flea markets to witness his art discoveries. Later we helped in his gallery in the eighth district. Art is in my blood thanks to this family introduction to the art world. In this regard, there was no seminal moment or experience, more like successive ones.

FS: For several years your collecting activity has focused on contemporary African art, particularly figurative painting, and portraiture. How did this develop?
AS: Many European painters, including Picasso, Matisse, or Modigliani, were deeply influenced by African art, especially sculpture. But I had not really explored African painting and African portraiture until very recently. A passion was born right away, the fruits of which can be seen at the Kunsthalle Krems.

FS: Alexandre Diop represents a central position in your collection. He's Franco-Senagalese, lives and works in Vienna, and studies at the Academy of Fine Arts there. How did you get to know him?
AS: I met Alexandre at the Academy of Fine Arts in Vienna during its open studios in January 2020, just two months before the world would change.

FLORIAN STEININGER: Amir, wie bist du zur Kunst gekommen? Gab es ein Schlüsselerlebnis?
AMIR SHARIAT: Als wir vor über 40 Jahren aus dem Iran nach Wien kamen, war mein Vater bereits über 60 und musste sein Leben neu ausrichten, um die Familie über Wasser zu halten. Denn wir hatten alles verloren, sowohl die Druckerei meines Vaters – er war Eigentümer und Herausgeber der größten Wirtschaftszeitschrift – als auch die Arztpraxis meiner Mutter. Also gab er sich seiner Leidenschaft hin, der Kunst, und wurde Kunsthändler. Mein Bruder und ich gingen oft mit zum Flohmarkt, um dort den Kunstentdeckungen unseres Vaters beizuwohnen. Später halfen wir in seiner Galerie im 8. Bezirk aus. Kunst habe ich dank dieser familiären Einführung in die Kunstwelt im Blut. Ein Schlüsselerlebnis gab es in diesem Sinne also nicht, eher mehrere Passagen.

FS: Seit ein paar Jahren hast du dich in deiner Sammlertätigkeit auf zeitgenössische afrikanische Kunst konzentriert, insbesondere auf figurative Malerei und Porträtkunst. Wie kam es dazu?
AS: Viele europäische Maler:innen, darunter Picasso, Matisse oder Modigliani, waren stark von der afrikanischen Kunst, insbesondere der Bildhauerei, beeinflusst. Ich hatte mich mit der afrikanischen Malerei und vor allem der afrikanischen Porträtmalerei aber bis vor Kurzem nicht wirklich auseinandergesetzt. Auf Anhieb entstand eine Passion, deren Früchte in der Kunsthalle Krems zu sehen sein werden.

FS: Alexandre Diop ist eine zentrale Position in deiner Sammlung. Er ist Franko-Senegalese, lebt und arbeitet in Wien und studiert dort an der Akademie der bildenden Künste. Wie hast du ihn kennengelernt?
AS: Ich lernte Alexandre beim Rundgang der Akademie der bildenden Künste im Januar 2020 kennen, nur zwei Monate, bevor unsere Welt sich verändern sollte. Ich war sofort von seinem Umgang mit Materialien und seinen erzählerischen Fähigkeiten

BASIL KINCAID, see cat. p. / siehe Kat. S. 111

I was immediately captivated by his use of materials and ability for storytelling. He clearly stands out as he is not only a gifted draftsman but despite his young age well versed in African and European philosophies. His practice tackles issues such as social inequalities and corruption in our societies.

FS: Amoako Boafo is the most prominent figure on the emerging painting scene in Ghana. Accra seems to be establishing itself as the new arts center in Africa. Boafo also initiated an artist-in-residence project there. The building is designed by star architect David Adjaye, who also designed the National Museum of African American History and Culture in Washington. You recently visited Boafo and Adjaye in Ghana. What was your impression of the new art hotspot Accra?
AS: The most impressive thing about the art scene in Accra and especially about Amoako and David is that they have created a community. The energy in the city and in many art studios is impressive and contagious. Amoako's studio is very centrally located, and six artists are currently working there. Artist Cornelius Annor, who like Boafo is represented in the exhibition, has also set up several studios in his large house in Amasaman, north of Accra, where nine artists are working. Similar things are happening with the art agency and collective Artemartis, run by Selasie Gomado, where artists like James Mishio have studios. The camaraderie among artists is admirable.

FS: Meanwhile, artists from Ghana also make up a large part of your collection, most with a focus on portraiture. This is also the focus of the exhibition at the Kunsthalle Krems. Will you continue specializing in this area?
AS: Contemporary African painting has not only won over my heart, but I think major collectors are starting to take notice and it is expanding our horizons enormously. Each generation produces a few incredible painters—now the big question is how this will continue to evolve. My collection and that of my brother's also feature other art movements, such as abstract painting from the 1960s, Austrian painters from the 1980s, and works by contemporary US artists. We will both continue to collect art and support artists. The exhibition at the Kunsthalle Krems is a great experience for the twenty-four exhibiting artists; most are very young—the youngest is just twenty-two, the oldest almost seventy.

fasziniert. Er sticht heraus, weil er nicht nur ein talentierter Zeichner ist, sondern trotz seines jungen Alters auch sehr bewandert in afrikanischen und europäischen Philosophien. Seine Arbeit adressiert Probleme wie soziale Ungleichheit und Korruption in unseren jeweiligen Gesellschaften.

FS: Amoako Boafo ist die prominenteste Figur der aufstrebenden Malereiszene in Ghana. Accra scheint sich als das neue Kunstzentrum in Afrika zu etablieren. Auch ein Artist-in-Residence-Projekt wurde von Boafo ins Leben gerufen. Das Gebäude wird von dem Stararchitekten David Adjaye geplant, der unter anderem das National Museum of African American History and Culture in Washington entworfen hat. Du hast unlängst Boafo und Adjaye in Ghana besucht. Welchen Eindruck hattest du vom neuen Kunsthotspot Accra?
AS: Das Beeindruckendste an der Kunstszene in Accra und vor allem an Amoako und David ist, dass sie eine Gemeinschaft geschaffen haben. Die Energie in der Stadt und in vielen Künstler:innenateliers ist beindruckend und ansteckend. Amoako hat ein sehr zentral gelegenes Atelier, in dem momentan sechs Künstler:innen arbeiten. Auch der Künstler Cornelius Annor, der wie Boafo in der Ausstellung vertreten ist, hat mehrere Ateliers in seinem großen Haus in Amasaman nördlich von Accra eingerichtet, wo neun Künstler:innen arbeiten. Ähnliches gilt für die Kunstagentur Artemartis, die von Selasie Gomado geführt wird, wo Künstler:innen wie James Mishio Ateliers haben. Die Kameradschaft unter den Künstler:innen ist bewundernswert.

FS: Mittlerweile nehmen die Künstler:innen aus Ghana auch einen großen Teil deiner Sammlung ein, die meisten mit dem Schwerpunkt Porträtmalerei. Das ist auch der Fokus der Ausstellung in der Kunsthalle Krems. Wirst du diese Spezialisierung weiterverfolgen?
AS: Ich glaube, dass die zeitgenössische afrikanische Malerei nicht nur mein Herz erobert, sondern auch die großen Sammler:innen erreicht hat und unser aller Horizont enorm erweitert. Jede Generation bringt eine Reihe unglaublicher Maler:innen hervor – die große Frage ist nun, wie sich das weiter entwickelt. Meine Sammlung und die meines Bruders umfassen auch andere Kunstrichtungen, etwa abstrakte Malerei der 60er-Jahre, österreichische Maler der 80er-Jahre oder auch Werke zeitgenössischer US-amerikanischer Künstler:innen. Wir werden beide weiterhin Kunst sammeln und Künstler:innen unterstützen. Die Ausstellung in der Kunsthalle Krems ist eine großartige Erfahrung für die 24 ausgestellten Künstler:innen; die meisten sind sehr jung – die jüngste ist gerade einmal 22, die älteste fast 70.

CORNELIUS ANNOR, see cat. p. / siehe Kat. S. 63

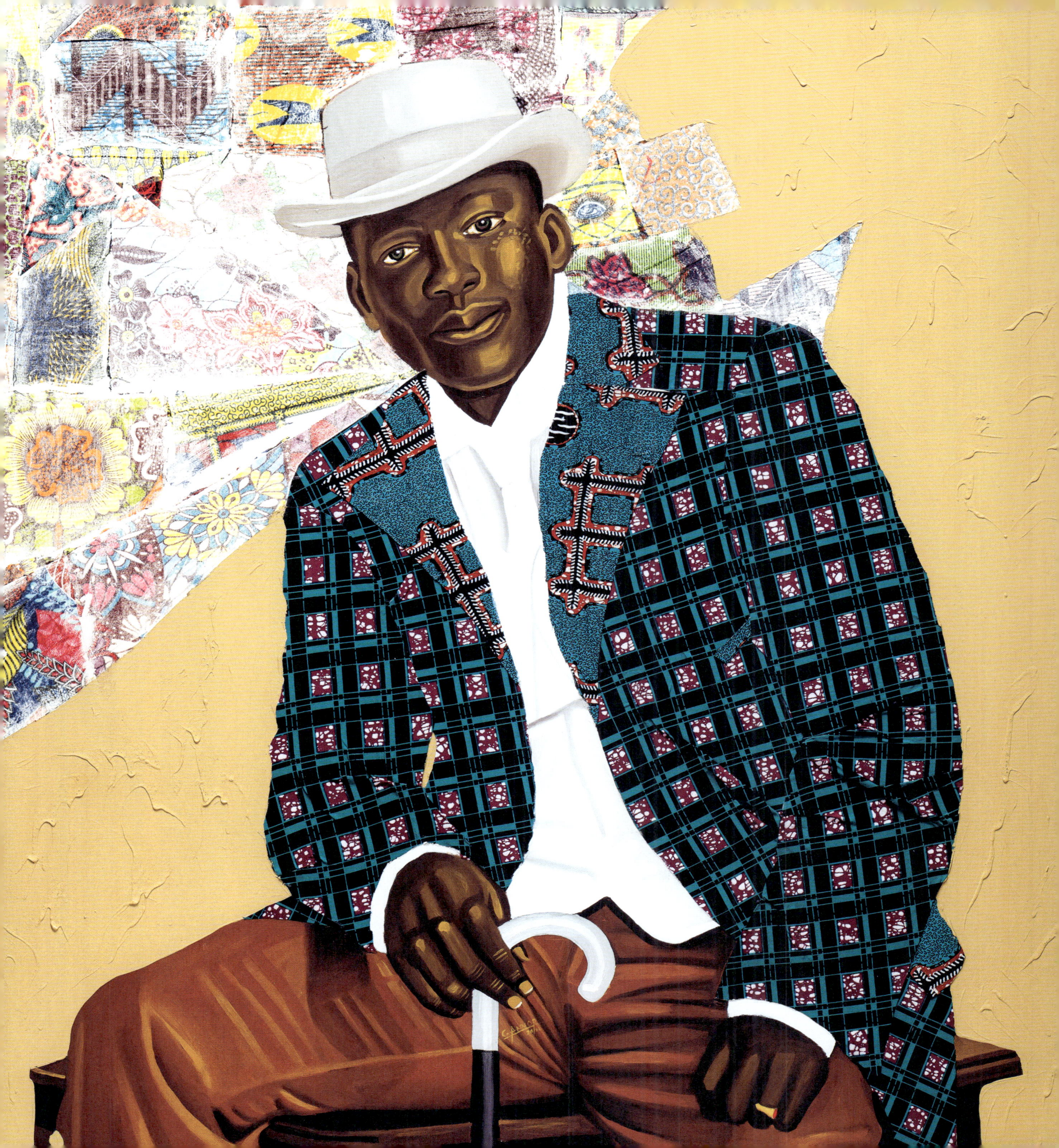

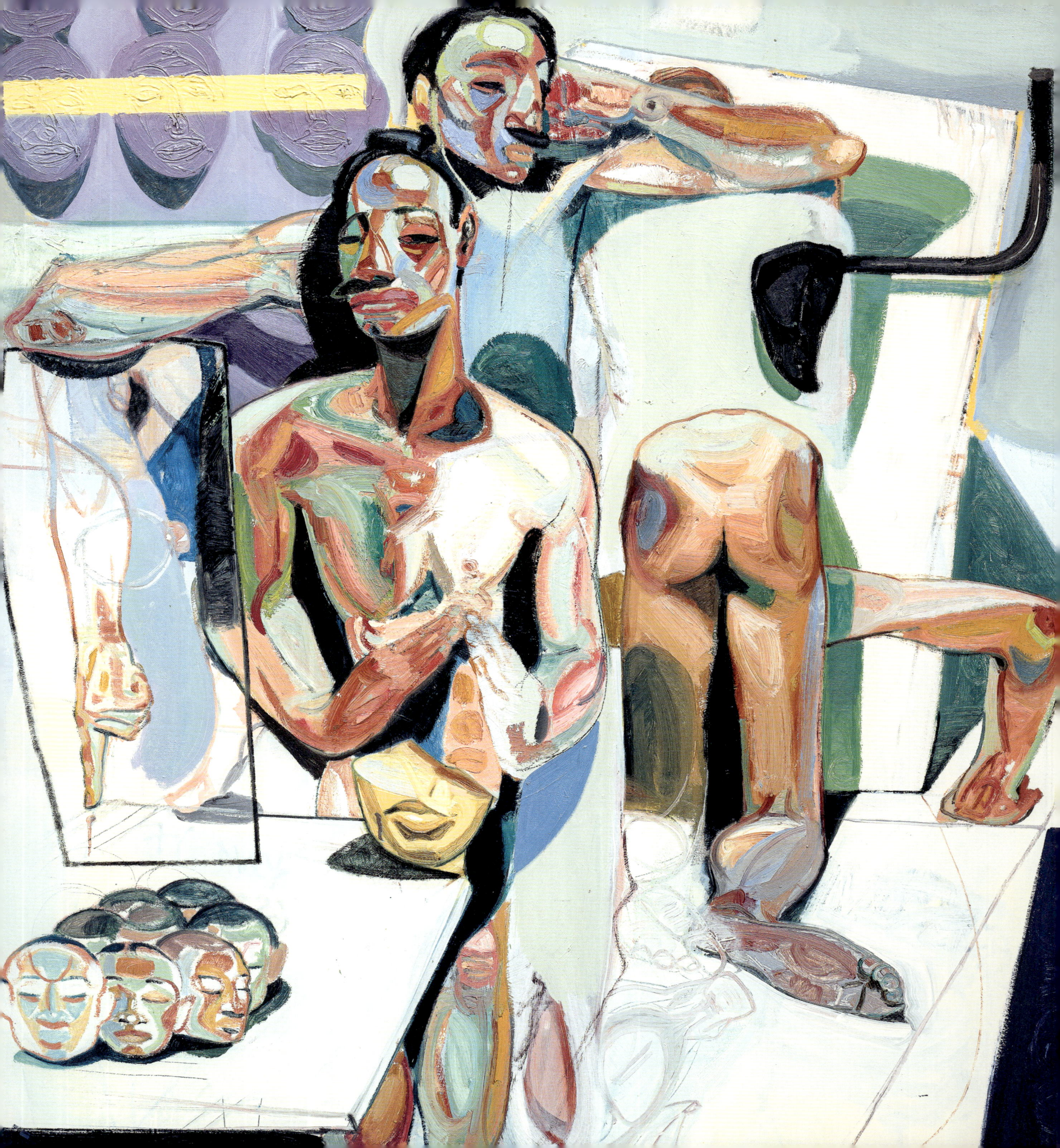

FS: In addition to paintings, your collection also features quilts. Many of these works were produced in Ghana or Luxor and are closely related to traditional African textile art. But their creators are US citizens. How did you come across this medium?

AS: As a native Persian, I have a personal and cultural connection to textiles. And I've always been an admirer of early modern European textile art. I have always been impressed by tapestries with biblical motifs, and exactly twenty years ago I had the fortune to see the one-of-a kind exhibition *Tapestry in the Renaissance: Art and Magnificence* at the Metropolitan Museum of Art in New York. During that period, collaborations between northern Europeans and Italians produced these impressive tapestries. The current collaboration between African—especially Ghanaian and Egyptian—and Afro-American artists is remarkable and is reminiscent of the synergies between Italian and Dutch artists. The interconnections between different cultures result in these incredible works of art.

FS: The artists are interconnected globally, many of them, like Tesfaye Urgessa, have moved to Western countries; some, like Basil Kincaid, feel rooted in Ghana and are active members of the new art community there. Kincaid really values the drive and energy in Ghana and feels very connected to the local scene, whereas in St. Louis he was more on his own. Did you also feel this local vitality?

AS: The energy on the west coast of Africa is exceptional and invigorating. I used to work in banking in Nigeria and always admired the energy, vitality, and business sense of the people there. The same can be said of Ghana, of course on a smaller scale. Basil Kincaid, for example, moved to Ghana a few years ago simply because he felt more comfortable there and the working conditions suited him. There are very good galleries in Africa, especially in South Africa, but also in all the other countries on this billion-strong continent. The number of private and public collectors of African art has increased enormously, as has the willingness to honor this art through exhibitions and to support the wonderful artists. For example US artist Kehinde Wiley, whose mother is Nigerian, has established a residency program in Senegal called Black Rock.

FS: Neben den Gemälden finden sich in deiner Sammlung auch Quilts, textile Kunstwerke. Viele dieser Werke wurden in Ghana oder Luxor produziert und sind eng mit traditioneller afrikanischer Textilkunst verbunden. Ihre Schöpfer:innen sind allerdings US-Staatsbürger:innen. Wie bist du auf dieses Medium gestoßen?

AS: Als gebürtiger Perser habe ich eine persönliche und kulturelle Verbundenheit mit Textilien. Und ich bin seit jeher ein Bewunderer der frühneuzeitlichen Textilkunst Europas. Ich fand schon immer die auf den Wandteppichen gezeigten Bibelmotive sehr ansprechend, und vor genau 20 Jahren konnte ich die einmalige Ausstellung *Tapestry in the Renaissance: Art and Magnificence* im Metropolitan Museum of Art in New York sehen. Damals führte die Zusammenarbeit von Nordeuropäern und Italienern zu diesen eindrucksvollen Wandteppichen. Die derzeitige Zusammenarbeit von afrikanischen – insbesondere ghanaischen und ägyptischen – und afroamerikanischen Künstler:innen ist beeindruckend und lässt an die Synergien zwischen italienischen und niederländischen Künstler:innen denken. Die Vernetzung unterschiedlicher Kulturen ergibt diese unglaublichen Kunstwerke.

FS: Die Künstler:innen sind global vernetzt, viele von ihnen sind in westliche Länder gezogen wie Tesfaye Urgessa; einige, wie Basil Kincaid, fühlen sich in Ghana verwurzelt und sind aktive Mitglieder der neuen Art Community. Kincaid schätzt an Ghana den Drive und die Energie und fühlt sich mit der lokalen Szene sehr verbunden, während er in St. Louis eher auf sich allein gestellt war. Hast du auch diese Vitalität vor Ort gespürt?

AS: Diese an der Westküste Afrikas anzutreffende Energie ist wirklich außergewöhnlich und mitreißend. Ich habe früher im Bankwesen in Nigeria gearbeitet und stets die Energie, Vitalität und den Handelssinn der Bevölkerung bewundert. Das Gleiche lässt sich von Ghana sagen, natürlich in kleinerem Maßstab. Basil Kincaid zum Beispiel zog vor einigen Jahren nach Ghana, weil er sich dort einfach wohler fühlte und die Arbeitsbedingungen ihm entsprachen. Es gibt viele sehr gute Galerien in Afrika, vor allem in Südafrika, aber auch in allen anderen Staaten dieses Milliardenkontinents. Die Anzahl der privaten und öffentlichen Sammler:innen afrikanischer Kunst ist enorm gestiegen und auch die Bereitschaft, diese Kunst durch Ausstellungen zu würdigen und die wunderbaren Künstler:innen zu unterstützen. Zum Beispiel hat der US-amerikanische Künstler Kehinde Wiley, dessen Mutter aus Nigeria stammt, ein Residency-Programm namens Black Rock im Senegal gegründet.

TESFAYE URGESSA, see cat. p. / siehe Kat. S. 93

FS: The official exhibition image is a portrait by Amoako Boafo of Kennedy Yanko, an US painter and sculptor. Boafo only paints people he knows personally. His portraits radiate individuality and beauty, are eloquent expressions of identity and empowerment. But they also attest to a painterly power that Boafo achieves by means of finger painting, which he mainly uses for creating faces and hands; this is how he achieves a psychological effect reminiscent of Schiele.
AS: Kennedy Yanko is not only a savvy artist, but also an amazing person with an eye for the long term. Amoako wanted to paint a picture for me, and I asked him if he could paint Kennedy. He immediately agreed because he has a lot of respect for Kennedy as a person and as an artist. The painting is based on a photograph Kennedy sent us. Amoako once again manages to bring out Kennedy's emotions with his wonderful finger painting.

FS: In contrast to European art, the portrait currently occupies a prominent position in contemporary African art, which is traditionally more representational. What do you think makes the portrait relevant today and where does your interest in portraiture come from?
AS: The first contemporary painting I purchased was a portrait by Andy Warhol. Familiarity with and the immediate recognizability of the person you are looking at on canvas are what drives an interest in portraiture generally. A familial relationship is established, as with Amoako Boafo's portrait of Kennedy Yanko, or Basil Kincaid's portrait of Kennedy Yanko and NAS. In both instances, I know the people portrayed, and this naturally creates a certain closeness to the paintings. Other works of art, such as those by Aplerh-Doku Borlabi, Millicent Akweley, or Atsoupé, are by comparison almost faceless in the sense that I do not know the people portrayed or that they do not even represent actual people. This adds mystery and allows the viewer to imagine their story.

FS: Das Titelbild der Ausstellung zeigt Kennedy Yanko, eine US-amerikanische Malerin und Bildhauerin, porträtiert von Amoako Boafo. Boafo malt ausschließlich Menschen, die er persönlich kennt. Seine Porträts strahlen Individualität und Schönheit aus, sind expressiver Ausdruck von Identität und Empowerment. Zum anderen zeugen sie von einer malerischen Kraft, die Boafo mittels Fingermalerei erzielt, die er vor allem bei Gesichtern und Händen einsetzt; damit erzielt er eine an Schiele erinnernde Psychologisierung.
AS: Kennedy Yanko ist nicht nur eine kluge Künstlerin, sondern auch eine absolut großartige Person, die sehr weitsichtig ist. Amoako wollte ein Bild für mich malen, und ich fragte ihn, ob er Kennedy malen könnte. Er war sofort einverstanden, da er Kennedy als Mensch und Künstlerin sehr schätzt. Das Gemälde basiert auf einem Foto, das Kennedy uns zugeschickt hat. Amoako schafft es hier einmal mehr, mit seiner wunderbaren Fingermalerei die Emotionen Kennedys zum Ausdruck zu bringen.

FS: Das Porträt ist in der zeitgenössischen afrikanischen Kunst, die traditionell eher gegenständlich geprägt ist, im Gegensatz zur europäischen stark vertreten. Was macht das Porträt deiner Meinung nach aktuell, und woher rührt dein Interesse für Porträtkunst?
AS: Das erste zeitgenössische Bild, das ich gekauft habe, war ein Porträt von Andy Warhol. Die Bekanntheit und die unmittelbare Wiedererkennbarkeit der Person, die man auf einer Leinwand betrachtet, sind ausschlaggebend für das allgemeine Interesse an Porträtmalerei. Es entsteht eine familiäre Beziehung, wie zum Beispiel mit Amoako Boafos Porträt von Kennedy Yanko oder dem von Basil Kincaid geknüpften Porträt von Kennedy Yanko und NAS. In beiden Fällen kenne ich die porträtierten Personen, und dadurch entsteht natürlich eine gewisse Nähe zu den Bildern. Andere Kunstwerke, etwa von Aplerh-Doku Borlabi, Millicent Akweley oder Atsoupé, sind wiederum fast gesichtslos in dem Sinne, dass die Personen mir nicht bekannt sind oder sogar keine realen Personen darstellen. Das verleiht den Porträts etwas Mysteriöses und regt die Betrachtenden dazu an, sich deren Geschichten vorzustellen.

ALEXANDRE DIOP, see cat. p. / siehe Kat. S. 71

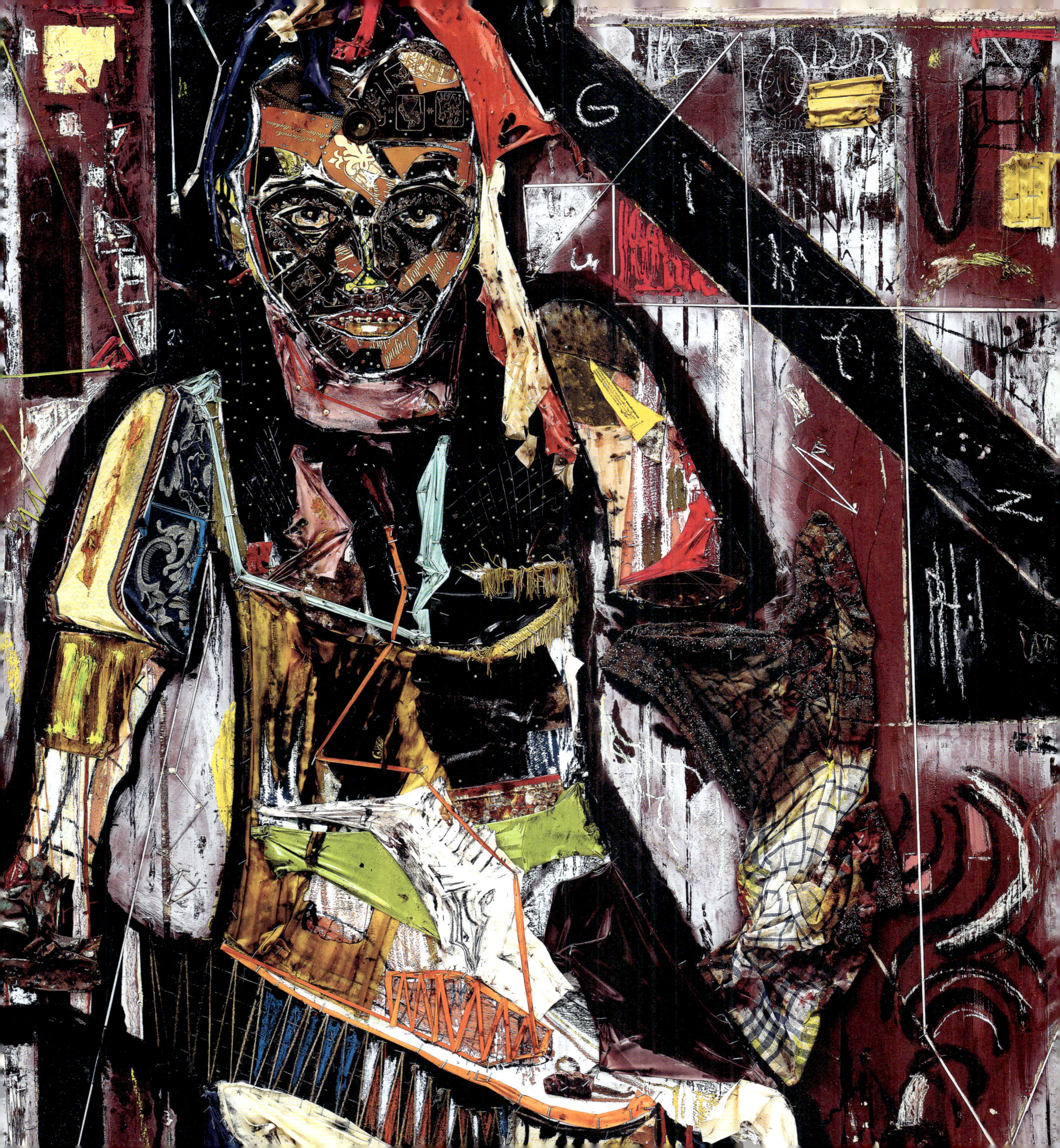

AUTHOR BIOGRAPHIES / AUTOR:INNENBIOGRAFIEN

SIR DAVID ADJAYE OBE

David Adjaye is a Ghanaian-British architect who has received international acclaim for his impact on the field. In 2000, Adjaye founded Adjaye Associates, which operates globally with studios in Accra, London, and New York. Adjaye's most well-known project to date is the National Museum of African American History and Culture, which opened in Washington DC in 2016.

MYRAH BROWN GREEN

Myrah Brown Green is an art historian, author, arts consultant, and independent curator, and holds a PhD in interdisciplinary studies. She is also a professional quilt maker and has taught textile arts for over thirty years. Her works can be found in prestigious collections such as the Smithsonian's and have been shown in Africa, Asia, Europe, and the US.

DIETER BUCHHART

Dieter Buchhart holds PhDs in art history and art restoration and has curated numerous exhibitions in renowned international museums and art spaces. Since 1999 he has worked as an art critic, and, as an art theorist, has authored numerous catalog texts, monographs, as well as interviews for *Kunstforum International* and others, in addition to his activities as a lecturer.

NIAMH COGHLAN

Niamh Coghlan is director at Richard Saltoun Gallery, London. She holds a master's in contemporary art history from Sotheby's Institute of Art and a bachelor of arts degree specializing in history of art & film studies. She works as a freelance writer and critic and has contributed to publications including *Textos sobre la obra de Abraham Cruzvillegas*.

ARMELLE DAKOUO

Armelle Dakouo has been active in the field of art in France and Africa since 2008. She has worked with several galleries including curating two exhibitions at Espace Commines, presenting artists from the African continent and diaspora. In 2020, Dakouo was appointed artistic director of the *AKAA* fair (*Also Known As Africa*) and is co-curator of the Congo Biennale 2022.

SIR DAVID ADJAYE OBE

David Adjaye ist ein ghanaisch-britischer Architekt, der für sein Schaffen international Anerkennung erhält. 2000 gründete er Adjaye Associates, das mit Studios in Accra, London und New York weltweit tätig ist. Adjayes bisher bekanntestes Projekt ist das National Museum of African American History and Culture, das 2016 in Washington, D. C., eröffnet wurde.

MYRAH BROWN GREEN

Myrah Brown Green ist Kunsthistorikerin, Autorin, Kunstberaterin und unabhängige Kuratorin mit einem Doktor in Interdisziplinären Studien. Sie ist zudem professionelle Quiltmacherin und unterrichtet seit über 30 Jahren Textilkunst. Ihre Werke sind in renommierten Sammlungen wie der des Smithsonians vertreten und wurden in Afrika, Asien, Europa und den USA ausgestellt.

DIETER BUCHHART

Dieter Buchhart ist Doktor der Kunstgeschichte und Restaurierung und Kurator zahlreicher Ausstellungen in renommierten internationalen Museen und Kunsträumen. Seit 1999 arbeitet er als Kunstkritiker und ist als Kunsttheoretiker Autor zahlreicher Monografien, Katalogtexte und Interviews, unter anderem für *Kunstforum International*, und auch als Vortragender tätig.

NIAMH COGHLAN

Niamh Coghlan ist Direktorin der Richard Saltoun Gallery in London. Sie hat einen Masterabschluss in zeitgenössischer Kunstgeschichte vom Sotheby's Institute of Art und einen Bachelorabschluss mit Schwerpunkt Kunst- und Filmgeschichte. Sie arbeitet als freie Autorin und Kritikerin und trug zu Publikationen wie *Textos sobre la obra de Abraham Cruzvillegas* bei.

ARMELLE DAKOUO

Armelle Dakouo ist seit 2008 in Frankreich und Afrika im Kunstbereich tätig. Sie arbeitete mit Galerien und kuratierte zwei Ausstellungen im Espace Commines in Paris, die Künstler:innen aus Afrika und der Diaspora vorstellten. Seit 2020 ist Dakouo künstlerische Leiterin der Messe *AKAA (Also Known As Africa)*, 2022 ist sie Ko-Kuratorin der Kongo-Biennale.

HEIKE DEMPSTER

Heike Dempster is an arts administrator and writer, and maintains a collaborative practice curating artist-talk series, exhibitions, and installations. In her writing, Dempster focuses on Africa, the Caribbean, and the diaspora. She has lived and worked in Germany, the UK, Jamaica, and the Bahamas, and has been based in Miami since 2012.

EKOW ESHUN

Ekow Eshun is a writer and curator. He is chair of the Fourth Plinth Commissioning Group and the former director of the ICA, London. He is the author of books including *In the Black Fantastic* and *Africa State of Mind*. He has contributed to numerous artist monographs as well as publications including the *New York Times* and the *Financial Times*.

PHILIPPE GODIN

After teaching philosophy, Philippe Godin became the editor of a blog hosted on *Libération* and later another on *Mediapart*. He worked as a press officer and art critic for various galleries including Anne de Villepoix. He has also written articles for magazines such as *Chimères*. As an author, Godin is currently working on a catalog on 100 Art Brut artists.

SELASIE GOMADO

Selasie Gomado, who worked as a mechanical engineer until 2021, co-founded the art collective Artemartis in 2018 and currently oversees operations both in Ghana and the rest of the world. He has seen numerous projects to fruition in multiple countries in both art and engineering fields.

MICHAËLA HADJI-MINAGLOU

Michaëla Hadji-Minaglou is an independent art curator. She also works as the gallery manager for AFIKARIS in Paris. After completing an MA in contemporary art, she decided to focus on the African art scene with the aim of deconstructing stereotypes and conveying the artists' messages.

HEIKE DEMPSTER

Heike Dempster ist Kunstmanagerin und Autorin und kuratiert mit anderen Gesprächsreihen mit Künstler:innen, Ausstellungen und Installationen. In ihren Texten konzentriert Dempster sich auf Afrika, die Karibik und die Diaspora. Sie hat in Deutschland, im Vereinigten Königreich, in Jamaika und auf den Bahamas gelebt und gearbeitet, seit 2012 lebt sie in Miami.

EKOW ESHUN

Ekow Eshun ist Autor und Kurator. Er ist Vorsitzender der Fourth Plinth Commissioning Group und ehemaliger Direktor des ICA, London. Er ist Autor mehrerer Bücher, darunter *In the Black Fantastic* und *Africa State of Mind*, und verfasste Beiträge zu zahlreichen Künstlermonografien und anderen Publikationen, darunter die *New York Times* und die *Financial Times*.

PHILIPPE GODIN

Nachdem er Philosophie unterrichtet hatte, wurde Philippe Godin Redakteur eines Blogs der *Libération* und eines weiteren bei *Mediapart*. Er arbeitete als Pressereferent und Kunstkritiker für verschiedene Galerien, darunter Anne de Villepoix. Zudem verfasste er Artikel für Zeitschriften wie *Chimères*. Derzeit arbeitet Godin an einem Katalog über 100 Art-Brut-Künstler:innen.

SELASIE GOMADO

Selasie Gomado, der bis 2021 als Maschinenbauingenieur arbeitete, war 2018 Mitbegründer des Kunstkollektivs Artemartis und leitet derzeit dessen Aktivitäten in Ghana und weltweit. In der Kunst wie im Ingenieurwesen führte er zahlreiche Projekte in vielen Ländern zum Erfolg.

MICHAËLA HADJI-MINAGLOU

Michaëla Hadji-Minaglou ist selbstständige Kunstkuratorin. Zudem arbeitet sie als Galeriemanagerin von AFIKARIS in Paris. Nach einem Masterabschluss in zeitgenössischer Kunst beschloss sie, sich auf die afrikanische Kunstszene zu konzentrieren, um Stereotype zu dekonstruieren und die Botschaften der Künstler:innen zu vermitteln.

CAROLYN L. MAZLOOMI

Carolyn L. Mazloomi is an historian, curator, author, lecturer, artist, and founder of the African-American Quilt Guild of Los Angeles and the Women of Color Quilters Network (WCQN). She has worked tirelessly to bring attention to the contributions of African American quilt artists and received many honors, among them being named a National Heritage Fellow.

CHARLES MOORE

Charles Moore is an art historian, curator, and author investigating abstraction, color theory, and social justice. Moore is the author of *The Black Market* (2020) and *The Brilliance of the Color Black* (2021). He received his master's degree in museum studies from Harvard University and is currently a doctoral student at Columbia University's Teachers College.

NIRU RATNAM

Niru Ratnam is a gallerist and writer who focuses on issues around cultural identity, postcolonial subjectivities and class in relation to contemporary art. He currently runs a gallery in Soho, London. He has published widely, including for *ArtReview*, *The Spectator*, *Garage,* and the *Financial Times*.

FLORIAN STEININGER

Florian Steininger is director of the Kunsthalle Krems. Until 2016 he was curator at the Bank Austria Kunstforum Wien. He has realized numerous exhibitions of modern and contemporary art, including *Roy Lichtenstein*, *Willem de Kooning*, *Frida Kahlo*, *Warhol & Basquiat*, *Per Kirkeby*, *Teresa Margolles*, *Patricia Piccinini*, *Andreas Werner,* and *Helen Frankenthaler*.

SARAH STENGEL

Sarah Stengel is a writer and arts administrator based in New York. She received her BA in art history from Wesleyan University, where she was the founding arts editor of *Method Magazine*. She is currently the director of communications at James Cohan Gallery in Tribeca.

CAROLYN L. MAZLOOMI

Carolyn L. Mazloomi ist Historikerin, Kuratorin, Autorin, Lehrende, Künstlerin und Gründerin der African-American Quilt Guild of Los Angeles und des Women of Color Quilters Network (WCQN). Sie setzte sich stets dafür ein, den Werken afroamerikanischer Quiltkünstler:innen Aufmerksamkeit zu verschaffen, und erhielt viele Ehrungen, darunter ein National Heritage Fellowship.

CHARLES MOORE

Charles Moore ist Kunsthistoriker, Kurator und Autor und befasst sich mit Abstraktion, Farbtheorie und sozialer Gerechtigkeit. Moore ist Autor von *The Black Market* (2020) und *The Brilliance of the Color Black* (2021). Er hat einen Masterabschluss in Museumsstudien der Universität Harvard und ist derzeit Doktorand am Teachers College der Columbia University.

NIRU RATNAM

Niru Ratnam ist Galerist und Autor und beschäftigt sich mit Fragen kultureller Identität, postkolonialer Subjektivitäten und sozialer Klasse in Bezug auf zeitgenössische Kunst. Derzeit betreibt er eine Galerie in Soho, London. Er veröffentlichte zahlreiche Texte, unter anderem in *ArtReview*, *The Spectator*, *Garage* und der *Financial Times*.

FLORIAN STEININGER

Florian Steininger ist künstlerischer Direktor der Kunsthalle Krems. Bis 2016 war er Kurator am Bank Austria Kunstforum Wien. Er kuratierte zahlreiche Projekte zur modernen und zeitgenössischen Kunst, darunter *Roy Lichtenstein*, *Willem de Kooning*, *Frida Kahlo*, *Warhol & Basquiat*, *Per Kirkeby*, *Teresa Margolles*, *Patricia Piccinini*, *Andreas Werner* und *Helen Frankenthaler*.

SARAH STENGEL

Sarah Stengel ist Autorin und Kunstmanagerin und lebt in New York. Sie machte einen Bachelor in Kunstgeschichte an der Wesleyan University, wo sie auch die Kunstredaktion des *Method Magazine* gründete. Derzeit ist sie Kommunikationsleiterin der James Cohan Gallery im New Yorker Stadtteil Tribeca.

Amir and Shahrokh Shariat dedicate this exhibition to their beloved father and his everlasting memory.

Amir und Shahrokh Shariat widmen diese Ausstellung ihrem geliebten Vater und seinem ewigen Andenken.

PUBLISHING INFORMATION / IMPRESSUM

Catalog for the exhibition
The New African Portraiture: Shariat Collections.
November 19, 2022 to April 10, 2023, Kunsthalle Krems

Katalog zur Ausstellung
The New African Portraiture. Shariat Collections.
19. November 2022 bis 10. April 2023, Kunsthalle Krems

Museumsplatz 5
3500 Krems an der Donau
www.kunsthalle.at

EXHIBITION / AUSSTELLUNG
Managing Directors / Geschäftsführung:
Julia Flunger-Schulz, Stefan Mitterer
Artistic Director / Künstlerischer Direktor:
Florian Steininger
Curator / Kurator: Ekow Eshun
Program Coordination / Programmkoordination:
AIR – ARTIST IN RESIDENCE Niederösterreich:
Klaus Krobath (Head / Leitung), Lisa Saahs
Exhibition Management / Ausstellungsorganisation:
Elke Pehamberger-Müllner (Head / Leitung),
Helene Heiß, Elisabeth Kainberger
Marketing and Communication / Marketing und
Kommunikation: Sigrid Wilhelm (Head / Leitung),
Matej Gajdos, Sabine Soban, Franziska Treml,
Elisabeth Zettl
Events: Martina Hackel and team / und Team
Development: Nicole Pröll and / und
Stephanie Schmitzer
Art Education and Research, Visitor Services, and
Artothek Niederösterreich / Kunstvermittlung,
Besucherservice und Artothek Niederösterreich:
Isabell Fiedler (Head / Leitung),
Claudia Pitnik and team / und Team
Shop and / und Ticketing: Sabine Mosgöller
(Head / Leitung) and team / und Team
Facility Management: Reinhard Kern (Head / Leitung),
Michael Huber, Markus Lehmerhofer, Lukas Rieder
Exhibition Setup / Ausstellungsaufbau: Andreas Frostl,
Filip Kadvanj, Marc Paget-Schanzl,
Konstantin Rössl, Karl Unterweger

CATALOG / KATALOG
Editors / Herausgeber: Ekow Eshun, Florian Steininger
Authors / Autor:innen: Sir David Adjaye OBE,
Myrah Brown Green, Dieter Buchhart, Niamh Coghlan,
Armelle Dakouo, Heike Dempster, Ekow Eshun,
Philippe Godin, Selasie Gomado,
Michaëla Hadji-Minaglou, Carolyn L. Mazloomi,
Charles Moore, Niru Ratnam,
Florian Steininger, Sarah Stengel
Managing Editor / Redaktion: Philipp Emanuel Missaghi
Production Manager / Produktionsleitung:
Elke Pehamberger-Müllner
Visual Concept, Graphic Design /
Visuelles Konzept, Grafik: Alexander Rendi
Assistance / Mitarbeit: Eugen Lejeune
Proofs / Lithografie: pixelstorm litho & digital Imaging
English Copyeditor / Englisches Lektorat: Erik Smith
German Copyeditor / Deutsches Lektorat:
Eva Luise Kühn (Preliminary editing of the texts
by Dieter Buchhart / Vorlektorat der Texte
Dieter Buchharts: Jürgen Geiger)
Translations / Übersetzungen: Michael Strand
(English–German / Englisch–Deutsch:
Sir David Adjaye OBE, Myrah Brown Green,
Niamh Coghlan, Ekow Eshun, Selasie Gomado,
Michaëla Hadji-Minaglou, Carolyn L. Mazloomi,
Charles Moore, Niru Ratnam, Sarah Stengel), Erik Smith
(German–English / Deutsch–Englisch: Dieter Buchhart,
Florian Steininger, Climate Imprint), Maria Schneeweiß
(French–German / Französisch–Deutsch:
Armelle Dakouo, Philippe Godin)
Printing and Binding / Gesamtherstellung: Holzhausen,
eine Marke der Gerin Druck GmbH
Publishing House / Verlag: Verlag der Buchhandlung
Walther und Franz König, Köln

The exhibition and catalog management would like to thank Eva Kovač, production manager at Shariat Collections, for her support of the exhibition project. / Ausstellungs- und Katalogmanagement danken Eva Kovač, Production Manager der Shariat Collections, für die Unterstützung des Ausstellungsprojekts.

First Edition / 1. Auflage

ISBN 978-3-7533-0306-2

Printed in Austria / Gedruckt in Österreich

Bibliographic information published by the Deutsche Nationalbibliothek: The Deutsche Nationalbibliothek lists this publication in the Deutsche Nationalbibliografie; detailed bibliographic data available on the Internet at http://dnb.de. / Bibliografische Information der Deutschen Nationalbibliothek: Die Deutsche Nationalbibliothek verzeichnet diese Publikation in der Deutschen Nationalbibliografie; detaillierte bibliografische Daten sind im Internet über http://dnb.de abrufbar.

DISTRIBUTION / VERTRIEB

Germany, Austria, Switzerland
Buchhandlung Walther König
Ehrenstraße 4
50672 Köln, Deutschland
Tel: +49 (0) 221 / 20 59 6 53
verlag@buchhandlung-walther-koenig.de

Unites States and Canada
D.A.P. / Distributed Art Publishers, Inc.
75 Broad Street, Suite 630
New York, NY 10004, USA
Tel: +1 (0) 212 627 1999
orders@dapinc.com

Outside the United States and Canada, Germany, Austria and Switzerland
Thames & Hudson Ltd., London
www.thamesandhudson.com

COPYRIGHT AND PHOTO CREDITS / COPYRIGHT UND BILDNACHWEIS

Reproduction Rights / Reproduktionsrecht: © Millicent Akweley: pp. / S. 33–35; © Cornelius Annor: pp. / S. 59–63, 131; © Crystal Yayra Anthony: pp. / S. 45–47; © Souleimane Barry: pp. / S. 81–83; © Bildrecht, Wien 2022: pp. / S. 23–27, 65–67, 125 (right / rechts); © Aplerh-Doku Borlabi: pp. / S. 29–31; Copyright the Artist: pp. / S. 85–89; © Alexandre Diop: pp. / S. 69–75, 135; © Kimathi Donkor: p. / S. 97; © Matthew Eguavoen: p. / S. 99; © Bouvy Enkobo: pp. / S. 103–105; © Basil Kincaid: pp. / S. 111–113, 128; © Turiya Magadlela: p. / S. 109; © Gastineau Massamba: pp. / S. 77–79; © James Mishio: pp. / S. 41–43; © Christopher Myers 2022: pp. / S. 115–117; © Jean David Nkot: p. / S. 107; © Boluwatife Oyediran: p. / S. 101; © Afia Prempeh: pp. / S. 55–57; © Otis Kwame Kye Quaicoe: pp. / S. 49–53; © Josie Love Roebuck: pp. / S. 119–123; © Eric Adjei Tawiah: pp. / S. 37–39; © Tesfaye Urgessa: pp. / S. 91–95, 132; © Kehinde Wiley: p. / S. 126 (right / rechts).

Photos / Fotos: © 2022@joritaust.com: pp. / S. 23–83, 91–115, 119–123, 128–135; © 2021 RMN-Grand Palais (musée du Louvre) / Mathieu Rabeau: p. / S. 125 (left / links); Courtesy of the Huntington Art Museum, San Marino, California: p. / S. 126 (left / links); Courtesy of the Kehinde Wiley Studio: p. / S. 126 (right / rechts); Courtesy of the National Portrait Gallery, London: p. / S. 125 (right / rechts); Courtesy Richard Saltoun Gallery London and Rome, photo: Ben Westoby: pp. / S. 85–89; Image courtesy the artist and James Cohan, New York: p. / S. 117.

Front Cover / Cover vorne: Amoako Boafo, *Kennedy*, 2021 (detail / Detail), © Bildrecht, Wien 2022, photo / Foto: © 2022@joritaust.com.

Back Cover / Cover hinten: Alexandre Diop, *Autoportrait of the Young Black Diable at the Age of 25*, 2021 (detail / Detail), © Alexandre Diop, photo / Foto: © 2022@joritaust.com.

Bundesministerium
Kunst, Kultur, öffentlicher Dienst und Sport

KULTUR NIEDERÖSTERREICH

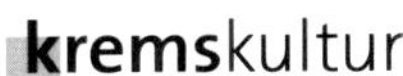

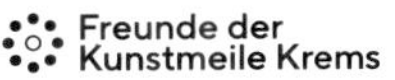

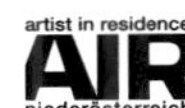

Kunstmeile Krems

CLIMATE IMPRINT / KLIMA-IMPRESSUM

Certificates are good—disclosure is better. In an effort to promote environmentally and climate-conscious production, the publisher of this book would like to provide the following product and production-specific information in the interests of transparency.

The MATERIALS used in the production of this art book have environmentally friendly properties. The uncoated paper used for the book block (Gerin REFORM, 120g) is a recycling paper made of 100% secondary fibers and has been awarded the Blue Angel ecolabel for outstanding environmental friendliness. The paper stock used for the cover (PEYDUR lissé, 135g) is an FSC-certified, uncoated printing substrate made from chlorine-free bleached, long-fiber sulphate pulp (FSC—the Forest Stewardship Council sets global criteria for ensuring that the wood used is sourced from sustainable and environmentally friendly forest management, complies with the social standards of the respective countries of origin, and as raw material was obtained legally). The paperboard used for the hardcover (Bookbinder gray paperboard, 3mm) is an environmentally friendly, solid fiberboard made from reclaimed paper pulp (waste paper). The water-based glue used for the binding (AQUENCE) is UZ 24-certified (Austrian Ecolabel), low-emission, and removeable.

The PRINT PRODUCTION was completed with a UV-sheetfed offset process (LE-UV/LED), certified by the German Printing and Media Industries Federation (BVDM) as safe for the health of producers and consumers. The printing INKS (SICURA LOW NRGY/LED ROCK) have excellent deinking and recycling properties; ink particles can be efficiently removed by flotation. This printing process does not require heating lamps for immediate ink curing, thereby saving energy. Since the printed sheets exit the press already dry, the use of a protective dispersion varnish is not required.

This publication bears the PRINTED IN AUSTRIA seal of approval from the Verband Druck Medien (Austrian print and media association), which stands for top-quality print products produced with Austrian know-how. TRANSPORT ROUTES related to the overall production (printing—binding—finishing) were kept as short as possible and restricted to a thirty-five-kilometer radius in Lower Austria and Vienna. The KLIMANEUTRAL (climate neutral) logo below indicates that the Product Carbon Footprint (PCF) has been calculated including the CO_2 emissions of a product or service from raw materials through production to delivery. Based on this calculation, a CO_2 offset payment was made; its use for a climate project is registered and can be viewed at climatepartner.com by entering the ClimatePartner ID 11582-2208-1007 listed under the logo.

Zertifikate sind gut – Offenlegung ist besser. Im Bemühen um eine umwelt- und klimabewusste Produktion möchte Ihnen der Herausgeber dieser Publikation nachstehende produkt- und produktionsspezifische Fakten im Sinn der Transparenz vermitteln.

Die zur Herstellung dieses Kunstbuchs eingesetzten MATERIALIEN besitzen umweltverträgliche Eigenschaften. Das ungestrichene Papier des Buchkerns (Gerin REFORM, 120 g) ist ein Recyclingpapier aus 100 % Sekundärfaserstoffen und ist mit dem Umweltzeichen Blauer Engel für besondere Umweltfreundlichkeit ausgezeichnet. Das Papier des Einband-Überzugs (PEYDUR lissé, 135 g) ist ein FSC-zertifizierter, ungestrichener Bedruckstoff aus chlorfrei gebleichtem, langfaserigem Sulfatzellstoff. (FSC – Forest Stewardship Council definiert weltweit gültige Kriterien, die gewährleisten, dass das verwendete Holz aus nachhaltiger und umweltgerechter Waldbewirtschaftung stammt, dabei soziale Standards der jeweiligen Herkunftsländer eingehalten werden und der Rohstoff Holz legal gewonnen wird.) Bei der für das Hardcover verwendeten Pappe (Buchbinder-Graupappe, 3 mm) handelt es sich um eine aus wiedergewonnenen Papierfaserstoffen (Altpapier) hergestellte umweltfreundliche Vollpappe. Der zur Bindung verwendete Kleber auf Wasserbasis (AQUENCE) ist nach UZ 24 (Österreichisches Umweltzeichen) zertifiziert, emissionsarm und entfernbar.

Die DRUCKPRODUKTION erfolgte im UV-Bogenoffsetverfahren (LE-UV/LED), dem vom Bundesverband Druck und Medien in Deutschland die gesundheitliche Unbedenklichkeit für Produzent:innen und Verbraucher:innen bestätigt wird. Die für den Druck verwendeten FARBEN (SICURA LOW NRGY/LED ROCK) haben ausgezeichnete Deinking- und Rezyklier-Eigenschaften, dabei können die Farbpartikel mittels Flotation effizient entfernt werden. In diesem Druckverfahren müssen zur unmittelbaren Farbhärtung keine wärmenden Strahler mehr eingesetzt werden, wodurch Energie eingespart wird. Da die bedruckten Bögen die Maschine bereits trocken verlassen, kann auf die Verwendung von Dispersionsschutzlack gänzlich verzichtet werden.

Die vorliegende Publikation besitzt mit PRINTED IN AUSTRIA das Gütesiegel vom Verband Druck Medien (Österreich), das für Printprodukte, die mit österreichischem Know-how und damit in Top-Qualität produziert wurden, steht. Die TRANSPORTWEGE im Rahmen der Gesamtherstellung (Druck – Bindung – Veredelung) wurden so kurz wie möglich gehalten und verliefen im Umkreis von 35 Kilometern zwischen Niederösterreich und Wien. Das untenstehende Zeichen KLIMANEUTRAL zeigt an, dass der Product Carbon Footprint (PCF) berechnet und die CO_2-Emissionen eines Produktes oder einer Dienstleistung von den Rohstoffen über die Herstellung bis zur Auslieferung dabei berücksichtigt wurden. Auf Basis dieser Berechnung wurde eine CO_2-Ausgleichszahlung geleistet, deren Verwendung für ein Klimaprojekt beurkundet und durch Eingabe der unter dem Logo angeführten ClimatePartner-ID 11582-2208-1007 auf climatepartner.com einsehbar ist.

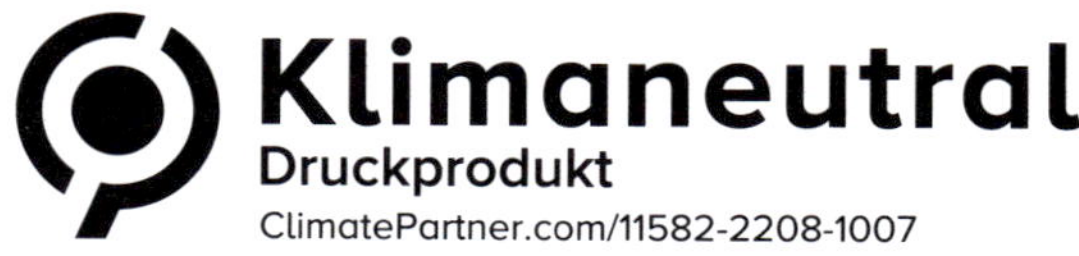